THE OPPORTUNITY

A BROOKINGS FOCUS BOOK

THE OPPORTUNITY

NEXT STEPS IN REDUCING NUCLEAR ARMS

Steven Pifer

Michael E. O'Hanlon

BROOKINGS INSTITUTION PRESS

Washington, D.C.

Library of Congress Cataloging-in-Publication data is available
ISBN: 978-0-8157-2429-2 (hardcover : alk. paper)

9 8 7 6 5 4 3 2 1

Printed on acid-free paper

Typeset in Sabon

Composition by Cynthia Stock
Silver Spring, Maryland

Printed by R. R. Donnelley
Harrisonburg, Virginia

CONTENTS

CONTENTS

FOREWORD

SHORTLY AFTER THE UNITED STATES conducted the Trinity test in 1945, President Truman confided to his diary, "We have discovered the most terrible bomb in the history of the world. It may be the fire destruction prophesied in the Euphrates Valley Era, after Noah and his fabulous Ark." When Albert Einstein—who had been indispensable in developing the physics that made the weapon possible but who had been cut out of the Manhattan Project—learned that Truman had approved use of Fat Man and Little Boy against Japan, he said, simply, "*Vey iz mir*" (Yiddish for "Woe is me").

Following the Soviet Union's "Joe One" test in 1949, Joseph Stalin remarked, "Atomic weapons can hardly be used without spelling the end of the world." In 1953, one of Stalin's immediate successors, Georgi Malenkov, said publicly that a war waged with "modern weapons" would be "the end of world civilization."

For all the antagonism between them, the superpowers spent decades working out a system that combined mutual deterrence with negotiated arms control to keep the Sword of Damocles from falling.

The string that holds that sword has remained intact since the end of the cold war, albeit frayed in places, because of the success in breaking what had been a defining cycle of earlier historical eras. Before the nuclear age, the story of war and peace followed a recurring and tragic pattern: first came catastrophic war, then came new mechanisms designed to better keep the peace, whose breakdown, in turn, resulted in new bouts of conflict. Following the destruction wrought by the Napoleonic Wars, the peacemakers of Vienna forged the Concert of Europe. When the balance of power undergirding it collapsed, mankind suffered through the "war to end all wars." In its aftermath, leaders created the League of Nations, which proved incapable of averting the onset of mankind's most destructive war, World War Two. Yet, out of the ashes of that conflict was created the League's more effective successor, the United Nations. In all of those cases, progress, to the extent it was achieved, was reactive.

During the nuclear age, however, progress has been proactive. Mechanisms to restrain the growth of atomic arms and conflict have been created without the world having to suffer through the ultimate cataclysm. With bitter memories of the destruction unleashed during the first half of the twentieth century, and an appreciation of the untold misery that would result from a nuclear exchange, world leaders, in many cases led by American presidents, had the foresight to establish a series of arms control mechanisms, including the Limited Test Ban Treaty; the Non-Proliferation Treaty; the Strategic Arms Limitation Treaty (SALT); the Strategic Arms Reduction Treaty (START); and the Comprehensive Test Ban Treaty (CTBT).

In April 2010, Presidents Barack Obama and Dmitry Medvedev met in Prague to sign the latest addition to this web of agreements, New START. It builds upon previous progress by requiring further cuts to U.S. and Russian arsenals, limiting both countries to a maximum of 1,550 deployed strategic nuclear warheads and 700 deployed strategic delivery vehicles. In that sense, New START represents a further step toward the long-term objective President Obama had announced one year earlier in Prague: a world free of nuclear weapons. Much clearly remains to be done before the world comes anywhere near attaining that goal. New START did not, for example, address the vast number of nonstrategic nuclear weapons held by the United States and Russia, nor did it place restrictions on the nuclear stockpiles of countries other than the world's two nuclear leaders.

With all of that history in mind, in this Brookings Focus book, Steve Pifer and Mike O'Hanlon explicate, in a concise and lucid way, the range of critical issues left outstanding in New START's wake. In the best tradition of Brookings scholarship, they also offer a series of pragmatic, fact-based recommendations. Nuclear policy will not be a major theme in this year's presidential election campaign given the pressing weight of economic and domestic challenges. But Steve and Mike explain how, with the 2012 U.S. presidential election behind us, new opportunities will exist to build a safer, more secure world. They outline a number of steps that could be taken by the U.S. president, whoever takes the oath of office on January 20, 2013, to make further progress in reducing nuclear weapons and bolstering the arms control regime.

Steve and Mike conclude by painting a portrait of the cumulative effect of their proposals come 2017—a world in which U.S. and Russian nuclear weapons have been further reduced, NATO and Russia have found a way to cooperate on missile defense, the nuclear test ban continues in force de facto, and the nuclear reductions process is beginning to involve third countries. For those who believe in a long-term goal of a world without nuclear weapons, Steve and Mike's vision would move us closer to that objective.

Not all readers will agree with the proposals. Some arms control advocates will lament that the authors do not suggest more radical steps. Meanwhile, arms control opponents will insist that Steve and Mike have gone too far. But their proposals represent a concerted attempt to advance the arms control agenda in a way that promotes the U.S. national interest while simultaneously strengthening the string that holds the Sword of Damocles above humanity's head, as well as increasing the probability that one day the sword will be removed entirely.

In writing this book, Steve and Mike have deployed to good effect their deep expertise in nuclear weapons issues and broader U.S. national security policy. Steve is director of Brookings's Arms Control Initiative, in which capacity he has written a number of widely praised policy papers on the full gamut of arms control issues. He served for twenty-five years as a foreign service officer, including as special assistant to Paul Nitze and as the American ambassador to Ukraine. Mike is director of research of the Brookings Foreign Policy program and is widely regarded as one of the world's foremost experts on U.S. defense and security policy. He has written several papers and books on missile defense, space weapons, and the future of arms control, as well as a previous Brookings book evaluating the goal of a nuclear-weapons-free world.

This book builds upon earlier work that Steve and Mike have done for the Arms Control and 21st Century Defense Initiatives, and they are grateful to their colleagues for the support they have received in those endeavors.

The authors would like to thank a number of people who reviewed all or part of earlier drafts of the book, including Bruce Blair, Avis Bohlen, Elbridge Colby, Thomas Donnelly, Harold Feiveson, Edward Ifft, Hans Kristensen, Jan Lodal, Bruce MacDonald, Jeffrey McCausland, Gary Samore, David Schwartz, Greg Thielmann, Frank von Hippel, Ted Warner, Richard Weitz, and Jon Wolfsthal. They are especially grateful to Theodore Piccone, who reviewed the entire text and oversaw the outside peer review process. Of course, the contents and conclusions remain solely the authors' work.

Thanks are owed to the excellent team under the direction of Bob Faherty at the Brookings Institution Press, especially copyeditor Marty Gottron, for moving this book forward on an expeditious basis. Steve and Mike are grateful to Ian Livingston for research assistance, to Christine Pifer for suggesting the cover design, and to Susan Woollen for the cover.

Finally, on behalf of Steve, Mike, and Brookings, I would like to express our deep gratitude to the Ploughshares Fund for its generous and continuing support that has made this book possible, along with so much of the Arms Control Initiative's work.

STROBE TALBOTT
President
Brookings Institution

September 2012

THE OPPORTUNITY

CHAPTER ONE

WHY NUCLEAR ARMS CONTROL SHOULD BE ON THE PRESIDENT'S AGENDA IN 2013

NUCLEAR ARMS REMAIN the ultimate weapon of mass destruction. As 2012 draws to a close, Iran and North Korea tend to dominate the headlines about nuclear arms issues. To be sure, the efforts to dissuade the regime in Tehran from achieving a nuclear weapons capability and to persuade North Korea and its new young autocrat to abandon its already established nuclear arms program are critical challenges facing the United States. They will rank high on the foreign policy agenda of the American president in 2013, be it Barack Obama or Mitt Romney, as will concerns about keeping nuclear weapons and fissile materials out of the hands of terrorist groups.

But the presidential in-box will also hold a number of issues related to more traditional nuclear arms control that must not be ignored. These issues, the subject of this book, set the basic international context for all discussions of nonproliferation. They address the 95-plus percent of all global nuclear weapons and weapons materials still held by the nuclear weapons states officially recognized by the nuclear Non-Proliferation Treaty—the United States, Russia, Britain, France, and China. They greatly influence the tens of billions of dollars still spent on nuclear arms annually by the major powers today—and the deterrent role those weapons still play in contemporary international politics. They are central to relationships between some of the great powers, notably Russia and the United States but also China and the United States, and can affect the broader character of those states' strategic interactions. These issues are, in short, still crucial to matters of global war and peace today.

In April 2009, President Obama and President Dmitry Medvedev of Russia met in London, where they agreed to launch a negotiation on strategic offensive arms, continuing a practice of nuclear arms limitation and reduction negotiations between Washington and Moscow that dates back more than forty years. One year later, they met in Prague to sign the New Strategic Arms Reduction Treaty (New START). The Obama administration considered the treaty a primary accomplishment of its policy to "reset" relations with Russia as well as the most important achievement in bilateral arms control in two decades. The treaty entered into force in February 2011; when its limits take full effect in 2018, it will constrain U.S. and Russian strategic nuclear forces to levels not seen since the late 1950s.

The arms control dialogue between Washington and Moscow over the past three years has addressed other questions as well, such as the relationship between offense and defense, the impact of missile defense, and nonstrategic nuclear weapons. But the tempo of discussions slowed greatly in the second half of 2011 and 2012, in large part because of presidential elections in the two countries.

Vladimir Putin's return as Russia's president in March 2012 surprised few, but the Russian bureaucracy nevertheless adopted a cautious stance during the election period and transition. Russian officials traditionally tend to display little creativity until they have a clear signal of direction from the top.

The American presidential election also had an impact. The Obama administration downplayed the vision of a world free of nuclear weapons that the president had painted in 2009 and followed a more careful line on arms control. Given other priorities and, in a heated presidential election campaign, the White House apparently wanted to avoid taking steps that would either complicate Obama's reelection drive or burden the future prospects for arms control. For their part, Russian officials quietly made clear as early as summer 2011 that they would not pursue new nuclear reduction negotiations with the United States until they knew who the American president would be in 2013, their experience being that Democratic and Republican administrations take very different approaches to arms control.

NUCLEAR QUESTIONS—AND THE ARMS CONTROL OPPORTUNITY

The U.S. president in 2013 will face an arms control opportunity. With good decisionmaking and a bit of luck on the negotiating front, he can help further reduce U.S. and Russian strategic arsenals while bringing nonstrategic and surplus warheads under controls for the first time. The two nuclear superpowers would still have 2,000 or more warheads each under the concepts we discuss—far more than the low hundreds likely required for even a fairly robust classic standard of deterrence—but far less than the 5,000 or so each has today. Associated steps could cap China's future arsenal and that of other powers too, at least through politically binding declarations, laying the basis for bringing those countries into the nuclear reduction process. This would be an unprecedented and highly useful accomplishment.

Taken together, these efforts might also make it easier for a future president to consider whether the global elimination of nuclear weapons would ever be possible or desirable. More immediately and more to the point, these efforts would improve nuclear safety considerably. The next president could, in the process, save substantial sums of money in nuclear accounts at a time when federal budget pressures are enormous. He might also reinvigorate the improvement in relations with Russia that occurred on President Obama's watch but that deteriorated somewhat more recently, while reducing the odds of future U.S.-China strategic nuclear competition. And he could lock in the very useful end to nuclear testing among the major powers that has enabled the international community to apply pressure on proliferating states such as Iran and North Korea.

Because Russia remains the other nuclear superpower, many of the key nuclear questions in the next presidential term will focus on the U.S.-Russian nuclear relationship. The yield—or destructive power—of each strategic nuclear warhead in the U.S. inventory today is six to as much as thirty times that of the atomic bomb that devastated Hiroshima in 1945. New START allows the United States and Russia each to maintain up to 1,550 deployed strategic warheads and up to 700 deployed strategic delivery vehicles—intercontinental ballistic missiles (ICBMs), submarine-launched ballistic missiles (SLBMs), and heavy bombers. With the dramatic changes that have taken place since the cold war, do the United States and Russia still need such large strategic forces? As the United States faces key modernization decisions, what kind of strategic forces does it want in the future? Should Washington attempt to negotiate further reductions in deployed warheads and delivery vehicles? If so, to what levels?

New START limits the number of deployed strategic warheads, that is, the warheads that physically sit atop deployed strategic ballistic missiles. But warheads that are held in reserve, referred to as nondeployed strategic warheads, and nonstrategic nuclear warheads fall under no constraints whatsoever. Indeed, New START limits only about 30 percent of the weapons in the current U.S. nuclear arsenal and a like or smaller percentage of the weapons in Russia's arsenal. American allies, particularly in Europe but also in Asia, would welcome reductions in Russian nonstrategic nuclear weapons. At the same time, some NATO allies question whether U.S. nonstrategic nuclear weapons must still be deployed in Europe to deter an attack on the Alliance. Should Washington try to constrain these weapons as well as the category of nondeployed strategic warheads? If so, how might arms control deal with these weapons?

Missile defense also will pose questions in 2013. U.S. policy going back to the early 1990s has been to defend the United States against *limited* ballistic missile attack. Moscow has expressed concerns that missile defense plans announced by the George W. Bush and Obama administrations could eventually degrade the Russian strategic nuclear deterrent. U.S. officials accept the interrelationship between offense and defense but argue that Russia currently has little ground for concern. The United States and NATO have suggested a cooperative NATO-Russian missile defense arrangement for Europe, but the Russians insist first on a legal guarantee that American missile defenses would not be directed against Russian strategic missiles. The Obama administration is unwilling to go there, understanding that the current Senate would refuse to consent to ratify anything that constrains missile defense. Will the sides be able to find a way around this impediment in 2013 and achieve a cooperative NATO-Russia arrangement? Or will missile defense pose a contentious issue on the agenda with Moscow that inhibits further nuclear reductions and undermines broader relations?

The nuclear questions go beyond the United States and Russia. Other issues that will face the president involve a wider spectrum of national actors.

The Comprehensive Nuclear Test Ban Treaty (CTBT) was signed by President Bill Clinton in 1996; the U.S. Senate debated it in 1999 but did not consent to ratification. China has not ratified the treaty either, although Britain, France, and Russia have. Going beyond previous bans on atmospheric testing and limits on the yield of weapons detonated underground, the CTBT would permanently prohibit all nuclear tests worldwide. The United States in any event has not conducted a nuclear test since 1992. Should the administration seek Senate consent to ratification of the treaty a second time? A verification system has been established that appears to make such a ban realistic; is that system sufficient to give the United States confidence that it could detect covert nuclear tests? Absent treaty ratification, does a continuation of the moratorium on nuclear testing observed by the five original nuclear powers (plus Israel) for a couple of decades still make sense for the United States? Are any changes needed in the means by which the U.S. Department of Energy, at its major weapons laboratories and other nuclear facilities, ensures the safety, effectiveness, and reliability of the American nuclear arsenal?

The United States and Russia are no longer producing highly enriched uranium or separated plutonium for nuclear weapons purposes. India and Pakistan are producing more fissile material; North Korea and Israel may be doing so in smaller quantities; and there is a modest amount of reprocessing of plutonium from the spent fuel of energy reactors in places like Japan. But with the superpowers out of the business of producing fissile material for weapons, it makes sense to ask if an accord could be reached to formalize and generalize the idea of cutting off the production of fissile materials. If a formal multilateral treaty regime cannot be established, would it be feasible to promote a moratorium—ideally not just on fissile material for weapons, but on all forms of fissile material, even those previously intended for commercial or scientific purposes?

As U.S. and Russian nuclear weapons inventories come down, two questions naturally arise. First, at what point does the arms control process potentially place the world on a serious trajectory toward zero (or very few) nuclear weapons, rather than simply constituting a continuation and extrapolation of classic arms control? Second, at what point must other countries be brought into the process so as not to create the potential for new arms races between one or more medium powers and the traditional nuclear superpowers, as the latter reduce their weapons holdings?

THE U.S. INTEREST IN NUCLEAR ARMS CONTROL

The president in 2013 will face a very busy agenda, with many issues, both domestic and foreign, competing for his attention. Why pursue further nuclear arms control when the cold war is more than twenty years in the past? Arms control is not and should not be considered an end in itself. It is a tool that, properly applied, can strengthen and enhance the security of the United States and America's allies. We believe that several reasons argue for going beyond the New START Treaty to pursue additional nuclear arms reduction steps that will make the United States and the American people safer and more secure.

First, the size of the Russian nuclear arsenal, even once New START's limits are fully met, will mean that Russia still retains the capability to physically destroy the United States several times over. No other country can do that. Much has changed since the end of the cold war and collapse of the Soviet Union, and the U.S.-Soviet nuclear showdown of the 1960s, 1970s, and 1980s is happily a thing of the past. A major Russian nuclear attack probably will not be placed high on the president's list of concerns. But, as a general proposition, we believe that the fewer the number of nuclear weapons that can strike the United States, the better America's security. Nuclear arms control offers a vehicle to achieve that.

Second, a stable nuclear balance is one in which neither side has a strong incentive to strike first in a crisis. The Russian military has begun developing a new heavy ICBM to carry multiple warheads. If Russia proceeds to deploy such a missile, it would sustain the threat to U.S. ICBMs in their silos that is now declining as older Russian SS-18 and SS-19 ICBMs are retired. In a crisis, a new heavy ICBM would pose an attractive target for U.S. attack, given the possibility of destroying many warheads by destroying one heavy ICBM. That development would not be healthy for strategic stability, even today. Further negotiated nuclear arms reductions that lowered the 1,550 limit on deployed strategic warheads could encourage Moscow not to go forward with a new heavy ICBM.

Third, with the exception of intermediate-range missiles, arms control has thus far left untouched nonstrategic nuclear weapons on both sides. Russia today maintains a sizable numerical advantage over the United States in these weapons. Although they generally lack the range to strike America, they pose a concern to U.S.

allies in Europe and Asia. NATO leaders have called for steps to reduce the Russian nonstrategic arsenal, as did the Senate during the debate on ratification of New START. Arms control offers a path to achieve that goal.

Fourth, a major benefit of arms control is increased transparency regarding the other side's military forces. New START, for example, requires a detailed data exchange, semiannual data updates, and notifications of changes regarding a side's strategic forces. The treaty also allows each side to conduct up to eighteen short-notice, on-site inspections a year of the other's strategic systems to check the data provided. This kind of transparency provides the U.S. intelligence community and military with a far better understanding of Russian strategic forces than would be possible with just national technical means—the euphemism for things such as surveillance satellites—by themselves. That allows the Defense Department to avoid worst-case assumptions and make smarter decisions regarding how to equip, staff, and operate U.S. strategic forces.

Fifth, strategic nuclear forces are expensive, and the United States is approaching the point when it must recapitalize all three legs of the strategic triad. In the coming years, the Defense Department will have to make decisions on a new ballistic missile submarine, a new ICBM, and a new heavy bomber. The new submarines may cost as much as $6 billion to $7 billion each, not counting the ballistic missiles, and the Pentagon seeks to cap the cost of a new heavy bomber at $550 million apiece. All of this comes at a time when growing concern about the federal budget deficit places enormous pressure on the U.S. defense budget. Arms control agreements that reduce the number of new strategic systems that must be built can free up scarce defense resources for operations that the U.S. military is far more likely to engage in than thermonuclear war.

Sixth, arms control and U.S. nuclear force reductions can bolster America's nonproliferation credentials. The United States and Russia between them maintain well over 90 percent of the nuclear weapons in the world. An active U.S. effort to reduce those stockpiles—an objective to which the United States is committed under the Non-Proliferation Treaty—will give Washington greater credibility in seeking to discourage nuclear proliferation. One should be realistic. A new U.S.-Russian nuclear arms treaty will not persuade Tehran or Pyongyang to alter course on nuclear weapons; Washington and its partners must pursue other strategies to achieve those goals. A new treaty—or other measures that produce further reductions in U.S. (and Russian) nuclear arsenals—would nonetheless strengthen the ability of U.S. diplomacy to secure third-country support to apply pressure against proliferation elsewhere, including against country X, the country after Iran that may consider attempting to acquire nuclear weapons.

Seventh, fewer nuclear weapons in the U.S. and Russian arsenals could reduce the risk that a weapon might be stolen or otherwise fall into the hands of a rogue state or nonstate actor.

Nuclear arms control has to be done in a smart way. It has to ensure that, as long as nuclear weapons exist, the United States maintains a secure, reliable, robust, resilient, and effective deterrent capable of preventing a nuclear attack on the United States, its allies, and partners, not just by Russia but by other potential nuclear adversaries. And arms control has to fit into the country's broader foreign and national security policies. With these caveats, it offers the president a potentially useful tool for strengthening U.S. security.

Let us address nuclear deterrence for a moment. We believe that, as long as nuclear weapons exist, the United States will require an effective nuclear deterrent. Nuclear deterrence played a key role during the cold war in preventing all-out conflict between the United States and Soviet Union, countries that opposed each other politically, ideologically, and militarily. Nuclear deterrence worked—with one major caveat: at several points, the world got lucky. For example, a Soviet attack on West Berlin, a different decision by President John Kennedy during the Cuban missile crisis, or a misreading of faulty computer alerts, such as the 1995 Russian misassessment of a Norwegian non-military rocket launch, could have plunged the world into a catastrophic thermonuclear nightmare.

Will we always be so lucky? That question, and concern about the growing number of states with nuclear weapons, some of whose governments are fragile and not necessarily predictable, leads us to conclude that working toward reducing and ultimately eliminating all nuclear weapons is a sensible goal. A world truly free of nuclear weapons could leave the United States—with friendly neighbors in Canada and Mexico, the protection offered by the Atlantic and Pacific Oceans, and the world's most powerful conventional forces—in a strong position. Washington would still need capabilities to extend deterrence to allies, but the end of nuclear weapons would not mean the end of deterrence, just the end of the nuclear component of it. U.S. conventional forces could threaten powerful punishment against a potential adversary.

We are realistic about this. Lots of things must happen: all nuclear weapons states must join in the reductions process; new verification methodologies must be developed and agreed; and, most important, progress must be made in resolving the underlying conflicts that motivate states to have nuclear weapons. Means of reconstituting an arsenal in extremis need to be explored, too. While it is far too soon to know if nuclear zero will someday be feasible, it is not too soon to take interim steps that could help clarify the choices. Carefully designed nuclear arms control steps can move us in that direction and improve U.S. security, even if the ultimate objective remains elusive.

As for nuclear deterrence in the meantime, we support the idea of making the circumstances in which the United States might resort to use of nuclear weapons more predictable and circumscribed. Ideally, the overarching purpose of nuclear weapons should be to deter a *nuclear* attack on the United States, its allies, and friends.

CHOICES FOR THE PRESIDENT

President Obama's views on nuclear arms control are well known. In an April 2009 speech in Prague, he laid out a vision of a world free of nuclear weapons and called for reducing the role and number of nuclear arms in U.S. security policy. At the same time, he made clear that, as long as nuclear weapons exist, the United States would maintain a reliable and effective nuclear deterrent. In April 2010, the administration issued its nuclear posture review, which codified the policy of seeking to reduce the number and role of nuclear weapons and specified an objective of creating conditions in which the sole purpose of U.S. nuclear weapons would be to deter nuclear attack on the United States, its allies, and partners.

Shortly after signing the New START Treaty with Medvedev, Obama called for further negotiated reductions with Russia. In addition to deployed strategic warheads, he suggested that future negotiations address nondeployed strategic warheads and nonstrategic nuclear weapons—raising the possibility that, for the first time, the United States and Russia might negotiate on the full range of weapons in their nuclear arsenals. He has also expressed support for ratification of the CTBT. If Obama is reelected, there is every reason to expect that his administration will pursue further steps in the area of nuclear arms control.

The GOP challenger, Mitt Romney, has taken a generally negative view of nuclear arms control and criticized New START in particular. His views reflect a broader skepticism among many Republicans about the value of negotiated limits on nuclear weapons, which the 2010 Senate debate over New START displayed vividly. A Romney presidency would likely bring to office that kind of wariness toward arms control. Several reasons, however, might move a Republican administration to consider efforts in this area.

First, the intense pressure on the defense budget may affect the resources available for strategic modernization. No one in the Defense Department believes that the current force of 400-plus Minuteman ICBMs will be replaced on a one-for-one basis. When Congress in 2011 asked the Pentagon to report on possible future ballistic missile submarine plans, it asked for options for a force of eight, ten, and twelve submarines, not the fourteen currently maintained by the U.S. Navy. Political pressure for reduced defense spending very likely will mean fewer resources and a smaller U.S. strategic force in the future. That could raise the value of an arms control agreement capping the Russian strategic force at a lower level.

Second, there is strong support in Congress for reducing the Russian numerical advantage in nonstrategic nuclear weapons. Indeed, the Senate resolution of ratification for New START called on the president to initiate within one year negotiations with Russia aimed at cutting that disparity. Romney himself criticized the treaty for not addressing nonstrategic nuclear weapons. Although most analysts anticipate some reduction in the number of Russian nonstrategic nuclear arms, because they are being replaced at a less than one-for-one rate, Moscow can still maintain a sizable advantage. Arms control could address that imbalance.

Third, a Republican administration might face a need to pursue arms control for alliance management purposes. NATO allies today are divided over whether deterrence requires the deployment of U.S. B61 nuclear gravity bombs in Europe. Some allies, such as Belgium, Germany, the Netherlands, and Norway, do not regard those weapons as necessary given the end of the cold war and the sweeping changes in the European geopolitical environment of the past twenty years. Those countries nevertheless are working with Washington and other allies that support the presence of American nuclear bombs to maintain a consensus position on NATO's nuclear posture. Keeping them on board—and away from unilateral action—has been easier because they recognize the Obama administration's desire to negotiate a reduction in nonstrategic nuclear weapons with Russia. Keeping allies on board would likely become more difficult if they concluded that Washington was not interested in negotiating reductions.

The need for Washington to pursue arms control in order to maintain consensus on NATO's nuclear position has an antecedent. When Ronald Reagan took office in January 1981, he wanted to redress what he considered to be dangerous trends in the nuclear balance against the United States. He was not especially interested in early negotiations with the Soviets on reducing nuclear arms. Yet by the end of the year, his negotiating team sat in Geneva to begin talks on reducing intermediate-range nuclear forces because the need to maintain the support of NATO allies for the 1979 "dual-track" decision demanded it.

Likewise, while NATO allies support U.S. missile defense plans for Europe, most also support the idea of a cooperative NATO-Russia missile defense arrangement. But allies do not want to see missile defense become a new point of contention with Russia and thus want Washington to explore a reasonable cooperative arrangement.

We are completing this book in the summer of 2012, six months before the next president is inaugurated. Even after the election is decided, however, the questions posed in these chapters will remain relevant. In our judgment, President Obama supports further nuclear arms reductions, and, if reelected, his administration would probably address many of the issues raised in the following chapters. It would do so while having to deal with Republicans in Congress who likely would remain skeptical about nuclear arms control. If Governor Romney is elected, he might find that arms control or alliance considerations lead him to address at least some of the same issues. And he might find that Democrats plus those in Congress pushing for deep budget cuts, including in the defense budget, would want to see continued arms control efforts.

THIS BOOK'S SCOPE

This book explores some of the key questions that the president in 2013 must consider regarding nuclear arms control. Our goal is to lay out the issues squarely, in a way that will inform the debate about future arms control questions, regardless of whether the next American president is named Obama or Romney, and to offer our recommendations on the next steps on nuclear arms reductions.

The book begins by examining past and current nuclear policy—the context in which any future negotiations will be set. It then focuses on possible steps to reduce and control strategic nuclear forces beyond those in New START and looks at ways to handle the nonstrategic nuclear weapons and missile defense issues. The book next discusses issues associated with the Comprehensive Nuclear Test Ban Treaty, questions surrounding a possible ban on the production of fissile material, and the potential for the multilateralization of the nuclear arms reduction process. The final chapter recaps our recommendations and describes how decisions and actions taken by the U.S. administration in 2013–17 could shape a safer and more secure world and perhaps open the prospect for a broader nuclear arms reductions process.

Our focus is first and foremost on decisions, treaties, and certain informal arms control steps that directly impinge upon American nuclear forces. To maintain that focus, we have purposefully chosen to omit some issues. The complex questions of how to handle today's major nuclear proliferation challenges—Iran and North Korea—are left to other analyses. Crisis management in regard to specific countries is not our focus, nor are the broader Nuclear Non-Proliferation Treaty and international export control regimes in sensitive nuclear-related technologies. Likewise, we do not address the nightmare scenario of a terrorist group gaining access to nuclear weapons or fissile materials. We have also chosen not to address the challenges of conventional arms control, particularly the fate of the Conventional Armed Forces in Europe Treaty regime, even though many analysts believe that decisions regarding nonstrategic nuclear weapons are linked to those relating to the conventional force balance. For example, many Russians suggest that, given Russia's conventional force disadvantages compared with the United States, NATO, or China, it must rely more on nonstrategic nuclear weapons. We note this possible linkage, but resolution of the many questions related to conventional arms control is beyond the scope of this book.

CHAPTER TWO

U.S. NUCLEAR POLICIES AND FORCES

THE UNITED STATES used nuclear weapons to bring an end to World War II with Japan. Nuclear weapons and nuclear deterrence subsequently formed a key foundation for U.S. security policy starting in the early 1950s, when substantial numbers of these weapons began to be introduced into the arsenal. Deterrence requires persuading a potential adversary that the risks and likely costs of aggression far outweigh any benefits that it might hope to achieve. U.S. strategists recognized early on that nuclear weapons posed great risks and massive potential costs.

NUCLEAR DETERRENCE DURING THE COLD WAR

In the aftermath of the Korean War, President Dwight D. Eisenhower sought to restrain defense spending and avoid competing with the Soviet Union in conventional forces—a race that neither the president nor the newly formed NATO Alliance wished to run. The Eisenhower administration chose to rely on its rapidly growing nuclear capability and advantage over the Soviet Union and, in January 1954, announced a policy of "massive retaliation," the main focus being to deter a Soviet attack on Western Europe. Secretary of State John Foster Dulles described the central tenet of the policy as "a great capacity to retaliate, instantly, by means and at places of our own choosing." As one author later put it, Dulles did not necessarily intend a large-scale use of nuclear arms for every aggression that might occur: "The important thing was to have the capacity to retaliate massively, because that would be the only fitting punishment to the greatest crime—an all-out attack on Western Europe. For lesser crimes, a more appropriate retaliation could be found. Dulles was thus talking about 'flexible retaliation.' This suggested a continuum of nuclear responses. . . ."[1]

The Eisenhower administration moved forward with building a nuclear force structure to support this doctrine, increasing the U.S. nuclear arsenal from 1,169 weapons in 1953 to 22,229 in 1961.[2] It deployed nuclear-capable aircraft such as the B-47 bomber to forward bases in Europe and North Africa, from where they could strike the Soviet Union, as well as a large number of tactical nuclear weapons on the territory of NATO members. The Defense Department also pursued true intercontinental strike capabilities, including the B-52 bomber, and intercontinental and submarine-launched ballistic missiles.

Questions quickly arose, however, about the credibility of the massive retaliation doctrine. Would Washington really respond to a relatively limited attack with massive use of nuclear arms? As the Soviet Union acquired its own intercontinental capabilities to strike the United States, would U.S. threats to use nuclear weapons remain credible?

These questions faced John F. Kennedy when he became president in 1961. The United States enjoyed a numerical advantage in long-range bombers and, with deployment of the Minuteman ICBM and Polaris SLBM, a ballistic missile advantage as well, but the Kennedy administration recognized that the Soviets had embarked on their own strategic nuclear buildup. The larger the Soviet strategic forces, the greater the doubts about the credibility of massive retaliation, especially for deterring a conventional invasion in Europe.

The Kennedy administration thus explicitly jettisoned the massive retaliation policy. Secretary of Defense Robert McNamara sought more flexible options that would concentrate on striking Soviet military forces and avoid cities. But doubts arose about the ability to control a conflict once nuclear weapons had been used, and McNamara became increasingly concerned about the costs of U.S. nuclear forces, particularly in an arms race with the Soviet Union. He shifted course and in 1964 introduced the term "assured destruction." He calculated that the U.S. ability to destroy 20–33 percent of the Soviet population and 50–75 percent of its industrial base would suffice to deter a Soviet attack on the United States.[3] He foresaw that, as Soviet strategic forces grew, the United States and Soviet Union would each have the capability to inflict enormous nuclear devastation on the other, even after having absorbed a first strike. This concept came to be described as mutual assured destruction (MAD).

The Kennedy administration also grappled with the more challenging task of extended deterrence. Assured destruction might well provide a credible deterrent against a Soviet attack on the United States. Whether it would deter the Soviets from attacking U.S. allies in Europe and Asia was less clear.

Washington discussed with NATO allies the possibility of providing U.S. nuclear-armed SLBMs that would be placed on ships or submarines operated by multinational NATO crews. This "multilateral nuclear force," which would have constituted a NATO deterrent, attracted interest in Europe, but the idea soon faded. Instead, under "programs of cooperation," the United States maintained nonstrategic nuclear weapons in Europe that in a conflict could be turned over to allies for use on their delivery systems (sometimes referred to as "dual-key" systems).

Ultimately, in 1967, NATO adopted the U.S. concept of "flexible response," which called on NATO commanders to "provide for the employment as appropriate of one or more of direct defense, deliberate escalation, and general nuclear response, thus confronting an enemy with a credible threat of escalation in response to any type of aggression below the level of a major nuclear attack."[4]

Flexible response aimed to give NATO military commanders a continuum of response options: conventional forces, Europe-based theater nuclear weapons, and—if all else failed—large-scale attack with U.S. (and British) strategic nuclear forces. Flexible response remained the basic NATO nuclear policy through the end of the cold war.

By the early 1970s, the United States deployed a mature mix of ICBMs, SLBMs, and intercontinental bombers—the strategic triad—and the Soviet Union was catching up by building its own triad. The two countries had also completed the first Strategic Arms Limitation Treaty (SALT) process in 1972. The negotiation resulted in two agreements. The Interim Offensive Arms Agreement capped the number of U.S. and Soviet strategic ballistic missile launchers at the numbers then deployed or under construction, and the Anti-Ballistic Missile (ABM) Treaty banned nationwide ballistic missile defenses and limited interceptor launchers and radars. By constraining both sides' missile defenses so that they could easily be overwhelmed by the strategic ballistic missile forces of the other, the SALT process appeared to fix MAD as a strategic reality (these treaties and other arms control agreements are discussed in greater detail in later chapters and in appendix A). The pairing of the two treaties reflected the interrelationship between offense and defense (table 2-1 shows operational strategic offensive forces in 1974).

The combination of the Interim Offensive Arms Agreement and ABM Treaty was seen by the Nixon administration and by many, but by no means all, analysts as contributing to strategic stability— a term that first emerged at this point—between the United States and Soviet Union. Improvements in survivable command and control, while they lagged the existing deployments of a survivable triad, ultimately added further confidence as well. Strategic stability had two components. First, crisis stability referred to a situation in which neither side had strong incentives to initiate use of nuclear weapons in a crisis, because the other side, even if it absorbed a first strike, would still be able to retaliate with a devastating

TABLE 2-1. Operational U.S. and Soviet Strategic Offensive Forces, 1974

	United States	Soviet Union
ICBM launchers	1,054	1,367
SLBM launchers	656	679
Intercontinental bombers	496	157

Sources: U.S. numbers from Thomas H. Wolfe, *The SALT Experience* (Cambridge, Mass.: Ballinger Publishing Company, 1979), p. 97. Russian numbers from National Resources Defense Council, Archive of Nuclear Data, "Table of USSR/Russian ICBM Forces" (www.nrdc.org/nuclear/nudb/datab4.asp#seventy); "Table of USSR/Russian Submarine Ballistic Missile Forces" (www.nrdc.org/nuclear/nudb/datab6.asp /); and "Table of USSR/Russian Strategic Bomber Forces" (www.nrdc.org/nuclear/nudb/datab8.asp).

response. The ABM Treaty constrained U.S. and Soviet missile defenses so tightly that each could be certain of its ability to devastate the other in a retaliatory strike. Second, arms race stability referred to a situation in which neither side had strong incentives to build up its forces. While both the United States and Soviet Union increased their strategic warhead numbers following SALT I (discussed below), this buildup was motivated largely by reasons other than a need to overwhelm a large ABM defense of the other side.

After having reached a peak of more than 31,000 in 1967, the number of nuclear weapons in the U.S. arsenal declined slightly, as older and less usable weapons were retired while the ICBM and SLBM force expanded and became more capable. As strategic nuclear capabilities grew, questions arose as to how they might be used. A key question was which targeting priorities should be incorporated in the highly classified Single Integrated Operational Plan (SIOP), the document that would guide the employment of the strategic triad should deterrence fail and nuclear war break out.

Two policy options defined the ends of a spectrum. One, to target a limited number of weapons at an adversary's cities and industrial targets, was referred to as a "countervalue" or "countercity" strategy. That option posed the most horrific potential costs to an adversary, but it raised ethical questions: Was attacking civilian populations the right way to respond if nuclear deterrence failed?

Would it in every case offer the most credible deterrent threat, including against a limited attack? Attacking Soviet cities, moreover, would almost invariably lead to nuclear strikes on American cities (had they not already been struck in an earlier attack).

At the opposite end of the spectrum was a "counterforce" strategy—to target strategic nuclear weapons at the adversary's strategic nuclear forces and their command and control systems (and perhaps the adversary's nonstrategic nuclear weapons systems and conventional armed forces as well). This option posed a more challenging task than a countervalue strategy. Cities provided large, fixed, "soft" targets, but both the United States and Soviet Union deployed ICBMs in hardened underground silos. Destroying them would require very accurate and large nuclear warheads. Other military forces were difficult to strike because of their mobility. The task of locating and attacking ballistic missile submarines hiding within the world's oceans was daunting, a reason why the United States chose to base so many of its strategic weapons on submarines.

The Nixon administration worried about the credibility of a nuclear deterrent based largely on the threat of countervalue retaliation. In a February 1970 report, Nixon asked, "Should a president in the event of a nuclear attack be left with the single option of ordering the mass destruction of enemy civilians, in the face of the certainty that it would be followed by the mass slaughter of Americans?"[5] Under the president's direction, James Schlesinger, who became secretary of defense in 1973, favored creating more options, including options for limited and selective nuclear strikes. According to one author, Schlesinger sought a nuclear policy that would have a wide range of nuclear options, "from the very small to the very large, and . . . the bias was on the development of the smaller strikes, which were to be counterforce rather than counter-city in character."[6] The Nixon administration believed that having such options would enhance the U.S. ability to deter a Soviet attack (or an attack by others, for that matter). In this sense, it followed in the steps of strategists going back to McNamara in seeking to incorporate more discriminating options in the SIOP.[7] The options also included means of targeting Warsaw Pact conventional military forces.

In reality, U.S. strategy postulated attacks against both countervalue and counterforce targets. The Joint Strategic Operations Plan for fiscal years 1969–77, prepared in 1968, instructed the Strategic Air Command to be able to "inflict unacceptable damage upon the war-supporting and urban-industrial resources of the enemy" and to be capable of "destroying a comprehensive military target system" and "limiting damage to the United States and its allies."[8] The 1974 "Policy Guidance for the Employment of Nuclear Weapons" laid out three main objectives: deterrence, escalation control (should deterrence fail), and general war. In the latter case, the U.S. goals were "destruction of those political, economic, and military resources critical to the enemy's post-war power and influence," "limitation of damage to the United States and its allies," and "maintaining a strategic force in reserve."[9]

Increasing numbers of strategic weapons made possible the wider options that Schlesinger desired. Although SALT capped the number of ICBM and SLBM launchers, the introduction of multiple independently targeted reentry vehicles (MIRVs) gave the U.S. military the capability to arm strategic ballistic missiles with multiple reentry vehicles (or warheads) that could strike different targets.[10] In part because putting MIRVs on missiles was relatively inexpensive, the number of U.S. strategic ballistic missile warheads dramatically increased in the early 1970s. The Soviets lagged five to seven years behind in MIRVing their ballistic missiles, but by the second half of the 1970s, they were rapidly increasing their warhead numbers as well. The United States also began developing air-launched cruise missiles (ALCMs) that could be deployed on its heavy bombers. These missiles effectively extended the range of the bomber and could be launched against heavily defended targets that the bombers themselves might not be able to reach. The Soviets also later equipped their heavy bomber force with ALCMs.

Some Soviet strategic systems gave U.S. military planners special concern. U.S. planners feared that the warheads on missiles such as the Soviet SS-19 ICBM and SS-18 heavy ICBM might be powerful and accurate enough to attack and destroy Minuteman ICBMs in their underground silos before they could be launched. For their part, Soviet military planners not too much later began to worry about the improving accuracy of U.S. strategic ballistic missile warheads, which enhanced the chances of Soviet ICBMs being destroyed in their silos, even with less powerful warheads than those deployed on Soviet missiles.

Harold Brown succeeded Schlesinger as secretary of defense when the Carter administration took office in 1977. He developed a "countervailing" strategy as the basis for strategic deterrence policy, the essence of which was to hold at risk those targets of greatest value in the view of the adversary's leadership. This approach led to placing greater priority on targeting the Soviet military and its command structure, as well as the structures through which the Kremlin maintained political control of the Soviet state. Many analysts saw this policy as moving toward a war-fighting concept and as mirroring what was believed to be Soviet policy and its focus on prevailing should a nuclear conflict occur. After a tortured debate over how to base the new MX ICBM to make it survivable against a possible Soviet strike, the Carter administration approved its deployment in silos. The missile could carry ten powerful and highly accurate warheads and enhanced the U.S. capability for striking Soviet ICBMs, including the SS-18, in their hardened silos. The Carter administration also agreed with NATO on the "dual-track" decision to deploy U.S. intermediate-range nuclear missiles in Europe while seeking negotiations with the Soviets on limiting such systems (discussed further in chapter 4).

President Carter and Soviet General Secretary Leonid Brezhnev concluded the SALT II Treaty in 1979, which constrained the United States and the Soviet Union to no more than 2,250 strategic nuclear delivery vehicles—ICBM launchers, SLBM launchers, and

TABLE 2-2. U.S. and Soviet Strategic Offensive Launchers, 1979

	United States	Soviet Union
ICBM launchers	1,054	1,398
MIRVed ICBM launchers	550	608
SLBM launchers	656	950
MIRVed SLBM launchers	496	144
Heavy bombers	573	156
Heavy bombers equipped to carry ALCMs	3	0

Source: U.S. and Soviet "Statement on Data on the Numbers of Strategic Offensive Forces as of the Date of the Signature of the Treaty," June 18, 1979.

intercontinental bombers (table 2-2 shows the strategic balance in 1979). After the Soviet Union invaded Afghanistan, however, the treaty ran into opposition in the U.S. Senate and was never ratified.

Ronald Reagan took office in 1981 believing that the Soviet Union had gained strategic advantages over the United States and determined to respond. He reversed the Carter administration's decision to cancel the B-1 strategic bomber, and he accelerated deployment of the MX missile in fixed silos, choosing to abandon more survivable mobile basing modes. The Reagan administration largely kept in place its predecessor's countervailing strategy, including targeting of the Soviet command structure, both military and political. The SIOP in the 1980s reportedly included some 50,000 designated ground zeros, or individual aim points for nuclear weapons (some targets, such as cities, contained multiple designated ground zeros).

Once in office, Reagan was distressed to find that the United States lacked even a minimal capability to defend against attacking Soviet ICBMs and SLBMs. He challenged the idea of nuclear deterrence and, in March 1983, launched the Strategic Defense Initiative (SDI), asking, "What if free people could live secure in the knowledge that their security did not rest upon the threat of instant U.S. retaliation to deter a Soviet attack, that we could intercept and destroy strategic ballistic missiles before they reached our own soil or that of our allies?"[11]

The Reagan administration invested substantial sums of money in SDI, exploring a variety of technologies to solve the challenge of protecting the United States against any—including a large-scale—ballistic missile attack. That effort, combined with the modernization of elements of U.S. strategic offensive forces, provoked deep concern in the Soviet Union that the U.S. military sought the capability to strike at Soviet nuclear forces and then defend effectively against a Soviet retaliatory attack. By 1986–87, however, the Soviets, while still concerned about U.S. missile defense efforts, recognized the difficult technical challenges and became less anxious about SDI.

In his second term, Reagan took a greater interest in arms control, in large part because he found a willing partner in Soviet leader Mikhail Gorbachev. Their October 1986 Reykjavik summit laid a foundation for their 1987 signing of the Intermediate-Range Nuclear Forces (INF) Treaty, which banned all U.S. and Soviet ground-launched INF missiles. The summit also produced major progress on a Strategic Arms Reduction Treaty (later referred to as START I), which President George H. W. Bush signed with Gorbachev in 1991. The provisions of START I required the United States and Russia to reduce their forces to no more than 1,600 strategic nuclear delivery vehicles capable of carrying no more than 6,000 accountable warheads (table 2-3 shows the START I–accountable forces in 1990). That meant substantial reductions on both sides, an unprecedented accomplishment even if the remaining arsenals would still retain the capacity to cause horrific damage far exceeding even the combined effects of all violence in World War II.

THE END OF THE COLD WAR

Bush and Gorbachev signed START I just before the Soviet Union collapsed at the end of 1991. In 1991 and 1992, the Bush administration announced a series of presidential nuclear initiatives, which

TABLE 2-3. U.S. and Soviet START I—Accountable Strategic Offensive Forces, 1990

	United States	Soviet Union
Deployed ICBM launchers	1,000	1,398
Warheads attributed to ICBM launchers	2,450	6,612
Deployed SLBM launchers	672	940
Warheads attributed to SLBM launchers	5,760	2,804
Deployed heavy bombers	574	162
Warheads attributed to heavy bombers	2,353	855
Total launchers and bombers	2,246	2,500
Total warheads attributed to launchers and bombers	10,563	10,271

Source: Data from the "Memorandum of Understanding on the Establishment of the Data Base Relating to the Treaty between the United States of America and the Union of Soviet Socialist Republics on the Reduction and Limitation of Strategic Offensive Arms" (http://dtirp.dtra.mil/tic/START/st_mou.htm).

accelerated implementation of some START I reductions and eliminated thousands of nonstrategic nuclear weapons—motivated in large part by a desire to encourage Russia to reduce and securely consolidate the former Soviet nuclear arsenal. Those initiatives included dismantlement of all nuclear artillery shells and nuclear warheads for short-range missiles and the removal of all nonstrategic nuclear weapons from U.S. Navy ships during normal peacetime circumstances. Largely as a result of these initiatives and implementation of the INF and START I treaties, the total U.S. nuclear stockpile declined from more than 21,000 weapons in 1990 to just under 11,000 weapons in 1994.[12] Russia reciprocated with a set of its own initiatives, which resulted in dramatic reductions in the Russian nuclear stockpile as well.

With the dissolution of the Soviet Union and the end of the cold war, public talk of countervalue, counterforce, and countervailing strategies in the United States largely subsided. Bill Clinton became president in 1993, and his administration conducted a nuclear posture review, the first in fifteen years. While placing importance on nuclear arms cuts, the review also cited "great uncertainty about the future," including about future developments in Russia, and the need to "hedge" against that uncertainty. It stated: "Two basic requirements necessarily guide U.S. planning for strategic nuclear forces: the need to provide an effective deterrent while remaining within START I/II limits, and the need to allow for additional forces to be reconstituted in the event of a reversal of currently positive trends."[13] The review also stressed the importance of dissuading other powers from seeking to obtain a nuclear advantage over the United States.

In January 1994, Clinton and President Boris Yeltsin, Gorbachev's successor, agreed that by May 30 neither country would target its strategic nuclear missiles at any country. While a useful step for improved atmospherics and in the event of an accidental launch, Defense Department officials quietly conceded that programming targets back into the missiles would be a relatively rapid process. The Clinton administration began implementation of the START I Treaty following its entry into force in December 1994, making decisions such as the one to remove the MX ICBM from the force, and secured ratification of the START II Treaty, although it never entered into force.

President George W. Bush took office in January 2001 and had a nuclear posture review conducted during his first year. Delivered to Congress at the end of 2001, the review announced a "major change in our approach to the role of nuclear offensive forces in our deterrent strategy." The report stated that the United States would no longer size its nuclear forces to those of Russia—the nearest peer competitor—but would instead shift to a "capabilities-based" approach. It described a new strategic triad, composed of "offensive strike systems (both nuclear and non-nuclear); defenses (both active and passive); and a revitalized defense infrastructure." It laid out four objectives: assure allies of the U.S. commitment to their security, dissuade competition in nuclear weapons, deter adversaries from attacking, and defeat the enemy should war occur.[14]

The nuclear posture review said the United States would move to maintain 1,700–2,200 operationally deployed strategic nuclear warheads, regardless of what other countries did with their nuclear forces. Russia's president, Vladimir Putin, sought a new strategic arms agreement, and in May 2002, Bush and Putin signed the Strategic Offensive Reductions Treaty (SORT), which limited each side to no more than 1,700–2,200 operationally deployed strategic warheads. Unlike previous accords, however, this agreement was minimalist in its stipulations and details, fitting in its entirety on two pages. One implication was that ongoing verification provisions were based on the START legacy rather than on any language in the SORT Treaty.

The Bush administration—like that of Bush's father—oversaw a major reduction of U.S. nuclear arms in the inventory, although the rate of dismantlement of old nuclear weapons slowed significantly. The U.S. nuclear stockpile, not counting weapons in the queue for dismantlement, declined from over 10,500 total weapons in 2000 to 5,113 in September 2009.[15] As part of this reduction, the Bush administration implemented the Clinton administration's decision to retire MX ICBMs and converted four of the U.S. Navy's eighteen Ohio-class ballistic missile submarines to carry only conventionally armed sea-launched cruise missiles and to provide support to Navy special operations forces.

While reducing the numbers of nuclear weapons, the Bush administration did explore new nuclear capabilities. It sought to develop the Robust Nuclear Earth Penetrator to destroy deeply buried targets. Congress, however, declined to fund the program, with many members fearing that it might make nuclear weapons more usable.

Given the aging of the weapons in the U.S. stockpile, the administration in 2005 also explored the possibility of building a Reliable Replacement Warhead. Secretary of Energy Samuel Bodman described the rationale:

It will be necessary to have the capability to replace most of the components in the weapons in the present stockpile. Therefore, we are beginning a program to understand whether, if we relaxed some of the warhead design constraints imposed on cold war systems (e.g., high yield to weight ratios), we could provide components for existing stockpile weapons that could be more easily manufactured and whose safety and reliability could be certified with assured high confidence, without nuclear testing.[16]

Congress, however, showed little enthusiasm. Some feared that the administration might use it as cover to develop new nuclear weapons capabilities.

The Bush administration also explored the possibility of quickly striking targets at long range with conventional weapons. It considered equipping two Trident SLBMs on each ballistic missile submarine with conventional warheads as part of the Conventional Trident Modernization Program, taking advantage of the increasing accuracy of the Trident II D5 missile. Armed with a conventional warhead or perhaps no explosive of any kind—the energy generated by the impact of an SLBM warhead traveling at more than 5 kilometers a second would be significant—the conventional Trident could hit targets 7,000–11,000 kilometers away in under thirty minutes. Congress did not support the program, in part out of concern that the Russians would not be able to tell the launch of a conventionally armed Trident from one carrying nuclear warheads.

Perhaps the most dramatic strategic policy move by the Bush administration was its decision to withdraw from the ABM Treaty, which it did in June 2002 after giving six months' notice in December 2001. Bush administration officials argued that, with the end of the cold war, the treaty and the offense-defense relationship that it codified no longer made sense. They worried about the potential of states such as North Korea and Iran to acquire ICBMs capable of reaching the United States and did not want to be constrained from deploying some capability to defend against that threat. In 2004, deployment of ground-based interceptors (GBIs) designed to defend the United States against rudimentary ICBMs began in Alaska and California—carrying forward a program that the Clinton administration had initiated but never actually decided to build. By 2012, thirty GBIs were in place.

Toward the end of Bush's second term, the question of the expiration of the START I Treaty arose. U.S. officials sought to negotiate with the Russians something to succeed START I, but the sides could not find agreement before the Bush administration left office in January 2009, particularly as the overall relationship deteriorated starting in 2006.

THE OBAMA ADMINISTRATION'S NUCLEAR POLICY

As part of his effort to "reset" relations with Russia, which had plummeted to a post–cold war low following the Russia-Georgia conflict in 2008, President Barack Obama approved a new arms control approach that would limit both strategic warheads and strategic delivery vehicles in negotiations on a new treaty, which he announced with Russian President Dmitry Medvedev in April 2009. Speaking a few days later in Prague, Obama outlined his objectives regarding nuclear weapons:

> So today, I state clearly and with conviction America's commitment to seek the peace and security of a world without nuclear weapons. I'm not naive. This goal will not be reached quickly—perhaps not in my lifetime. It will take patience and persistence. . . . To put an end to Cold War thinking, we will reduce the role of nuclear weapons in our national security strategy, and urge others to do the same. Make no mistake: As long as these weapons exist, the United States will maintain a safe, secure, and effective arsenal to deter any adversary, and guarantee that defense to our allies. . . . But we will begin the work of reducing our arsenal.[17]

TABLE 2-4. U.S. and Russian START I-Accountable Strategic Offensive Forces, July 2009

	United States	Russia
Deployed ICBM launchers	550	465
Warheads attributed to ICBM launchers	1,600	2,001
Deployed SLBM launchers	432	268
Warheads attributed to SLBM launchers	3,264	1,288
Deployed heavy bombers	206	76
Warheads attributed to heavy bombers	1,052	608
Total launchers and bombers	1,188	796
Total warheads attributed to launchers and bombers	5,916	3,897

Sources: Department of State Fact Sheet, "START Aggregate Numbers of Strategic Offensive Arms (as of July 1, 2009), as compiled from individual data submissions of the Parties."

Note: The START I counting rules significantly overstated the total numbers of U.S. and Russian strategic offensive forces, for three reasons. First, a number of ICBM silos and SLBM launch tubes were empty but had not been eliminated according to START I's procedures, so they still counted as carrying ICBMs and SLBMs with their attributed warheads. Second, four U.S. ballistic missile submarines had been converted to carry conventionally armed sea-launched cruise missiles, and a number of U.S. B-1 bombers had been converted to carry conventional weapons only, but these systems continued to count under START I rules. Third, most U.S. ICBMs and SLBMs carried fewer warheads than the numbers attributed to them. On the other hand, START I undercounted the number of bomber weapons.

U.S.-Russian negotiations soon got under way. During their July 2009 Moscow summit, Obama and Medvedev issued a joint statement outlining the parameters for what later became known as the New START Treaty. At just about the same time, the sides conducted the last data exchange required by the START I Treaty before its expiration (table 2-4).

The U.S. government also began work on a new nuclear posture review. At the time, the U.S. strategic war plan—Operations Plan 8010, formerly referred to as the SIOP—was based on guidance issued during the Bush administration and reportedly held strike plans focusing on Russia and China but also addressing North Korea, Iran, Syria, and a response to an attack by some other actor using weapons of mass destruction.[18] The Obama administration did early work in the context of its review to prepare a position for the New START negotiations in 2009, but the final review was not completed and released until April 2010.[19]

Released as an unclassified document, the nuclear posture review stated that as long as nuclear weapons exist, the United States would maintain a nuclear deterrent that was safe, secure, and effective. It articulated four other objectives for U.S. policy: "preventing nuclear proliferation and nuclear terrorism; reducing the role of U.S. nuclear weapons in U.S. national security strategy; maintaining strategic deterrence and stability at reduced nuclear force levels; [and] strengthening regional deterrence and reassuring U.S. allies and partners."

The review said that the "fundamental" role of U.S. nuclear weapons was "to deter attack on the United States, our allies, and partners." It set the goal of creating the conditions in which the "sole" purpose of U.S. nuclear forces would be to deter nuclear attack but noted that, for the time being, there was "a narrow range of circumstances" in which nuclear weapons could be useful in deterring a conventional, chemical, or biological attack by a state possessing nuclear arms.

The review announced a modified "negative security assurance": the United States would "not use or threaten to use nuclear weapons against non-nuclear weapons states that are party to the Nuclear Non-Proliferation Treaty (NPT) and in compliance with their nuclear nonproliferation obligations." The new assurance meant that the United States would not respond with nuclear weapons to an attack by a non-nuclear weapons state in compliance with its NPT obligations, even if the attack involved the use of chemical or biological weapons, but the United States could instead inflict a "devastating conventional military response." Some criticized this change in policy for reducing the deterrent effect of U.S. nuclear weapons against other kinds of weapons of mass destruction.

The nuclear posture review also outlined the strategic forces that the United States would maintain under the New START Treaty. Signed the same week that the review was released, New START limited the United States and Russia each to no more than 700 deployed ICBMs, SLBMs, and heavy bombers; no more than 1,550 deployed strategic warheads; and no more than 800 deployed and nondeployed ICBM and SLBM launchers plus heavy bombers. The review noted that U.S. strategic forces in 2010 consisted of 14 Trident ballistic missile submarines, each with 24 SLBM launch tubes; 450 Minuteman III ICBMs; and 76 B-52H and 18 B-2 heavy bombers that were equipped to carry nuclear weapons. The report added that, once the New START limits were fully implemented, the United States would maintain a strategic triad, including:

—A total of 240 deployed SLBMs (20 missiles on 12 Trident ballistic missile submarines, with two other submarines normally in long-term maintenance and carrying no missiles). The 240 deployed SLBMs could carry up to 1,090 warheads.

—Up to 420 deployed Minuteman ICBMs, each carrying a single warhead.

—Up to 60 deployed heavy bombers, each of which would count as one warhead under the New START deployed strategic warhead limit, regardless of how many weapons the bombers might carry.

Together, these total 720 deployed strategic delivery vehicles. As of July 2012, the Defense Department had yet to decide on how to draw down to 700, which would require reducing 20 ICBMs or bombers, or a combination of both.

With regard to nonstrategic nuclear weapons—sometimes referred to as tactical or substrategic nuclear weapons—the nuclear posture review stated that the warheads that had been kept in storage for sea-launched cruise missiles would be retired and placed in the queue for dismantlement. That would leave the B61 gravity bomb as the only nonstrategic nuclear weapon in the U.S. arsenal. The review said that the F-35 Joint Strike Fighter would be given the capability to deliver nuclear as well as conventional weapons, ensuring that the U.S. Air Force maintained a dual-capable fighter-bomber after the retirement of the F-15 and F-16. To strengthen regional deterrence, the Air Force would retain the ability to forward deploy F-15s, F-16s, F-35s, B-2s, and B-52Hs, if necessary.

The nuclear posture review indicated that, as a matter of policy, the United States would not develop new nuclear warheads and would not improve the military capabilities of nuclear warheads going through life extension programs. U.S. policy would seek to maintain the arsenal by refurbishing existing weapons, reusing nuclear components, and, if necessary, replacing nuclear components, with a policy preference for the first two courses of action.

As directed by the review, the Obama administration launched an implementation study, one objective of which was to consider presidential guidance regarding the use of nuclear weapons. In essence, the president must articulate what he wants U.S. nuclear weapons—which Pentagon officials refer to as "the president's weapons"—to accomplish should deterrence fail. This guidance will be a key determinant of the number of nuclear weapons that the United States needs to maintain in the stockpile.

For example, were the president to adopt a minimal deterrent posture requiring that U.S. strategic nuclear forces be capable of holding at risk only a few dozen of a potential adversary's urban centers or key industrial and infrastructure installations, Strategic Command might require a relatively small number of strategic nuclear warheads. Most analysts believe it unlikely, for the foreseeable future, that a president would adopt such a dramatic change in nuclear posture. Among other things, it would raise questions about the effectiveness of the deterrent and the ethics of a counter-value targeting plan.

Should the president set a higher bar for the damage he seeks to have inflicted on an adversary in a conflict, the number of weapons needed would be greater. The more demanding the objective, the larger the number of survivable warheads the operational plan would need. The required level of damage expectancy can also affect the number of warheads. A high damage expectancy requirement might require assigning multiple warheads to strike a particular target, where a lower damage expectancy requirement might need only one warhead.

The president's guidance will ultimately be translated into U.S. war plans (the plans existing in July 2012 were based on the guidance prepared under the Bush administration). Once the president issues his presidential policy directive on strategic force guidance, it will go to the Defense Department, where the guidance for the employment of force will be prepared, laying out targeting goals and strike options that can range from a small number of warheads to a large-scale attack. The next step in the process is preparation by the Joint Chiefs of Staff of the joint strategic capabilities plan (nuclear supplement). The commander of Strategic Command will take these three documents and add his own guidance. Planners at Strategic Command will then produce a new Operations Plan 8010, which among other things would provide the number of strategic weapons that the U.S. Air Force and Navy need to deploy to carry out the guidance—and which Defense Department officials stress will ensure a nuclear deterrent that is "safe, secure, and effective." That number would also set a baseline for any future negotiation seeking to reduce strategic weapons to levels below those in New START. Among the questions to be considered in this process, beginning with the presidential guidance, are whether the target categories should be reduced, whether damage expectancy requirements can be relaxed, whether the number of attack options can be reduced, and whether strategic alert levels can be relaxed. Options for using nuclear forces against the conventional military capabilities of a nuclear-armed adversary will also clearly be part of the discussion. Ultimately, the Secretary of Defense must approve the operations plan.[20]

Arms control advocates engaged officials at the National Security Council, Defense Department, and State Department with recommendations for the review in 2011 and early 2012. They suggested that the review take a "zero-based" approach to the target plan, that is, rather than looking at the existing target plan and scaling it back, planners should start from scratch and build a new set of targets that U.S. strategic forces should hold at risk in order to maintain an effective deterrent. Reducing target categories could result in a smaller target set, which would require a reduced number of warheads.

For example, does it make sense for Strategic Command to target Russian ICBM silos? If the Russians launch first, the silos would be empty. If, in an intense crisis, the United States launches first, the Russians would likely launch their ICBMs on tactical warning, leaving the silos empty by the time that U.S. warheads arrived. Targeting Russian ICBM silos appears to make sense only if one plans for the possibility of a U.S. "bolt-from-the-blue" attack on Russian strategic forces, a most unlikely scenario.

A second recommendation passed to U.S. officials was that Strategic Command be told that it no longer had a requirement for "prompt launch," which was understood to be the capability to launch ICBMs within twenty minutes of confirmation of Russian missile launches. While ICBMs can be launched in just a few minutes, the full twenty minutes would likely be needed to inform and make a recommendation to the president, get his decision, and transmit an order to launch U.S. ICBMs before Russian warheads struck ICBM fields. Prompt launch gives the president the option of letting U.S. ICBMs fly before they could be destroyed in their silos.

While giving up the prompt launch requirement would leave those ICBMs at risk, the U.S. military has or has almost completed the process of downloading each U.S. ICBM to carry only one warhead. A Russian attack planner would have to target at least one and, if he were conservative, two warheads on each U.S. silo. In the conservative case, the Russians would expend well over half of the ballistic missile warheads they are permitted under the New START Treaty to attack about 25 percent of the U.S. deployed strategic warheads. Such an attack might have been an option to consider, at least theoretically, in a severe cold war crisis when

Minuteman III and MX ICBMs carried multiple warheads, because the Russians would use one or two warheads to destroy three or ten. It would make little sense, however, when U.S. ICBMs carry only one warhead. The large number of warheads that would have to be used to attack the ICBMs in their silos is a unique characteristic of the ICBM leg of the triad. Attacking U.S. ballistic missile submarines in port, or heavy bomber air bases and nuclear storage facilities, on the other hand, would require a relatively small number of nuclear warheads, perhaps a few dozen.

Elimination of the prompt launch requirement could be accomplished by a directive without requiring steps such as removing warheads from missiles. Eliminating the requirement would remove an option whose execution would require a presidential decision in minutes. While more conservative analysts would question whether the president in all cases would wish to forgo the prompt launch option, as a general rule, it would be preferable if the president had hours and perhaps days to consider what would be the most monumental decision of his (or her) presidency, if not all of human history. Eliminating the requirement might also reduce the number of ballistic missile submarines the United States needed, if the primary day-to-day operating criterion for the ballistic missile submarine force became the number of submarines safely at sea rather than the number of submarines on station and capable of launching promptly at their targets.

By spring 2012, it was believed that most of the work for the presidential review had been completed and that the review contained several options. A February Associated Press report asserted that the review included three options for reducing deployed strategic warhead numbers below the level in New START, to 1,000–1,100, 700–800, and 300–400.[21] White House officials publicly responded that no options had been presented to the president and privately denied that the White House had requested specific numbers. Secretary of Defense Leon Panetta told a congressional hearing that maintaining the status quo was also an option. He downplayed the idea that the administration might unilaterally reduce U.S. strategic forces.

The president's guidance presumably will reflect the main principles of the 2010 nuclear posture review, including reducing the role of nuclear weapons, maintaining deterrence and stability at lower levels, and sustaining a safe, secure, and effective nuclear arsenal. One of the challenging questions will be how to maintain strategic stability—particularly crisis stability, that is, to minimize incentives to strike first in a crisis—if or as the number of U.S. strategic nuclear weapons is reduced.[22]

Speaking in Seoul in late March 2012, the president seemed to foreshadow the possibility of further cuts. "We can already say with confidence that we have more nuclear weapons than we need. . . ," he said. "I firmly believe that we can ensure the security of the United States and our allies, maintain a strong deterrent against any threat, and still pursue further reductions in our nuclear arsenal."[23]

In April, Assistant Secretary of Defense Madelyn Creedon told the House Armed Services Committee that, as part of the review, the Defense Department was asking "what are the guiding concepts of employing nuclear weapons to deter adversaries, and what are the guiding concepts for ending a nuclear conflict on the least catastrophic terms if one has already started?" The review process aimed to "inform the presidential direction that guides force structure, force posture, and stockpile requirements needed to protect the United States and our allies and partners, as well as to inform plans for the employment of nuclear weapons in the event that deterrence fails."[24] As of mid-July 2012, it was unclear when the president would finalize and release his guidance. Some suggested that the White House might wait until after the presidential election to do so.

POLICY AND FORCE MODERNIZATION CHOICES

The president in the term beginning in 2013 will face choices regarding strategic nuclear deterrence policy. He will also face major decisions about the content and pace of modernizing the U.S. strategic triad, as well as about how to ensure sufficient funding for the nuclear weapons complex responsible for maintaining safe and reliable nuclear weapons to carry out its mission. He will have to deal with Congress to secure funding, which may not be a straightforward process. In 2012, the House of Representatives threatened to deny funding for implementing the New START reductions; the White House threatened a veto, but that would mean no budget and no funding for implementing the reductions.*

---

* If President Obama is reelected, he presumably will go forward with implementation of his guidance regarding strategic forces and nuclear weapons employment. How far implementation of that guidance will have proceeded will depend in large measure on when he issues it; the process for moving from his presidential decision directive to a new Operations Plan 8010 approved by the Secretary of Defense will take time.

If Mitt Romney is elected president, he could decide to put a hold on the Obama decision and consider guidance of his own. This is not necessarily a foregone conclusion, as presidents in the past have sometimes accepted, at least initially, the nuclear guidance of their predecessor—or at least they have not moved quickly to change it. However, given Romney's very critical attitude toward New START and concerns expressed by Republicans in Congress about Obama's interest in further nuclear force reductions, a Romney administration could well be dubious about the Obama administration's policy of reducing the role and number of U.S. nuclear weapons. Much would likely depend on whether Romney administration officials believed that the Obama plan allowed sufficient nuclear forces to, in their judgment, deter the full spectrum of potential threats to the United States and its allies.

As Bryan Bender reported in an April 30, 2012, *Boston Globe* article, Robert Joseph, an under secretary of state in the George W. Bush administration and an adviser on Romney's foreign policy team, laid out his concern about the Obama approach: "The problem with the president's approach is that he has stated we are going to go lower even before this [nuclear posture review implementation] study is completed. It is still a very dangerous security environment, and we need to be prudent and realistic. Russia is increasing its nuclear arsenal. China is modernizing. Iran is pursuing nuclear weapons and long-range missiles." Romney advisers might argue for revising Obama's guidance and offer different views as to what should guide U.S. nuclear deterrence policy. A Romney administration might also reconsider whether to try to revive the Robust Nuclear Earth Penetrator and Reliable Replacement Warhead programs.

The president must make these modernization decisions as the Russians and, to a lesser extent, the Chinese are modernizing their strategic forces. Before we describe the Russian programs, it should be noted that the United States and Russia (and the Soviet Union before it) take different approaches to modernizing their strategic nuclear forces. U.S. systems typically are designed and built to last longer than their Russian counterparts—certainly that has become the norm in recent years, at least. The U.S. practice is to put existing nuclear warheads through life extension programs and maintain them in the inventory, while Russian warheads—which are generally believed to have a shorter service life to begin with—usually are retired and replaced with new warheads.

The same is true for delivery systems. For example, the Minuteman III ICBM was first deployed in the early 1970s and, with various modernizations and life extension programs, is expected to remain in service until 2030. Some even suggest that its service life could be extended further. By contrast, the Russian SS-25 ICBMs were first deployed in 1988—fifteen years after the Minuteman III—but all are expected to be retired from service by 2020.

Economic difficulties following the collapse of the Soviet Union had a negative impact on Russian modernization and overall force structure; the Russians did very little in this regard during the 1990s. Fueled in large part by revenues from exports of oil and natural gas, Moscow's fiscal situation improved significantly after 2003. Russia is now operationally modernizing the ICBM and SLBM legs of its strategic triad. The Russians appear to place greater reliance on nuclear forces in general, given the deterioration of their conventional force capabilities over the past two decades and the fact that those conventional forces are stretched by the need to defend Russia's long land borders. The Russian military's 2010 defense doctrine reserved "the right to utilize nuclear weapons in response to the utilization of nuclear and other types of weapons of mass destruction against it and (or) its allies, and also in the event of aggression against the Russian Federation involving the use of conventional weapons when the very existence of the state is under threat."[25]

Russia's Strategic Rocket Forces are undergoing a significant transformation as older SS-18, SS-19, and SS-25 ICBMs are retired and will likely be out of the force by 2021. Deployment of the SS-27 Mod 2 Yars mobile ICBM, believed to carry up to six warheads, began in 2010, and the Yars is expected soon to be deployed in silos as well. The Russians, moreover, have begun development of a new heavy ICBM that might carry as many as ten warheads, although it is not expected to enter the force until 2018 or possibly 2022. The Russian Navy is also being modernized, with two new Borey-class ballistic missile submarines (out of an eventual total of eight to ten) expected to begin operational service in 2012 or 2013. The Russians appear to have worked out the problems with the new six-warhead SS-NX-30 Bulava SLBM, which had a troubled test history but now appears ready for service.[26]

In February 2012, during his campaign to be elected for a third term as president, Putin described a major military modernization program that included the production of more than 400 modern ICBMs and SLBMs and eight ballistic missile submarines by 2022. Some analysts question whether the program will be achievable, given other demands on the Russian budget. A production rate averaging 40 strategic ballistic missiles a year would appear well above the average capacity demonstrated by the Russian missile industry over the past fifteen years.

In the future, the United States may need to take greater account of Chinese strategic force developments. China continues to modernize its strategic forces, at a modest but not insignificant pace, and currently deploys 55–65 single-warhead silo-based and mobile ICBMs; the status of its single ballistic missile submarine and nascent SLBM program is uncertain.[27] The U.S. military must also take account of developments in other countries, particularly regarding nuclear weapons and long-range ballistic missiles, that could pose a threat to the United States and vital U.S. interests.

While Russia is now deploying new ICBMs, SLBMs, and ballistic missile submarines, Washington over the next several years faces decisions about building strategic systems that will enter service around 2030.[28] The first of the fourteen Ohio-class ballistic missile submarines (SSBNs) is scheduled to be retired from the fleet in about 2027, with subsequent Ohio-class SSBNs due for retirement at the rate of about one a year thereafter. Partially to save money in the near term, the Defense Department has decided to begin construction of the first new SSBN in 2021—a two-year slip in the earlier plan to begin construction in 2019—with the objective of having it ready for its first operational patrol in 2031.

Of the fourteen Ohio-class SSBNs, twelve are normally loaded with missiles while two are in long-term overhaul (their missiles are removed before the overhaul process begins). Five of the twelve submarines are typically believed to be at sea on station in range of possible targets, two or three are in transit between their home ports (Kings Bay, Georgia, and Bangor, Washington) and their at-sea stations, and the remainder are in or near port.

The Defense Department currently plans to replace the Ohio-class submarines with twelve new SSBNs—the SSBN(X) class—each with sixteen SLBM tubes as opposed to the twenty-four tubes on the Ohio-class. The SSBN(X) submarines will have nuclear reactors that should last the forty-year life span of the boats without requiring refueling. The current need to refuel reactors, a lengthy process, is a primary reason why, at any given time, two of the Ohio-class SSBNs are in long-term overhaul; the new submarines will still need to enter shorter, midlife overhaul for general maintenance. (A caveat to the point on nuclear reactors: as discussed in a subsequent chapter, it is at least conceivable that a fissile material cutoff treaty could lead to pressures to lower the uranium-235 content of the reactor fuel; were that to happen, admittedly a remote prospect at the moment, refueling might be necessary in the course of the new submarine's lifetime.) The U.S. Navy currently is examining how to reduce the costs of the new submarines, originally estimated at $6 billion–$7 billion each and with a total life-cycle program cost estimated at $350 billion through 2080.

In December 2011, Congress asked the Defense Department to examine four options for the number of replacement submarines: twelve submarines with sixteen SLBM launch tubes each, ten submarines with sixteen launch tubes each, ten submarines with twenty launch tubes each, and eight submarines with twenty launch tubes each (which, in theory, could be satisfied by the Ohio-class submarines or by a replacement class of submarines). By adjusting the average number of warheads deployed per SLBM, it is possible to design SLBM loadings so that each of these options results in the same total number of warheads.

As for the Trident II D5 SLBM itself, the missile is still being produced, and the Navy plans to begin deploying a new life-extended variant (Trident D5LE) beginning in 2015. Initially, the SSBN(X) will carry the Trident D5LE. The Trident D5 missile, which has recorded more than 130 successful launches, is expected to remain in service until at least 2040, so it will not be necessary for some time to begin development of a replacement.

The Minuteman III ICBMs were deployed in the early 1970s, and the U.S. Air Force currently deploys about 450 of the missiles at ICBM fields in Montana, North Dakota, and Wyoming. The Minuteman III is expected to remain in service until 2030. Should the Defense Department decide to replace this missile, it would likely have to begin design development within the next five years and begin purchasing new missiles around 2025. It appears unlikely that funding would permit replacement of the Minuteman III on a one-for-one basis; indeed, a Defense Department official remarked privately in 2011 that, given budget constraints, no one in the Pentagon expected a one-for-one replacement. Alternatively, the U.S. Air Force might consider whether the life of the Minuteman III could be extended beyond 2030 in order to postpone the procurement costs of a new ICBM.

Although the Air Force plans to keep B-2s and B-52Hs flying through 2040—by which time the latter will be seventy-five years old—it also would like to procure 80–100 new long-range bombers, primarily for conventional missions. The Air Force has said that it would later add the capability for the new bomber to carry out nuclear strike missions. Some in Congress want the Air Force to build a nuclear delivery capability into the new bomber from the beginning.

These strategic modernization programs could stress the Defense Department budget, particularly if the Pentagon in the 2020s is concurrently procuring new SSBNs, new long-range bombers, and new ICBMs, not to mention missile defense systems. In July 2011, James Cartwright, the vice chairman of the Joint Chiefs of Staff, warned that "the challenge here is that we have to recapitalize all three legs and we don't have the money to do it."[29] Since that statement, the dilemma has only grown more acute, as the August 2011 Budget Control Act mandated that Defense Department budgets decline by almost $500 billion more over the next decade than previously planned. Further defense budget cuts, whether happening through the sequestration process or a more orderly (and probably less severe) legislative vehicle, are quite possible in the coming years as well, depending on electoral outcomes and economic and fiscal conditions.

The president will have to bear that set of circumstances in mind as he makes decisions regarding the timing of the individual modernization programs. The Pentagon favors maintaining a strategic triad, as do many in Congress. The Obama administration's nuclear posture review said that it would maintain the triad. However, given pressures on the defense budget, some ask whether it is time to consider a step such as giving up one of the legs of the triad and converting to a strategic dyad to save money for more urgent defense needs.

Each leg of the triad makes a different contribution and offers different advantages and disadvantages. ICBMs, once built, are by far the cheapest leg to operate per dedicated launcher. Virtually the entire force is on day-to-day alert, is within range of targets, can be quickly launched, and has a strong command and control system. An adversary in a crisis would have to understand that any nuclear attack on ICBM silos—resulting in hundreds of nuclear detonations in the continental United States—would be certain to draw a nuclear retaliatory strike. The drawback to U.S. ICBMs is that they sit in fixed silos, the coordinates of which are well known, and many or most could be targeted and destroyed in a nuclear strike by an adversary with a large number of highly accurate and powerful warheads (currently, only Russia has the means to consider this even theoretically). The decision to download the Minuteman III so that each will carry only a single warhead makes them less attractive targets, however.

The primary advantage of ballistic missile submarines and SLBMs is the SSBNs' ability to roam the world's oceans and preserve their survivability. Over fifty years of U.S. operations, no case has been publicly reported of another country successfully tracking a U.S. ballistic missile submarine. The Trident D5 equals the Minuteman III in accuracy, and some Trident missiles now carry the Mk-5 reentry vehicle, which contains the most powerful ballistic missile warhead in the U.S. inventory—the W88, which is believed to have a yield of some 450 kilotons. The drawback to ballistic missile submarines is that they are expensive to build and operate and may not always be in range of targets. Communications with these systems from central command authorities are also somewhat more challenging to ensure than for other legs of the triad. There is also the worry that a breakthrough in antisubmarine warfare might compromise the SSBNs' survivability; although that is a low-probability development, it would have a huge impact on the U.S. strategic nuclear force and thinking.

The advantage of bombers is that they can perform conventional as well as nuclear missions; indeed, the U.S. Air Force interest in a new bomber is driven mainly by conventional requirements.

The long flight times required before they can deliver their weapons—measured in hours rather than the twenty or thirty minutes an intercontinental ballistic missile would require—would allow time for a possible halt to hostilities. Bombers can have their alert status raised in ways that would signal seriousness of U.S. intent in a crisis. Drawbacks are that bombers are expensive to build and operate and are vulnerable while at air bases. And their ability to penetrate modern air defenses depends greatly on stealth and associated characteristics. The B-2's stealth permits it to carry nuclear gravity bombs, because it is more likely to penetrate to its target. The B-52H, on the other hand, is armed with air-launched cruise missiles, because it is considered likely to have great difficulty evading modern air defenses.

If the United States decided to move to a strategic dyad, ballistic missile submarines and SLBMs constitute the leg most likely to be maintained. A number of analysts argue that the logical combination for a dyad would be SLBMs and bombers, because the United States will in any case maintain a fleet of bombers for conventional strike missions. Others have suggested maintaining a dyad of SLBMs and ICBMs, with the possibility to convert conventional bombers to nuclear missions if that later proved necessary. Adding a nuclear capability to existing bombers in order to reconstitute a third leg of the triad would be much cheaper and faster than if the dyad consisted of SLBMs and bombers, and a decision were taken to reconstitute the ICBM leg.

The Pentagon strongly prefers to maintain a triad, as a way of hedging against technological failure or surprise. For example, maintaining a substantial ICBM force and some bombers hedges against either a failure in the Trident D-5 SLBM (however unlikely) or a Russian breakthrough in antisubmarine warfare. The United States will likely maintain a triad for the foreseeable future.

CHAPTER THREE

STRATEGIC NUCLEAR FORCE REDUCTIONS AFTER NEW START

THE UNITED STATES and the Soviet Union (or Russia) have engaged in negotiations to control and reduce strategic nuclear forces for more than forty years. However, only since the mid-1980s have Washington and Moscow pursued genuine nuclear reductions. The 1990 Strategic Arms Reduction Treaty (referred to as START I) required real cuts in both sides' strategic forces. The New START Treaty that entered into force in early 2011 will build on START I and the Strategic Offensive Reductions Treaty to cut U.S. and Russian strategic nuclear warheads to about one-fifth of the number that were in each side's inventories at the end of the cold war.

Yet when the New START limits are reached in 2018, the United States and Russia will each deploy as many as 1,550 strategic nuclear warheads, not counting reserve warheads or weapons for bombers over and above the one warhead officially counted for each deployed bomber. Each of those warheads will be larger—some will be thirty times larger—than the weapons that decimated Hiroshima and Nagasaki. One issue that the president will face in 2013 is whether to seek further reductions and how. President Barack Obama made clear in 2010 that he would like to negotiate a follow-on agreement to New START; Mitt Romney expressed a far more skeptical view of the value of strategic arms control.

If the president wishes to pursue further reductions, and the Russians are prepared to engage (possible but not a given), Washington will have to address several questions. How far below the limits in New START should new reductions go? Should the negotiation be broadened to include nondeployed (or reserve) strategic warheads, which thus far have not been limited? Is it time to reconsider some of the previous counting rules, which could undercount bomber weapons and capture conventional warheads on strategic ballistic missiles? What new monitoring requirements might be needed? Alternatively, would it be sensible for the United States to consider unilateral steps to reduce its nuclear forces?

We believe that further reductions are in the U.S. interest and recommend that the U.S. government seek to engage Russia in a negotiation that would draw down the number of deployed strategic warheads to no more than 1,000. We would also limit nondeployed strategic warheads, which will entail new verification challenges. These reductions would be part of an effort—addressed in this chapter and the next—to move to a limit that would cover all U.S. and Russian nuclear warheads.

NEW START

Strategic nuclear arms control negotiations between the United States and Soviet Union began in 1969. They produced the Anti-Ballistic Missile Treaty and the Interim Offensive Arms Agreement. The latter, referred to as SALT I, essentially froze the number of U.S. and Soviet intercontinental ballistic missile and submarine-launched ballistic missile launchers. The 1979 SALT II Treaty, which never formally entered into force but was informally observed for a period by both sides, capped the number of ICBM and SLBM launchers plus heavy bombers at equal levels. The SALT treaties did not constrain warhead levels, which rose dramatically between 1969 and the mid-1980s by equipping ballistic missiles with multiple independently targeted reentry vehicles (MIRVs) and by deploying air-launched cruise missiles (ALCMs).

President Ronald Reagan launched the Strategic Arms Reduction Treaty talks in 1982. START I, signed by Presidents George H. W. Bush and Mikhail Gorbachev in 1991, mandated significant reductions of both launchers and warheads. It was followed by START II, which provided for further reductions but which never entered into force. The 2002 Strategic Offensive Reductions Treaty, signed by Presidents George W. Bush and Vladimir Putin, applied further reductions compared with START I but lacked agreed definitions, counting rules, and verification measures. These agreements set the context for the New START Treaty. (See appendix A for a more detailed discussion of the SALT, START I and II, and SORT treaties.)

When President Obama assumed office in January 2009, one of his early foreign policy priorities was to "reset" relations with Russia. When Obama held his first meeting with Russian President Dmitry Medvedev in April, the two agreed as a matter of priority to begin negotiations on a replacement for START I, which was due to expire in December 2009. Their joint statement said the presidents "agreed to pursue new and verifiable reductions in our strategic offensive arsenals in a step-by-step process."[1] A START-specific joint statement noted that the new treaty would address the "reduction and limitation of strategic offensive arms," that it would "seek to record levels of reductions in strategic offensive arms that will be lower than those in the 2002 Moscow [SORT] Treaty," and that it would contain "effective verification measures drawn from the experience of the Parties in implementing the START Treaty."[2]

When negotiations got under way shortly thereafter, U.S. negotiators indicated early on that they were prepared to limit strategic delivery vehicles as well as strategic warheads, meeting one of the Russians' main concerns.[3] The negotiators also agreed early on that the new treaty would contain no sublimits but would allow each side full freedom to choose its mix of ICBMs, SLBMs, and bombers.

When Obama and Medvedev met in Moscow in July 2009, they issued a joint understanding that reflected the first months of negotiations. Each side would "reduce and limit its strategic offensive arms so that seven years after entry into force of the treaty and thereafter, the limits will be in the range of 500–1,100 for strategic delivery vehicles, and in the range of 1,500–1,675 for their associated warheads." The document laid out nine other elements that would be recorded in the new treaty.[4] Later leaks disclosed that the Russians wanted limits of 500 strategic delivery vehicles and 1,675 associated warheads, while the United States proposed limits of 1,100 and 1,500.

Subsequent work in the autumn of 2009 included verification measures and drafting treaty text. The sides agreed to limit deployed strategic delivery vehicles—ICBMs, SLBMs, and heavy bombers—with a "deployed" ICBM or SLBM being a missile in a silo, on a mobile ICBM launcher, or in a submarine launch tube. In addition to this and the limit on warheads, the sides explored a third limit, which would cover deployed and nondeployed ICBM and SLBM launchers and deployed and nondeployed heavy bombers. Deployed missile launchers are those containing ICBMs or SLBMs; nondeployed launchers are empty missile silos or SSBN launch tubes; nondeployed heavy bombers are test aircraft or those at repair or production facilities.

The sides failed to conclude a new treaty before START I expired in December 2009. Negotiations picked up again in January 2010, when National Security Adviser James Jones and Chairman of the Joint Chiefs of Staff Mike Mullen went to Moscow. Their meetings produced agreement on the numerical values for the treaty limits and resolved most of the open verification issues. Negotiators finalized the treaty text in February and March, and Obama and Medvedev met in Prague in April to sign it.

New START has a duration of ten years—which can be extended for up to five years—and specifically supplanted SORT. It provides for three limits. Under the treaty's terms, seven years after entry into force, the United States and Russia will each be limited to:

—No more than 700 deployed ICBMs, SLBMs, and heavy bombers.

—No more than 1,550 deployed strategic warheads, with each warhead on a deployed ICBM and SLBM—regardless of whether it is nuclear or conventional—counting, and with each deployed heavy bomber being counted as a single deployed strategic warhead.

—No more than 800 deployed and nondeployed ICBM and SLBM launchers and heavy bombers.

Because of the warhead counting rule for bombers, the United States and Russia may deploy more than 1,550 strategic ballistic missile warheads, bombs, and air-launched cruise missiles. U.S. bombers can carry more than one weapon apiece; indeed, B-52Hs at one time could carry 20 ALCMs, though they would carry significantly fewer today. The U.S. Air Force reportedly maintains 100 B61 and B83 nuclear gravity bombs for its B-2 force and has 528 air-launched cruise missiles, of which some 200 are at operational heavy bomber bases, for its B-52H bombers.[5]

New START contains detailed verification measures—a data exchange, regular data updates, and the possibility for each side to conduct up to eighteen short notice, on-site inspections per year—augmented by requirements to provide notifications to the other of changes in strategic forces. New START's actual-load counting rule for ICBMs and SLBMs is monitored by a requirement that, when an inspection team arrives at an ICBM base or ballistic missile submarine base, it is given a list of all deployed ICBMs or SLBMs at that location and the number of warheads on each missile; it may then choose one missile for inspection to confirm the number of warheads mounted on it. As inspections are conducted, the sides are building a fairly good picture of the number of warheads on ICBMs and SLBMs across the other side's entire force.

New START simplifies the rules for eliminating strategic delivery vehicles so that they no longer count under the treaty. For example, where START I had required that heavy bombers be eliminated by having their fuselage cut in two places and each wing severed as well, New START requires only that the fuselage be cut or one wing severed. New START also provides for simplified conversion procedures. This was of particular interest to the U.S. Navy, which plans to convert four SLBM launch tubes on each Trident SSBN so that the tubes cannot contain a ballistic missile and thus would not count under New START.

The Senate ratification debate over New START proved more difficult than anticipated. Critics raised numerous questions. Some noted that the treaty's preamble recognized the interrelationship between strategic offensive and strategic defensive weapons and expressed concern that the treaty would constrain U.S. missile defenses. The preamble, however, does not constitute a limit, and New START's only constraint on missile defense is a ban on placing interceptor missiles in converted ICBM or SLBM launchers, something the Missile Defense Agency and Air Force said they would not do in any case (for one reason, converting ICBM silos is more expensive than building new silos to house the interceptor missiles). Critics worried that Moscow might threaten to withdraw from New START if the United States built up its missile defenses and thereby blackmail Washington into scaling back its missile defense plans. In part to address this concern, Obama wrote to the Senate that his administration planned to deploy all four phases of the European phased adaptive approach to missile defense.

Others criticized the treaty for requiring greater reductions from the United States than from Russia. That was true, although at the time of the treaty's signing, Russia was building new ICBMs, SLBMs, and ballistic missile submarines, while the United States only had its Trident D5 production line operating. The treaty will cap the Russian strategic force level. (As explained in chapter 2, the United States and Russia are on different cycles for the modernization of their strategic delivery systems.) Another criticism was that New START did not limit nonstrategic—or tactical— nuclear weapons, a category in which the Russians have a significant numerical advantage. New START, however, was intended to replace START I, which covered only strategic offensive forces.

New START was also criticized for limiting conventional warheads on ICBMs and SLBMs as deployed strategic warheads. The administration responded that, were it to decide to place conventional warheads on strategic ballistic missiles, this would be a "niche" capability entailing a very small number of weapons under the 1,550 deployed strategic warhead limit. Still, some analysts worried that, by accepting limits on conventional weapons in a treaty on strategic nuclear arms, the administration had set a precedent that could prove problematic in the future.

Some critics noted that New START's verification measures were, on some issues, less rigorous than those in START I, for example, on ensuring access to telemetry from missile test flights. Administration officials countered that New START contained all the monitoring measures needed for verifying its provisions and noted that, with their START I experience, the militaries on both sides had sought to simplify the verification regime.

One very important issue turned on the administration's commitment to modernize both the nuclear weapons complex that supports nuclear warheads and the delivery systems that make up the strategic triad. The Bush administration had underfunded the nuclear weapons complex during its term; the Obama administration in 2010 said that it would address that problem. Its funding plan over the following decade allocated $85 billion for the nuclear weapons complex as well as $100 billion for U.S. strategic delivery systems. Given the deficit and pressures to reduce the budget, some analysts expressed concern over whether these commitments would be met. (Indeed, the House of Representatives reduced the administration's fiscal year 2012 request for modernizing the nuclear weapons complex.)

Some Democrats felt that the New START ratification process became overly politicized. They pointed out that New START represented a modest reduction in strategic forces compared with the SORT limit and that its implementation was verifiable, whereas SORT had no monitoring provisions. The Senate had voted 95-0 to consent to ratification of SORT. In the end, the Senate voted

71-26 to consent to ratifying New START in December 2010. The Russians ratified in January 2011, and the treaty entered into force in February.

From February 2011 through July 2012, implementation appeared to have gone smoothly. As of May 2012, each side had conducted its eighteen permitted on-site inspections in the first treaty year and five of its permitted on-site inspections in the second year. The sides had exchanged more than 2,300 treaty notifications.[6]

CURRENT AND POSSIBLE FUTURE STRATEGIC FORCE STRUCTURES

The United States and Russia exchanged data in February 2011 and update the data every six months under New START. According to the February 2012 data update, the Russians were already below New START's limits on deployed strategic delivery vehicles and deployed strategic warheads (it is possible for one side to go below a limit and later come back above it; the limits do not become binding until February 2018) (table 3-1).

In a May 2010 statement, the Defense Department described its planned strategic force once New START reductions are fully implemented: 240 deployed Trident D5 SLBMs on 12 ballistic missile submarines; up to 420 deployed Minuteman III ICBMs; and up to 60 deployed B-2 and B-52H heavy bombers equipped for nuclear armaments. (The Pentagon must still decide whether to reduce an additional 20 ICBMs or 20 bombers, or some combination, to reach the deployed strategic delivery vehicle limit of 700.)

Since the Minuteman III ICBMs will be downloaded so that each carries a single warhead and since New START counts each deployed heavy bomber as a single warhead, the combination of 460 ICBMs and bombers will mean 460 deployed strategic warheads. The U.S. Navy thus can deploy up to 1,090 warheads on its 240 deployed SLBMs and still allow the total U.S. force to fit within the overall deployed strategic warhead limit.

As for the 800 limit on deployed and nondeployed launchers, the U.S. Navy plans to convert four SLBM launch tubes on each of

TABLE 3-1. U.S. and Russian Strategic Forces, February 2012

	United States	Russia
Deployed strategic delivery vehicles	812	494
Deployed strategic warheads	1,737	1,492
Deployed and nondeployed ICBM/SLBM launchers and heavy bombers	1,040	881

Source: Department of State, Bureau of Arms Control, Verification and Compliance, "New START Treaty Aggregate Numbers of Strategic Offensive Arms," Fact sheet (April 6, 2012).

its fourteen ballistic missile submarines so that they cannot carry an SLBM. Those submarines thus will account for a total of 280 launchers—240 deployed (that is, holding SLBMs) and 40 nondeployed (launch tubes with no SLBMs on two submarines in long-term overhaul). The U.S. military will be able to have up to an additional 60 nondeployed launchers and bombers; the Defense Department is considering maintaining some ICBM silos after the missiles have been removed (this would allow the possibility, should the treaty break down, for placing ICBMs in those silos).

The Russians have not said how they will structure their strategic force once New START limits take full effect. In 2009, they initially proposed a limit of no more than 500 deployed ICBMs, SLBMs, and heavy bombers, which suggests their planned number of deployed strategic delivery vehicles is significantly less than the 700 that the treaty permits; in fact, the Russians are already well below the 700 limit. Some nongovernmental analysts expect the number of Russian deployed strategic warheads to fall well below 1,550 and project that the number of deployed Russian strategic delivery vehicles may decline to around 400 (table 3-2).

Many current Russian warheads are on SS-18 and SS-19 ICBMs, which are near the end of their service life and should soon be retired. Russian production of new ICBMs and SLBMs has proceeded at a relatively modest pace in recent years. Some analysts question whether the Russian military will be able to deploy new missiles at a rate matching the retirement of older missiles. Russian

TABLE 3-2. Notional U.S. and Russian Strategic Offensive Forces under New START

	United States[a]	Russia[b]
Deployed ICBMs	420	192
Warheads on deployed ICBMs	420	542
Deployed SLBMs	240	128
Warheads on deployed SLBMs	1,090	640
Deployed heavy bombers	40	76
Warheads attributed to deployed heavy bombers	40	76
Total deployed ICBMs, SLBMs, and heavy bombers	700	396
Total warheads on or attributed to deployed ICBMs, SLBMs and heavy bombers	1,550	1,258

a. The figures for U.S. weapons assume that the United States chooses to keep 420 deployed Minuteman III ICBMs, which will require the number of deployed U.S. nuclear-capable bombers to be reduced to 40. If the Defense Department were to choose to keep more than 40 bombers (it has said it may keep up to 60), it would have to reduce 1 deployed Minuteman III for each bomber over 40.

b. The Russian figures are based on calculations by Pavel Podvig, Russian Strategic Nuclear Forces, "New START Treaty in Numbers" (russianforces.org/blog/2010/03/new_start_treaty_in_numbers.shtml). A different calculation provided to the authors by Hans M. Kristensen in July 2010 projected a total of 403 Russian-deployed ICBMs, SLBMs, and heavy bombers attributed with 1,349 warheads under New START. The Russian government has not stated its planned strategic nuclear force structure under New START, and the U.S. government has not produced an unclassified estimate of the Russian strategic nuclear force structure under New START.

analyst Aleksey Arbatov has projected that the number of Russian deployed strategic warheads could fall to as low as 1,000–1,100. He described this decline as a key factor behind the Russian decision to develop a new heavy ICBM to replace the SS-18 and SS-19; with a relatively small number of such missiles, the Russians could maintain 1,550 warheads.[7]

Defense Department officials, on the other hand, doubt that the Russian strategic force will decline this low or as low as suggested in table 3-2. They point out that Russia currently produces the Yars ICBM and Bulava SLBM and is developing a new mobile ICBM and new heavy ICBM; they thus believe that the Russian military will be able to make full use of its permitted 1,550 deployed strategic warheads. They also note that U.S. negotiators originally proposed a limit on deployed strategic warheads of 1,500, but the Russians would only go as low as 1,550, suggesting that the Russian military will be able to maintain 1,550 warheads.

AFTER NEW START: TO REDUCE FURTHER OR NOT TO REDUCE?

One arms control question facing the president in 2013 will be whether the United States and Russia should pursue further reductions in strategic forces. Obama articulated the goal of a world free of nuclear weapons and, when signing the New START Treaty in April 2010, indicated that the next step should be a follow-on agreement that would limit not only deployed strategic warheads but also nondeployed (or reserve) strategic warheads and nonstrategic nuclear weapons, both deployed and nondeployed.

In such a negotiation, a key question would be the level of the limits the United States would seek. The level presumably would be shaped by the outcome of the nuclear posture review implementation study and the resulting determination of the number of strategic nuclear weapons needed. Although the results of the implementation study had not been made public as of mid-July 2012, Obama and the Defense Department had already indicated a view that some reductions could be made beyond those in New START. The scale of the reductions was not clear.

Assuming that a new negotiated agreement with Russia would—like its START I, SORT, and New START predecessors—reflect equality of limits, the United States could ensure that it would have parity in strategic nuclear weapons with its nearest peer competitor. Some analysts will likely caution that Washington must also take careful account of China's nuclear forces, as well as possible developments by other third countries. China currently maintains a relatively small nuclear arsenal of up to 300 nuclear warheads of all types and 55 to 65 ICBMs. Some analysts nevertheless worry that Beijing might in the future be tempted to build a larger nuclear force commensurate with its growing geopolitical weight and status or to address concerns about the impact of U.S. missile defense on China's minimal deterrent.

More conservative analysts would argue against seeking further negotiated strategic force reductions with Russia. Given global uncertainties, they would take the position that U.S. strategic forces have been reduced as low as is sensible, particularly given the limits imposed by the New START Treaty. Some might express concern that another round of negotiations with Russia on strategic forces would turn administration attention away from more pressing nuclear problems, such as the need to prevent further proliferation.*

---

*As of July 2012, Romney had not indicated a specific view on further nuclear reductions or on a new negotiation. Given his negative reaction to the New START Treaty and more wary skepticism about Russia in general, he presumably would be less interested than Obama in pursuing negotiations aimed at further nuclear reductions. Or perhaps, even if willing to accept lower numbers (like Republican and Democratic presidents before him), he might be more ambitious about deploying missile defenses—which could itself lead Russia to lose interest in any further accords on nuclear reductions. His campaign's October 2011 white paper, "An American Century: A Strategy to Secure America's Enduring Interests and Ideals," said that Romney would "review the implementation of the New START Treaty and other decisions by the Obama administration regarding America's nuclear posture and arms control policies to determine whether they serve the best interests and national security of the United States," but it offered no detail.

One possible course for a Republican administration would be to exercise the right to withdraw from the New START Treaty, although Romney has not indicated, as of July 2012, that he would pursue such a course. It would have serious implications for the broader U.S.-Russia relationship and might raise concerns on the part of U.S. allies, who generally support New START. Another course would be to allow implementation of New START to go forward—the treaty will be in force until 2021—but not seek further reductions in strategic offensive forces. Nonstrategic nuclear weapons may be a separate issue—Republicans have called for action to reduce the Russian numerical advantage in this category (see chapter 4). A Republican administration might well decide to conduct a nuclear posture review of its own before making any decisions about further arms control steps and could conceivably halt implementation of Obama's new nuclear planning guidance, pending completion of such a review.

Of course, the Russians would have a key voice in any further negotiated reductions. They have agreed, at least in principle, to work toward further cuts. In addition to language on step-by-step reductions and a nuclear-free world in the April 2009 Obama-Medvedev joint statement, the preamble to New START notes that the sides seek "to preserve continuity in, and provide new impetus to, the step-by-step process of reducing and limiting nuclear arms, while maintaining the safety and security of their nuclear arsenals, and with a view to expanding this process in the future, including to a multilateral approach."

That said, since completion of New START in April 2010, Moscow has shown little enthusiasm for engaging in new negotiations. While U.S. and Russian officials have quietly conducted strategic stability talks, Russian officials have linked further reductions in nuclear weapons to other issues, such as missile defense. For example, Foreign Minister Sergey Lavrov on March 1, 2011, told the UN Conference on Disarmament in Geneva:

> We insist that there is a clear need to take into account the factors that negatively affect strategic stability, such as plans to place weapons in outer space, to develop non-nuclear armed strategic offensive weapons, as well as unilateral deployment of a global BMD [ballistic missile defense] system. Nor could we ignore the considerable imbalances in conventional arms, especially against the backdrop of dangerous conflicts persisting in many regions of the world.[8]

Over the course of 2011, it became apparent that, of these issues, Moscow's position regarding missile defense and how it might affect reduced Russian strategic forces posed the biggest obstacle to a new round of bilateral nuclear reduction negotiations (missile defense is discussed further in chapter 5). Moreover, senior Russian officials in summer 2011 privately indicated that Moscow would wait until after the U.S. presidential election in November

2012 to decide whether and how to pursue further reductions.[9] That reflected a view in Moscow that a Republican president might pursue a very different approach to arms control than Obama.

Moscow may not be eager for further strategic force reductions for several reasons. Strategic nuclear weapons constitute Russia's strongest claim to a superpower position on par with the United States. Some Russian officials may worry that further strategic cuts that narrow the gap between Russia and the United States, on the one hand, and third countries with nuclear weapons, on the other, would diminish Russia's status. Moreover, the deterioration of Russian conventional force capabilities since 1991 and the uncertain prospects for their modernization over the coming decade have likely increased Russian reliance on nuclear weapons.

Still, the Russians may have incentives to engage in a further round of arms reduction negotiations. As of March 1, 2012, Russian strategic forces were already below two of the three New START limits. Should Russian strategic force levels continue to decline, as some nongovernmental analysts project, while the U.S. military maintains 700 deployed strategic delivery vehicles and 1,550 deployed strategic warheads, Moscow may have a reason to negotiate a reduction in the New START limits. That could allow the Russians to preserve strategic parity and save the cost of developing and deploying a new heavy ICBM.

A second incentive for Moscow stems from the "upload" issue—the ability to put additional warheads on strategic missiles that carry less than their maximum capacity. It appears that, as they implement New START, the Russians are maintaining full warhead sets on the missiles that they retain. They thus have little or no capacity to upload warheads onto existing missiles should the treaty break down. The United States, on the other hand, has a significant upload capability. With 240 deployed Trident II D5 missiles carrying 1,090 warheads, the U.S. SLBM force would still have room for an additional 830 warheads, since each Trident II D5 can carry up to 8 warheads. Likewise, a number of Minuteman III ICBMs could be uploaded as well. Of the 450 deployed Minuteman III ICBMs in the force, 150 were downloaded to a single warhead and had the "bulkhead"—the platform on which the warheads rest—replaced, with the old one destroyed. Those missiles now can carry only a single warhead. Other Minuteman III ICBMs, however, have been downloaded, but the old bulkhead is not being replaced, so they could be uploaded with one or two additional warheads were the treaty to break down.[10] Nuclear-equipped heavy bombers also provide a significant upload capability.

This imbalance may give the Russians an incentive to negotiate, in order to seek constraints on nondeployed strategic warheads and limit the U.S. upload advantage. Obama indicated as early as 2010 a readiness to include nondeployed strategic warheads in a next round of negotiations.

The Russian position on further nuclear reductions will not become clear until at least 2013. For its part, the U.S. government could weigh other steps regarding strategic nuclear forces. With the Russian military on track to meet its New START limits well ahead of the February 2018 treaty deadline, Washington might consider accelerating implementation of its New START reductions as well. Since the Defense Department has concluded that 1,550 deployed strategic warheads on 700 deployed strategic delivery vehicles will suffice to meet U.S. security interests in 2018, it would seem that those numbers would also suffice if reached earlier.

There are reasons for the United States to consider early implementation. The effort could be cited by the U.S. delegation to the 2015 Non-Proliferation Treaty review conference as an additional demonstration of Washington's commitment to meet its obligation under Article VI to move toward disarmament. Early implementation of New START might also signal Moscow of Washington's seriousness in reducing nuclear arms and help secure Russian agreement to a further round of negotiations.

Some would question the value of early implementation by the United States. They might argue that maintaining U.S. strategic forces at current levels for as long as possible is desirable in an uncertain world or that U.S. advantages over Russia in the numbers of deployed strategic delivery vehicles and deployed strategic warheads could give Moscow greater incentives to engage in a follow-on round of negotiations.

The president might direct early implementation, but he would have to consider that accelerating reductions—particularly to achieve the limits of 700 deployed strategic delivery vehicles and 800 deployed and nondeployed launchers and heavy bombers—could pose cost and scheduling issues for the U.S. military. For example, accelerating implementation of the 700 limit would require early removal of some SLBMs and ICBMs from their launch tubes and silos. That could raise questions of pace of removal and available storage space for nondeployed missiles. Accelerating implementation of New START's 800 limit could prove more difficult. To meet this limit, the U.S. Navy plans to convert four launch tubes on each of fourteen ballistic missile submarines so that they are incapable of containing or launching an SLBM. The Navy plans as much as possible to perform the conversions when submarines are in scheduled long-term overhaul to minimize the impact on submarine operations. The U.S. Air Force must complete the elimination of over 100 ICBM silos, a process involving significant environmental requirements.

It would appear easiest to accelerate implementation of the deployed strategic warhead limit, which would require only that warheads be removed from deployed ICBMs and SLBMs. It would be possible to leave missiles in their silos or launch tubes without warheads. For example, the U.S. Air Force might remove warheads from some Minuteman III ICBMs but leave the missiles in their silos, pending later removal. The ICBMs would still count as deployed missiles but would be declared to a visiting Russian inspection team as having zero warheads. The Russians would have the option of choosing one of those missiles for inspection to confirm that it indeed carried no warheads.

Warheads downloaded from Trident and Minuteman missiles would need to be placed in storage, either at military or Department of Energy installations. Given the backlog in eliminating U.S. nuclear weapons—a few thousand weapons are believed to be in the dismantlement queue—it would be some years before they would be dismantled. Downloading warheads to accelerate implementation of the 1,550 limit thus would be a reversible process. If the Russians went back above 1,550, warheads in storage could be uploaded on to Trident and Minuteman missiles that had been downloaded. If the U.S. government decided to adopt a policy of early implementation of the deployed strategic warhead limit, it might make a policy statement to the effect that it would proceed with early implementation so long as Russia kept the number of its deployed strategic warheads below 1,550. Alternatively, Washington and Moscow might jointly state their commitment to early implementation of the deployed strategic warhead limit.

A more dramatic step was proposed in April 2011 by former secretary of state Madeleine Albright and former Russian foreign minister Igor Ivanov. They noted the possibility that the level of Russian deployed strategic warheads would fall significantly below 1,550. They suggested that the U.S. government could announce, as a matter of unilateral policy, that it would reduce its deployed strategic warheads to 1,300, provided that Russia did not exceed the 1,300 level.[11] An alternative approach would be for both governments to declare that, as a matter of national policy, they would not exceed the level of 1,300. The sides could use New START rules to monitor a level of 1,300 just as well as they can use those rules to monitor the 1,550 limit.

Albright and Ivanov suggested that the U.S. government consider such a step to encourage the Russians to enter new negotiations and create conditions in which the Russians no longer would pursue a new heavy ICBM. Some may caution against such an offer, however, arguing that it could yield leverage that Washington could apply in a follow-on negotiation itself, including to bring the Russians to put nonstrategic nuclear weapons on the table.

Other nongovernmental analysts have expressed interest in unilateral U.S. strategic force reductions, in part because they believe that engaging Moscow in a new round of nuclear negotiations will be difficult or that unilateral reduction measures, perhaps coordinated with Russia, could be implemented more quickly. They argue that, if the U.S. government determines that it can safeguard U.S. security with a number of deployed strategic warheads below New START's 1,550 level, the United States should move to that lower level, even if it does so unilaterally. Such a step could produce budget savings—at a time when the Defense Department's budget is under pressure—and might, as did President George H. W. Bush's unilateral presidential nuclear initiatives in 1991 and 1992, prompt reciprocal reduction steps by Russia. Such a unilateral approach would be reminiscent of the nuclear posture review conducted by the George W. Bush administration in 2001; it set a level for U.S. strategic forces of 1,700–2,200 operationally deployed warheads, *regardless* of what Russia and other countries might deploy.

Some quarters in the U.S. Congress, however, would take a negative view of unilateral U.S. reductions. The House of Representatives in May 2012 passed amendments to the fiscal year 2013 defense authorization bill that barred unilateral reductions by the United States and even applied limits on steps to implement the New START Treaty. The White House threatened a veto.

STRATEGIC ISSUES IN A FOLLOW-ON NEGOTIATION

If the United States and Russia agree to a follow-on negotiation to further reduce strategic nuclear forces, they would likely have to deal with eight key issues: a new deployed strategic warhead limit; conventional warheads on strategic ballistic missiles; other long-range conventional strike systems; the bomber weapon counting rule; limits on strategic delivery vehicles and launchers; possible sub-limits; limits on nondeployed strategic warheads; and verification.

Deployed Strategic Warhead Limit

One issue Washington would have to consider in a follow-on negotiation would be how much to lower the 1,550 limit on deployed strategic warheads. A key factor in determining that level would be the presidential guidance that flows from the nuclear posture review implementation study and the targeting guidance that results, which would in turn indicate the number of deployed strategic warheads the United States needs.

U.S. negotiators in New START originally proposed a deployed strategic warhead limit of 1,500 on the basis of then-current nuclear weapons employment policy, based on analysis that used the targeting guidance developed following the Bush administration's 2001 nuclear posture review. The Obama administration's review gave priority to developing numbers that U.S. negotiators could table in the New START negotiations in June 2009 but was not completed until April 2010. Some reports suggested that the U.S. military's absolute bottom line for the New START negotiation was 1,300 deployed strategic warheads.

One possible objective for a follow-on negotiation would be to reduce the limit on deployed strategic warheads to 1,000. According to a February 2012 Associated Press story, 1,000–1,100 was the most modest limit on warheads of the three options the White House asked the Pentagon to study.[12] Some in the Obama administration reportedly were interested in the 1,000 warhead limit in 2009, but 1,500 was seen as allowing a quicker deal, when time was of the essence given START I's looming expiration. In discussions during 2010, some Russian analysts suggested 1,000 deployed strategic warheads as a bottom line for a bilateral U.S.-Russia treaty, below which the Russian government would not reduce without some limits on third-country nuclear forces or constraints on missile defense.

Stanford professor emeritus Sidney Drell and former senior U.S. government official James Goodby have suggested a quick way to achieve a lower deployed strategic warhead limit. They have proposed that the United States and Russia agree to amend the New START Treaty to replace the 1,550 limit on deployed strategic warheads with 1,000, leaving the rest of the treaty intact, including the February 2018 deadline for achieving the reductions.[13]

Others have proposed deeper reductions, including a total of 1,000 deployed and nondeployed strategic warheads or even 1,000 total nuclear weapons. In May 2012, Global Zero, which favors the ultimate elimination of all nuclear weapons, released a report prepared by a commission chaired by James Cartwright, a former Strategic Command commander and former vice chairman of the Joint Chiefs of Staff. The report advocated reductions to 900 total strategic warheads and the elimination of all nonstrategic nuclear weapons by 2022. Of the 900 warheads, 360 would be reentry vehicles deployed on Trident SLBMs and 90 would be gravity bombs deployed at the B-2 bomber base. An additional 360 Trident warheads and 90 gravity bombs would be held in reserve. All ICBMs and their warheads would be eliminated.[14] (The U.S. Air Force chief of staff and the commander of Strategic Command both promptly expressed their disagreement with the proposal.)

The scale of future reductions may have at least as much to do with symbolic and perceptual matters, such as what is seen as necessary by Washington and Moscow to maintain a clear nuclear superpower status vis-à-vis other countries, and less with formal targeting requirements established by the "nuclear priesthood." In any event, this debate will surely continue across multiple dimensions.

Another factor a U.S. administration must weigh is the reaction to the proposal in the U.S. Senate, which ultimately must approve ratification of any new treaty (or an amendment of the existing New START Treaty). For the foreseeable future, Senate Republicans likely will remain skeptical of radical reductions, particularly those that result from an agreement negotiated by a Democratic president. Unless that attitude could be changed, it would argue for a more modest approach to the next treaty. That said, a treaty negotiated by a Republican president could expect an easier time during Senate consideration of its ratification. One unknown factor is whether the pressure to reduce the defense budget could constrain funds for modernization of U.S. strategic forces and thus prompt wider interest in reduced strategic forces.

Conventional Warheads on Strategic Ballistic Missiles

If Washington and Moscow decided to negotiate a follow-on agreement, the question of revisiting the rule of counting conventional warheads on ICBMs and SLBMs could arise. Neither side now deploys conventional warheads on strategic ballistic missiles, and the Pentagon has indicated that it is focusing more on pursuing other technologies for long-range conventional strike weapons.

However, some strategic analysts are uncomfortable with a treaty on strategic nuclear forces that limits conventional capabilities. They question whether counting conventional warheads might prove problematic were a future agreement to lower the total number of deployed strategic warheads and the United States to decide that it wanted to arm ICBMs and SLBMs with conventional warheads. As one former senior Bush administration official put it, the concern was with the principle: it would be no problem to have 40 conventional warheads on ICBMs and SLBMs under New START's 1,550 limit, but what would the U.S. view be in the future if the total warhead limit were 500 and the United States wanted to deploy 100–200 conventional warheads on its strategic ballistic missiles?

Long-Range, Conventional Strike Weapons

In a new negotiation, the Russians may raise the question of long-range, conventionally armed, precision-guided weapons other than those on ICBMs and SLBMs. Currently, the main focus of Russian concern appears to be U.S. conventional air- and sea-launched cruise missiles. The tactical, conventionally armed Tomahawk land-attack missile is highly accurate, capable of landing within a few meters of an aim point, and can deliver a 1,000-pound warhead to a range of 1,600 kilometers (1,000 miles).[15] The U.S. Navy deploys many hundreds of these missiles on a variety of platforms: surface warships, attack submarines, and four Trident submarines previously used for ballistic missiles. Each of the latter can carry up to 154 sea-launched cruise missiles (SLCMs). Russian analysts have postulated a conventional cruise missile attack on Russian strategic forces, including ICBM silos, but they acknowledge that Russia would have tactical warning of an attack as SLCM-armed surface ships moved into range (although they might not detect submarines coming close). One nongovernmental analysis estimated that a conventionally armed U.S. SLCM would have a 37 percent single-shot kill probability against a Russian ICBM silo hardened to withstand an overpressure of 1,000 pounds per square inch, while a conventional U.S. ALCM would have a 17 percent single-shot kill probability.[16]

It is difficult to imagine circumstances in which the United States would agree to limit conventional cruise missiles in a new strategic arms treaty, given their importance to U.S. conventional power projection. U.S. military officers, moreover, doubt that conventional warheads on U.S. cruise missiles have the explosive power to destroy a hardened ICBM silo.[17] How each side assesses this probability might be a question for informal consultations between the two militaries to see if there really is an issue.

Another potential issue is the hypersonic glide vehicle, which both the U.S. and Russian militaries are exploring. The Defense Department is interested in using such a vehicle to rapidly strike targets at intercontinental distances with conventional weapons. The hypersonic glide vehicle would be launched on a ballistic missile and "fly" at hypersonic speeds along the upper reaches of the atmosphere. Because it would not follow a ballistic course, it would not be captured by the definitions of the New START Treaty, even though it might be capable of performing ICBM and SLBM-type missions. Thus, should either the United States or Russia make substantial progress in developing such a vehicle, the other may raise it as an issue in New START's Bilateral Consultative Commission.

Bomber Weapon Counting Rule

Closely related to the deployed strategic warhead limit would be the question of the rule for counting bomber weapons. Under New START counting rules, each deployed heavy bomber is counted as one warhead under the 1,550 limit, continuing the preferential treatment that previous strategic arms control agreements have accorded bombers. The problem is the question of "uncounted weapons"—any weapon more than one that a heavy bomber might carry—which is why the sides will in reality likely field more than 1,550 deployed strategic weapons under New START. If the U.S. Air Force maintains 300 nuclear gravity bombs and air-launched cruise missiles at bases for its B-2 and B-52Hs, the number of uncounted U.S. weapons will be about 250.

The logic underpinning this counting rule is understandable, but counting bombers as having only one warhead represents a large discount regarding bomber weapons delivery capability. The issue of changing the rule might arise in a follow-on negotiation. One approach would keep the discount rule in principle but reduce the amount of the discount; for example, the sides might agree to count each heavy bomber as three or four strategic warheads per aircraft rather than one. That would still give bombers preferential treatment but would reduce the number of uncounted weapons. By contrast, if the sides continued to count bombers as one weapon but reduced the overall deployed strategic warhead limit, the number of uncounted weapons could increase as a percentage of the number of deployed strategic warheads, hardly a desirable outcome.

An alternative approach would return to a U.S. proposal during the New START negotiations: count all nuclear bombs and air-launched cruise missiles stored at or very near the bases where deployed bombers are located as deployed strategic warheads. That would eliminate the discount for bomber weapons and end preferential treatment for bombers.

A third approach—since neither the United States nor Russia normally maintains nuclear weapons on board heavy bombers—would treat all nuclear weapons for heavy bombers as "nondeployed" strategic warheads (discussed below). The deployed strategic warhead limit then would cover only warheads on ICBMs and SLBMs. This approach might not be attractive to either side, however.

The approach Washington would choose could hinge on the projected numbers of U.S. and Russian heavy bombers equipped for nuclear armaments. The United States long had a lead in this area and regularly sought, and achieved, preferential discounted treatment for bombers. Under New START, however, Russia possibly may have more heavy bombers equipped for nuclear armaments, even though the U.S. Air Force would still maintain a numerical lead in total heavy bombers.

Limits on Strategic Delivery Vehicles and Launchers

If the sides decided to further limit deployed strategic warheads in a follow-on negotiation, the question of reducing the limits on deployed strategic delivery vehicles and on deployed and nondeployed launchers and heavy bombers would need to be addressed. The Russians almost certainly would seek to lower the two limits, in particular the limit on deployed strategic delivery vehicles. Since the Russian military is already at about 500 deployed strategic delivery vehicles and its current strategic modernization programs, which emphasize MIRVed strategic missiles, seem unlikely to produce a force of more than 400–500, any tightening of this limit would initially fall solely on U.S. strategic forces.

The Russian military might also see value in lowering the limits on deployed strategic delivery vehicles to constrain U.S. upload capacity. The fewer the number of deployed U.S. ICBMs and SLBMs, the fewer the platforms onto which nondeployed warheads could be uploaded.

The U.S. military, while following through on the de-MIRVing of the Minuteman III ICBM force, favors maintaining a larger number of strategic delivery vehicles. A stability argument can be made for leaving the limit at 700 or possibly 600 while bringing down the limit on deployed strategic warheads. Doing so would encourage the sides, especially the Russians, to de-MIRV their ICBMs and lower the ratio of warheads to missiles.

The Russians, however, appear to be less concerned about the stability argument and reconciled to deploying a smaller number of strategic delivery vehicles. It is cheaper for them (and the United States) to deploy a set number of warheads on MIRVed missiles rather than on single-warhead missiles, and MIRVs offer benefits in overwhelming missile defenses. In a follow-on negotiation, U.S. negotiators should expect a Russian press to reduce the 700 limit.

In weighing a lower strategic delivery vehicle limit, Washington would want to consider its ability to maintain the strategic triad; the 2010 nuclear posture review stated that the United States would maintain a triad for the foreseeable future. Doing so should be possible under a limit of 600 or even 500. Assume a deployed strategic delivery vehicle limit of 500, as opposed to 700 in New START. The U.S. Air Force could reduce the number of Minuteman III ICBMs, and the U.S. Navy could further "detube" Trident submarines, that is, remove SLBMs and convert the missile tubes so that they would not fall under New START's limits. A limit of 500 would allow for a notional U.S. force of 40 deployed heavy bombers, 144 deployed Trident II D5 SLBMs (12 each on 12 submarines) and 320 deployed Minuteman III ICBMs. This would maintain the triad, but it would involve difficult decisions among constituencies that favor different legs.

A new agreement on further limiting deployed strategic delivery vehicles would raise the question of whether the New START limit of 800 deployed and nondeployed ICBM and SLBM launchers and heavy bombers equipped for nuclear armaments should be lowered. If U.S. strategic forces could live with 500–600 deployed strategic delivery vehicles, cutting the number of launchers and heavy bombers from the 800 limit to 600–700—which would still allow each side to have 100 nondeployed ICBM and SLBM launchers and heavy bombers—should not pose a major problem. They might even agree to a lower limit.

Sublimits on Strategic Delivery Vehicles

The question of sublimits might arise if there were interest in encouraging the sides to move away from certain types of strategic systems, such as MIRVed ICBMs. Some strategists may worry that the Russians will maintain a significant number of their permitted warheads on MIRVed ICBMs in silos. Trying to resurrect the idea of sublimits on MIRVed or heavy ICBMs, however, could be a difficult proposition, since U.S. negotiators dropped those sublimits in both the SORT and New START negotiations. Because the Russians favor MIRVed ICBMs in part as a means to maintain a larger number of warheads with a smaller investment in strategic ballistic missiles, persuading them to accept a sublimit that required them to increase production of single-warhead ICBMs to maintain rough parity in overall warhead numbers would be difficult.

Limits on Nondeployed Strategic Warheads

It will be increasingly problematic for the United States and Russia to reduce the permitted number of deployed strategic warheads in a follow-on negotiation while leaving nondeployed (or reserve) strategic warheads untouched. This issue could be particularly important for the Russians. Although the Defense Department has not disclosed a breakdown of its strategic arsenal, it appears that the U.S. military maintains at least one nondeployed strategic warhead for every deployed strategic warhead (table 3-3). This number provides for much more than maintenance spares—it is a hedge against technological failure in a warhead type or geopolitical surprise, such as a significant buildup in Russian strategic nuclear forces.

TABLE 3-3. Estimated U.S. and Russian Nuclear Warhead Numbers

	United States	Russia
Warheads on/for deployed strategic delivery vehicles	~1,950	~2,430
Nonstrategic nuclear warheads	~500	~2,000
Nondeployed (reserve) strategic warheads	~2,500	?
Warheads in queue for dismantlement	~3,000	~5,500
Total	~8,000	~10,000

Source: This table is drawn from the data in Hans M. Kristensen and Robert S. Norris, "U.S. Nuclear Forces, 2012;" and Hans M. Kristensen and Robert S. Norris, "Russian Nuclear Forces, 2012," both in the *Bulletin of the Atomic Scientists* 68, no. 2 (2012): 87–97. Note that the number of deployed strategic warheads in this table differs from the numbers in table 3-1, which shows the number of deployed strategic warheads as declared per New START counting rules, which count only one warhead for each deployed bomber. Kristensen and Norris estimate the number of weapons actually designated for deployed bombers. The number for warheads on/for deployed strategic delivery vehicles on the Russian side appears to count maximum loads for Russian bombers and thus may overstate the actual number. It is possible that the 5,500 figure may overstate the number of Russian warheads in the dismantlement queue and may include some weapons that might be put in the nondeployed (reserve) strategic warhead or nonstrategic nuclear warhead categories.

The U.S. ICBM and SLBM force has a far greater capacity for uploading—in excess of 1,000 warheads—than does the Russian force. If the Russians build more than 500 strategic delivery vehicles, and particularly if they build a new heavy ICBM, they might create their own upload capacity. But that will depend on many factors, including the sustainability of Russian defense spending, and such a buildup would not be complete for a number of years.

The most obvious way to constrain nondeployed strategic warheads would be to impose a numerical limit on them. Washington would need to decide what limit to seek. The number would be affected by considerations such as the need for spares, the need for warheads to hedge against catastrophic warhead design failure, and progress on revitalizing the U.S. nuclear weapons complex. With regard to the latter two points, modernization of the nuclear weapons complex should enable the U.S. military to reduce its nondeployed stockpile, as a more robust complex will be more capable of identifying and responding to issues regarding the stockpile (including by building new warheads more quickly than the United States can today, should that be deemed important).

A variation of this approach would be to set a single limit covering all strategic warheads—deployed and nondeployed—perhaps with a sublimit on deployed strategic warheads. For example, a follow-on treaty might limit each side to 1,500–2,000 total strategic warheads, of which no more than 1,000 could be deployed. This approach could be broadened further to include nonstrategic nuclear weapons, a move that would place all nuclear warheads under a single aggregate limit. (This approach is addressed in chapter 4.)

An alternative approach would simply limit nondeployed strategic warheads to certain declared locations, away from ICBM, SSBN, and heavy bomber bases, and require data exchanges and regular updates. There might be other conditions that would make moving significant numbers of nondeployed warheads to ICBM, SSBN, or heavy bomber bases more difficult and detectable.

If the sides decided to limit nondeployed strategic warheads—either as a separate category or under a single limit that covered all nuclear weapons—they would need to agree on what to do about nuclear warheads removed from the inventory and placed in the queue for dismantlement to ensure against a buildup of a covert stockpile of nondeployed weapons. Difficult monitoring challenges would be involved in providing assurance that all weapons removed from the inventory for dismantlement would not be able to reenter the inventory (U.S. and Russian officials in the early 1990s discussed techniques for verifying the elimination of nuclear weapons, but more work would be needed in this area). Alternatively, the implementation period for eliminating excess warheads could be made longer than the period past accords have typically granted the two countries for reducing their excess delivery vehicles.

As a corollary to limits on nondeployed strategic warheads, in a follow-on negotiation the sides might explore the value of limits on nondeployed strategic ballistic missiles. Devising workable limits, however, could prove difficult. A side producing a new ICBM or SLBM may produce a lot of nondeployed missiles during the production run, which would be maintained for years for tests as well as for maintenance spares. If nondeployed strategic warheads were to be constrained, and the number of deployed and nondeployed ICBM and SLBM launchers remained limited, there might be less need for a separate numerical limit on nondeployed strategic missiles.

Verification Issues

Verification would be a critical aspect of any new U.S.-Russian strategic nuclear arms agreement. Presumably, measures for monitoring limits on deployed delivery vehicles, deployed warheads, and deployed and nondeployed launchers would build on those contained in New START, including a detailed data exchange with regular updates, notifications, unique identifiers for strategic missiles and heavy bombers, and on-site inspections. With such measures, the intelligence community likely could, as with New START, monitor with high confidence Russian compliance with the limits on deployed strategic delivery vehicles and warheads.

U.S. negotiators might consider some amendment to the monitoring provisions. As the numbers of strategic forces are reduced, the benefits of cheating, and thus the temptation to do so, could rise. Concern about this could prompt interest in increased numbers of inspections or greater transparency measures in a new treaty. For example, under New START rules, the data exchanged do not include the number of warheads deployed on individual missiles, but the sides gather that information as they conduct inspections. A more straightforward approach would be to require that the data exchange include the number of warheads on each deployed ICBM or SLBM. That would allow for better decisions about where to conduct inspections and would raise the risk that cheating would be discovered.

The far more complex monitoring challenge would be posed by limits on nondeployed strategic nuclear warheads, which are not mounted on deployed ICBMs or SLBMs. The same considerations would apply to nuclear gravity bombs and to air-launched nuclear cruise missiles, whether located at operational heavy bomber bases or elsewhere.

An essential building block for monitoring any limit on nondeployed strategic warheads would be a requirement that those warheads be maintained at declared storage facilities, except during prenotified transfers and perhaps temporary deployments. Under such a regime, any strategic nuclear warhead spotted outside of an ICBM, SSBN, or heavy bomber base or declared storage facility whose movement had not been prenotified would constitute a violation. Detecting such violations would be exceedingly difficult, although the care with which the United States and Russia handle movement of nuclear weapons might create some possibility of discovery.

Given the heavy security and other unique features at nuclear weapons storage sites, the United States and Russia likely already know most, if not all, of the locations where the other side maintains its nuclear weapons. In 2009, experts from the Federation of American Scientists estimated that the United States maintained nuclear weapons at 21 storage facilities, 15 in the continental United States, and 6 on the territory of 5 NATO allies in Europe. They estimated that Russia had 48 storage sites, all on Russian territory. They noted that the Defense Department's Threat Reduction Program in 2000 had counted 123 nuclear weapons locations in Russia, based on where it had been requested to provide Cooperative Threat Reduction assistance to upgrade security, while the Department of Energy's National Nuclear Security Administration had counted 73 locations. (These totals may reflect a count of separate areas within secure storage sites that are counted as a single storage site in the 48 total.)[18]

Declaring their nuclear weapons storage areas might not be that large a hurdle for the two sides. The tougher question would be their willingness to declare the number of nuclear weapons maintained at each storage site and to agree on procedures for inspections. Access to the entire site in one inspection might not be required. For example, a data exchange could include site diagrams for each nuclear weapons storage area, showing the location of storage bunkers, bays, or chambers. The sides might agree on a procedure whereby an arriving inspection team would be informed of the number of nuclear weapons in each bunker, bay, or chamber and would then have the opportunity to choose one for inspection to confirm the number, much in the same way that deployed strategic warhead inspections are carried out at ICBM and SLBM bases.

Inspectors entering storage bunkers or chambers would require equipment to confirm that observed weapons, many of which would almost certainly be stored in protective containers, were indeed nuclear weapons, that is, that they contained a mass of highly enriched uranium or plutonium consistent with a nuclear explosive device. The equipment would have to operate in a manner that did not reveal sensitive design details of the weapons. U.S. and Russian officials explored these kinds of technical challenges in the early 1990s.

Working out procedures to accomplish this monitoring requirement would be a daunting but perhaps not impossible task. The militaries on both sides would have to provide a degree of transparency that they have not had to in the past. Some Russian analysts believe that such transparency would not be possible in the near term and advocate that the two sides monitor storage sites to ensure that weapons do not leave without prior notification rather than try to monitor the number of weapons within storage sites. Monitoring the storage sites would not be easy, because in the course of normal events, some nuclear weapons would necessarily be moved between storage areas and ICBM, SSBN, and heavy bomber bases.

With political will and some creativity, the sides might be able to work out provisions to allow monitoring of the number of nondeployed strategic warheads at declared storage sites in parallel with monitoring the number of deployed strategic warheads on individual ICBMs and SLBMs. That would be critical for any attempt to limit nondeployed strategic warheads (as well as non-strategic nuclear weapons). The question then would turn to the possibility of nuclear warheads stored covertly at undeclared locations. If either side tried to hide some of its nuclear warheads, it would always run some risk of detection, especially if a defector or other source provided relevant intelligence. While the risk of detection might be quite minimal, the political consequences of such a treaty violation would be very significant and thus might deter cheating.

At this point, it is unlikely that either side in a follow-on negotiation would be prepared to propose or accept an "anytime, anywhere" challenge inspection system that would allow inspectors to travel immediately to any location where they suspected covert undeclared storage of nuclear weapons. How would the U.S. government react, for example, to a Russian challenge inspection request to check the buildings at the secret Area 51 test facility in Nevada for covert nuclear weapons? And the Russians traditionally are far more sensitive than the Americans about permitting access to their military sites.

The best that might be achieved would be a two-tier verification system, in which the sides would have high confidence in their ability to monitor the limits on deployed strategic delivery systems, deployed strategic warheads, and deployed and nondeployed strategic launchers, as they do under New START, but less confidence in their ability to monitor limits on nondeployed strategic warheads, particularly given questions about storage at undeclared sites. Such a two-tier verification regime would allow the sides to monitor with high confidence the most readily usable nuclear warheads and strategic delivery vehicles but could also leave many, including members of the Senate, uneasy about the ability to monitor the entirety of the treaty's limits.

In the end, an argument could be made that the United States could safely accept the lesser monitoring confidence regarding nondeployed strategic warheads, as long as it had high confidence in its ability to verify the number of deployed strategic warheads and as long as that number remained fairly high. If a follow-on treaty to New START limited each side to 1,000 deployed strategic warheads and, for example, 500 nondeployed strategic warheads, the covert storage of an additional 200 nondeployed strategic warheads would be a major political problem, but would it have much effect on the overall strategic balance?

The lower confidence in the ability to monitor nondeployed strategic nuclear warheads would have to be offset against the value of gaining some transparency on these weapons—and, as is discussed in the next chapter, on nonstrategic nuclear weapons, most or all of which are nondeployed. An intelligence community assessment that it could not have high confidence in its ability to monitor some aspects of the treaty would raise issues in the Senate, although the question could depend in part on whether the treaty was negotiated by a Democratic or Republican administration. A Republican president's treaty might well have an easier time securing the two-thirds majority in the Senate needed for approval of ratification.

An additional advantage of even an imperfect monitoring protocol for nuclear warheads is that both sides would gain experience and expertise in this new area of arms control—making it easier to know if more rigorous regimes could be developed in the future (as they surely would have to be, for example, in any worldwide nuclear zero accord, discussed further in chapter 8). Whether or not the experience improved the prospects for a reliable future warhead accord, the information gained could be highly instructive.

CONCLUSIONS AND RECOMMENDATIONS

We believe that further reductions in U.S. and Russian strategic nuclear weapons below the levels in New START are in the U.S. national interest. While Washington might at some point want to consider the wisdom of unilateral reductions, with the possibility that Moscow could follow suit, we believe that treaty limits provide a stronger and more durable arms control regime. We thus recommend that the United States seek one more bilateral nuclear negotiation with Russia, the objective of which would be to reduce deployed strategic warheads to no more than 1,000. In such an agreement, the United States could accept limits on deployed strategic delivery vehicles of no more than 500 and on deployed and nondeployed launchers and heavy bombers of no more than 575–600. A prohibition on new heavy ICBMs would be desirable, but it would require negotiating capital that U.S. negotiators could better apply elsewhere. The sides should also constrain nondeployed strategic warheads and limit these, along with deployed strategic warheads and all nonstrategic nuclear weapons under a single aggregate limit, as discussed in chapter 4.

As for counting rules, we recommend that the actual-load counting rule for warheads on deployed ICBM and SLBMs be maintained but that the bomber weapon counting rule be modified. While bombers continue to merit preferential treatment, as overall limits are reduced, it is more difficult to justify counting only one weapon for each deployed nuclear-capable heavy bomber. The number should be increased to three or four. Should the sides deploy conventional warheads on ICBMs or SLBMs, they should, as under New START, count under the deployed strategic warhead limit. Washington should resist proposals to limit conventionally armed cruise missiles but should consider consultations to discuss how much of a threat they pose to strategic systems.

We recognize that monitoring limits on nondeployed strategic nuclear warheads will pose new verification challenges. Moreover, even if the sides are prepared to accept very intrusive measures, they likely will have less confidence in their ability to verify limits on nondeployed strategic warheads than on deployed warheads. Some degree of lesser confidence is an acceptable risk in order to begin to gain a measure of control of those weapons. Moreover, with 1,000 deployed strategic warheads—which could be monitored with high confidence—it is difficult to see how Russian cheating on nondeployed strategic warheads could significantly affect the broader strategic balance.

Such an agreement as a follow-on to New START would leave the United States with a nuclear deterrent that would be safe, secure, effective, and capable of deterring any potential adversary from a major attack on the United States, its allies, or forces. Negotiating such an agreement would take time, likely two to three years, but it would position the United States to demonstrate at the 2015 Non-Proliferation Treaty review conference its continued commitment to nuclear reductions and perhaps set the stage to seek more direct involvement in the reductions process by other nuclear weapons states. While this proposal might seem to some as a modest step, it is likely to be as far as the United States can go in a bilateral format with Russia. Moreover, bringing in nondeployed strategic warheads (and nonstrategic nuclear weapons) would be a major step.

CHAPTER FOUR

ADDRESSING NONSTRATEGIC NUCLEAR WEAPONS

UNLIKE STRATEGIC NUCLEAR WEAPONS, nonstrategic nuclear weapons have not been subject to arms control efforts, with one very successful exception—the 1987 U.S.-Soviet intermediate-range nuclear forces treaty banned all U.S. and Soviet land-based missiles with ranges between 500 and 5,500 kilometers. Still, thousands of nonstrategic nuclear weapons exist today, particularly in the Russian inventory. Making a case for further cuts in strategic nuclear forces is becoming increasingly difficult while this category remains outside limits. Indeed, when consenting to ratification of the New START Treaty, the U.S. Senate made clear its desire to see an effort to address nonstrategic nuclear weapons.

As a result of unilateral policy decisions over the past twenty years, the United States and Russia have each greatly reduced their stockpiles of nonstrategic nuclear weapons. But the president in 2013 may find himself under some pressure to consider the issue, particularly from many NATO countries, which expect Washington to make a serious effort to engage Russia in arms control on nonstrategic weapons. The president has three possible approaches to consider: confidence-building measures, such as transparency regarding numbers and locations; unilateral measures, such as parallel percentage reductions; and negotiated limits.

We recommend the pursuit of transparency measures as a starter but also suggest that the United States seek to engage Russia in a negotiation that would reduce and set limits on nonstrategic nuclear weapons. The best approach would be to seek a single aggregate limit that would cover all U.S. and Russian nuclear warheads—strategic and nonstrategic, deployed and nondeployed—with a sublimit on the warheads of greatest concern, deployed strategic warheads.

NATO AND NONSTRATEGIC NUCLEAR WEAPONS

Nonstrategic nuclear weapons have made up part of the U.S. arsenal for sixty years. These weapons, or subcategories of them, are sometimes referred to as battlefield, tactical, theater, or substrategic nuclear weapons. There is no agreement in the West, let alone between the West and Russia, on these terms or exactly which weapons they cover. For purposes of the following discussion, the term "nonstrategic nuclear weapons" includes all nuclear warheads except those for use on delivery systems constrained by the New START Treaty—that is, all nuclear warheads except those on or stored in reserve for strategic ballistic missiles, and nuclear gravity bombs and nuclear-armed cruise missiles launched from heavy bombers. This inclusive definition captures nuclear warheads for systems such as Russian missile defense interceptor and anti-aircraft missiles as well as gravity bombs for nonstrategic aircraft. Its advantage is that this term, combined with strategic nuclear warheads (as defined by New START), would cover all nuclear weapons in the U.S. and Russian arsenals except for those that have been retired and are awaiting dismantlement.

Even as the Eisenhower administration built up strategic nuclear forces capable of holding at risk targets in the Soviet Union rather than competing with the Soviets in conventional forces, the U.S. military began deploying a wide range of nonstrategic nuclear weapons in Europe, starting in 1955. By 1961, the year Eisenhower left office, the United States had deployed almost 3,000 of these weapons on the territory of seven NATO allies in support of its Article 5 commitment.[1] These weapons included nuclear warheads for surface-to-surface missiles, antiaircraft missiles, air-to-surface missiles and air-to-air missiles; nuclear gravity bombs for tactical aircraft; nuclear artillery shells; and atomic demolition munitions (later in the 1960s, the U.S. Navy introduced nuclear depth charges in Europe as well).[2] A number of these weapons deployed in Europe were capable of striking targets in the Soviet Union, prompting Moscow to argue for many years that they were "strategic."

In 1967, the year that NATO formally adopted the policy of flexible response, the number of U.S. nonstrategic nuclear weapons in Europe had climbed to almost 7,000. The number would peak at just over 7,300 in 1971. A bit over 60 percent of these weapons were for use by U.S. delivery systems. The remaining weapons were maintained by U.S. forces under "programs of cooperation" and would, in a conflict, be provided to Allied military forces for use by their delivery systems. The Soviets also deployed thousands of nonstrategic nuclear weapons in the European USSR and on the territory of Warsaw Pact countries, including warheads for delivery by artillery, surface-to-surface missiles, and tactical aircraft.

In the context of NATO's policy of flexible response, the deployment of nonstrategic nuclear weapons in Europe gave NATO military commanders multiple options for deliberate escalation to use of nuclear weapons against invading Soviet and Warsaw Pact forces, should direct defense with conventional forces fail. NATO viewed nonstrategic nuclear weapons as having both military and political utility. A nuclear weapon certainly could inflict significant damage on an attacking force; even the possibility of nuclear use could significantly affect conventional force operations. For example, a Soviet tank division that massed to break through NATO forces would present an inviting target for a nuclear strike. Soviet conventional operations could be slowed if commanders had to disperse their forces to avoid presenting targets for such strikes. The United States made many of its nuclear weapons relatively small—with a yield of a few kilotons, less than the bombs dropped on Hiroshima and Nagasaki—to increase at least somewhat the plausibility of their usability against such targets.

NATO allies, however, placed far more importance on the political utility of nonstrategic nuclear weapons: the Alliance's use of these weapons would signal to Moscow that the conflict had reached a hugely dangerous point, with a growing risk of escalation to general nuclear response involving strategic nuclear strikes against the Soviet homeland. Nonstrategic nuclear weapons deployed in Europe were thus seen as linking U.S. strategic nuclear forces to the defense of NATO and thereby strengthening the over-all deterrent impact of NATO.[3] European allies favored nonstrategic systems that had the range to strike targets in the Soviet Union, believing that they would provide a more effective deterrent in Moscow's eyes and regularly worrying that shorter-range systems might mean that a NATO-Warsaw Pact nuclear exchange would be limited to the countries of Central Europe, such as East and West Germany.

In addition to deterring a Soviet–Warsaw Pact attack, U.S. nuclear weapons in Europe also assured NATO allies that U.S. military power, including strategic nuclear forces, was fully committed to their defense. Successful assurance often seemed more difficult than deterrence; Washington had to persuade its allies that it really was prepared to risk a Soviet nuclear attack on the United States in order to defend Europe.

In the late 1970s, the Soviets began deploying the SS-20 intermediate-range ballistic missile at bases in the Soviet Union; this missile could carry three independently targeted reentry vehicles to a range of 5,000 kilometers. The SS-20 was not captured by the SALT II Treaty, which defined ICBMs as having a range of greater than 5,500 kilometers. The combination of the rapid and ongoing production of the SS-20 and Soviet achievement of strategic nuclear parity with the United States—as codified by SALT II—raised concern among NATO allies in Europe. They worried that, with Soviet strategic forces in effect "balancing out" U.S. strategic forces, the growing Soviet advantage in intermediate-range missiles could make NATO's threat of a first use of nonstrategic nuclear weapons in response to conventional attack less credible, thus undermining NATO's entire deterrence continuum.

At the end of 1979, NATO agreed to what became known as the "dual-track" decision. To counter the Soviet buildup in intermediate-range nuclear force missiles, the Alliance decided that the United States would deploy 464 nuclear-armed ground-launched cruise missiles (GLCMs) and 108 Pershing II ballistic missiles on the territory of five NATO allies beginning in 1983. This was thought of as the deployment track. From their planned deployment sites, the GLCMs and Pershing IIs could reach targets in the Soviet Union, an important criterion for NATO allies. At the same time, NATO expressed willingness to discuss with Moscow possible limitations on intermediate-range nuclear force (INF) systems and to begin those negotiations before GLCM and Pershing II deployments began. This was the negotiation track.

The two tracks were closely linked. U.S. and NATO officials regarded progress along the deployment track as essential to motivate the Soviets to engage in serious negotiations in which they would be asked to give up a sizable existing military advantage. U.S. commitment to the negotiation track was also essential, to maintain the support of NATO governments for proceeding with the missile deployments, which were very unpopular with European publics.

The Reagan administration originally proposed the "zero-zero" option, under which the United States would forgo deployment of the GLCMs and Pershing IIs if the Soviets agreed to eliminate all of their SS-20, SS-4, and SS-5 ballistic missiles, resulting in a global ban on all U.S. and Soviet longer-range INF missiles. The Soviets showed no interest in the idea—indeed, there was little expectation in Washington that the Soviets would agree—and instead offered proposals that would have codified a Soviet numerical advantage.

Moscow broke off the negotiations in late 1983 following the deployment of the first U.S. INF missiles in Europe. Negotiations resumed in 1985, shortly after Mikhail Gorbachev came to the helm in Moscow, and two years later produced the INF Treaty, which banned all U.S. and Soviet land-based ballistic and cruise missiles with ranges between 500 and 5,500 kilometers. By June 1991, the United States had eliminated 846 INF missiles, the Soviets 1,846.[4] (For a more detailed description of the INF negotiations and treaty, see appendix A.)

With the end of the cold war, the dissolution of the Warsaw Pact, and the collapse of the Soviet Union by the end of 1991, the number of U.S. nuclear weapons in Europe—which had trended downward from their peak in 1971—declined dramatically: from some 4,000 in 1990 to about 600 in 1993. This reduction coincided with a steep decline in the overall number of U.S. nonstrategic nuclear weapons, from around 8,000 in 1990 to about 2,000 in 1996.[5]

The U.S. reductions were driven in large part by the presidential nuclear initiatives announced by President George H. W. Bush in September 1991, a set of unilateral reductions—to which Gorbachev responded shortly thereafter. These initiatives set in motion a process that, among other things, left the U.S. nonstrategic nuclear arsenal with only nuclear gravity bombs and warheads for sea-launched cruise missiles; the latter were removed from U.S. Navy ships and placed in storage sites ashore, leaving only nuclear bombs in the actively deployed inventory. (Bush announced a second set of presidential nuclear initiatives in January 1992, but they dealt solely with strategic systems.)

As the number of nuclear weapons assigned to NATO declined and Europe adapted to the end of the cold war, NATO's declared policy regarding nuclear weapons evolved as well. The 1991 strategic concept released by NATO leaders stated that "the fundamental purpose of the nuclear forces of the Allies is political: to preserve peace and prevent coercion and any kind of war" and observed that "the circumstances in which any use of nuclear weapons might have to be contemplated by them [the Allies] are therefore even more remote." It noted that NATO nonstrategic nuclear forces would consist solely of nuclear gravity bombs delivered by dual-capable aircraft—aircraft capable of delivering nuclear as well as conventional weapons.[6]

The 1999 strategic concept contained much of the same language but added that "NATO's nuclear forces no longer target any country."[7] The Alliance relaxed its readiness requirements for dual-capable aircraft, some of which during the cold war had been maintained on quick-reaction alert and could have taken off with nuclear weapons in minutes. By 2003, the readiness requirements for dual-capable aircraft operated by Alliance members were "being measured in months."[8]

U.S. NONSTRATEGIC NUCLEAR WEAPONS IN ASIA

Just as the number of U.S. nonstrategic nuclear weapons deployed forward in Europe surged in the 1950s, so too did their number in Asia. By 1961, U.S. military forces had deployed 1,700 nonstrategic nuclear weapons in Asia (not counting those on board U.S. Navy ships at sea). They were located on Okinawa, Guam, and Taiwan and in South Korea and the Philippines, intended for possible use against the Soviet Union, China, and North Korea. The U.S. military also deployed non-nuclear components for nuclear weapons at bases in Japan before withdrawing them in the mid-1960s, out of sensitivity to Japan's "nuclear allergy." (Okinawa was under U.S. control until 1972; when it reverted to Japan, the United States withdrew all nuclear weapons from the island.) The number of weapons deployed ashore in the Pacific region rose to a peak of more than 3,200 in the 1960s and then declined to about 1,100 in 1977, when they were deployed only on Guam and in South Korea.[9]

The United States deployed nonstrategic nuclear weapons in the Pacific region under very different arrangements than it did in Europe. First, whereas the U.S. deployments in Europe were thoroughly interwoven with America's commitment to NATO, in

Asia, bilateral security commitments to countries such as Japan, South Korea, and Australia formed the basis for U.S. security relations. Second, U.S. nuclear weapons in the Pacific region were for use solely by U.S. delivery systems. The United States maintained no weapons for use by Asian allies' delivery systems, as it did in Europe. And third, NATO's declared public policy stressed not only the commitment of U.S. nuclear weapons to the defense of NATO allies but also the physical presence of those weapons in Europe (although specific locations were not revealed). U.S. allies in the Western Pacific generally welcomed the nuclear presence as underpinning their security but were much more reticent about acknowledging that presence publicly.

The earlier and more rapid drawdown of nonstrategic nuclear weapons from bases in the Western Pacific compared with the drawdown in Europe stemmed from several factors. First, Washington concluded that potential conflicts in Asia were far less likely to escalate to use of nuclear weapons than was a major conflict in Europe. In Vietnam, the United States had eschewed use of nuclear weapons. Second, in Europe, NATO faced superior conventional Soviet and Warsaw Pact forces that could attack over a broad front. U.S conventional forces had a more advantageous position in the Western Pacific, where U.S. sea and air power dwarfed that of potential adversaries, and most of the allies that they would have to defend were island states or South Korea, which faced a limited front from North Korea.[10]

The presidential nuclear initiatives announced by Bush in September 1991 effectively curtailed the presence of nonstrategic nuclear weapons in the Western Pacific. The remaining land-based weapons were withdrawn from South Korea—although given North Korea's recent belligerent attitude, some in Seoul suggest that nuclear weapons should perhaps be returned—while all nonstrategic weapons were removed from U.S. warships globally. Thereafter, U.S.-based strategic nuclear forces provided the nuclear umbrella that extended nuclear deterrence to America's

Asian allies. If necessary, nuclear-armed sea-launched cruise missiles could be returned to U.S. ships at sea. Given the collapse of the Soviet Union, however, along with a North Korea apparently mired in stagnation, and the prowess demonstrated by U.S. conventional forces in the 1991 conflict with Iraq, allies in Asia appeared comfortable with the changed U.S. posture. (This was true even though the early 1990s marked the point at which U.S. intelligence first assessed that North Korea might be on a path to a functional nuclear weapons capability.)

U.S. allies in East Asia closely follow U.S.-NATO discussions on nonstrategic nuclear weapons, in part because they see the credibility of a U.S. nuclear deterrent that is forward-deployable to Asia to be bolstered by the forward deployment of U.S. nuclear weapons in Europe. Allies in Asia are also concerned that any U.S.-Russia negotiations regarding nonstrategic nuclear weapons not cause Russian weapons to be relocated out of Europe into the Asian part of Russia, which could degrade their security.

THE NUCLEAR POSTURE REVIEW, NATO'S STRATEGIC CONCEPT, AND THE DETERRENCE AND DEFENSE POSTURE REVIEW

The U.S. nuclear posture review released in April 2010 announced that the nuclear warheads for sea-launched cruise missile (SLCMs) would be retired from the inventory. Some analysts worried that this decision could unnerve Asian allies, but those governments evinced little public concern. The review also stated that the U.S. military would "retain the capability to forward-deploy U.S. nuclear weapons on tactical fighter-bombers (in the future, the F-35 Joint Strike Fighter) and heavy bombers (the B-2 and B-52H), and will proceed with full scope life extension . . . for the B61 nuclear bomb, which will be able to be carried by the F-35 and B-2." The United States maintains dual-capable F-16 aircraft and B61 bombs in Europe, and B-2 and B-52 aircraft periodically deploy to Guam. The review essentially punted, however, on the question of nonstrategic nuclear weapons deployed in Europe, noting that "these [nuclear posture review] decisions do not presume what NATO will decide about future deterrence requirements, but are intended to keep the Alliance's options open and provide for capabilities to support other U.S. commitments." It also stated that "any changes in NATO nuclear posture should only be taken after a thorough review within—and decision by—the Alliance."[11]

The nuclear posture review could leave aside NATO nuclear issues, because NATO leaders at their 2009 summit had requested preparation of a new strategic concept, to be adopted at the Alliance's summit in Lisbon in November 2010. President Obama's April 2009 Prague speech had helped to precipitate a public discussion about NATO's role in nuclear reductions and about moving toward a world free of nuclear weapons. Seeking removal of nuclear weapons became part of the October 2009 coalition agreement between the Free Democratic Party and Christian Democratic Union in Germany. Dutch politicians called for removal of U.S. nuclear arms, and the Belgian parliament took up legislation to ban storage of nuclear weapons on Belgian territory. As the debate gathered steam, other NATO allies, especially those that had joined the Alliance after 1999, such as Poland and the Baltic states, argued that NATO should maintain nonstrategic nuclear weapons as part of its defense posture.

NATO foreign ministers met informally in April 2010 in Tallinn to discuss how the strategic concept might apply to nuclear weapons issues. Secretary of State Hillary Clinton set out five principles for nuclear weapons and arms control:

—"As long as nuclear weapons exist, NATO will remain a nuclear alliance;

—"As a nuclear alliance, widely sharing nuclear risks and responsibilities is fundamental;

—"The broader goal of the Alliance must be to reduce the number and role of nuclear weapons and recognize that NATO has already dramatically reduced its reliance on nuclear weapons;

—"The Alliance must broaden deterrence against 21st century threats, including missile defense, strengthen Article 5 training and exercises, and draft additional contingency plans to counter new threats; and

—"In any future reductions NATO's aim 'should be to seek Russian agreement to increase transparency on nonstrategic nuclear weapons in Europe, relocate these weapons away from the territory of NATO members, and include nonstrategic nuclear weapons in the next round of U.S.-Russian arms control discussions alongside strategic and nondeployed nuclear weapons.'"[12]

These principles helped shape the emerging strategic concept, although European allies had divided into two groups. One group questioned whether deterrence in the post-cold-war world required deployment of U.S. nuclear weapons in Europe. The most prominent advocate of this view was Germany. Other allies, such as Belgium, Denmark, Greece, Luxembourg, the Netherlands, Norway, Spain, and Portugal, shared or leaned toward this view. The second group of allies held that NATO should continue to maintain nonstrategic nuclear weapons in Europe, which they saw as continuing to contribute to deterrence of outside attack. This group included the Baltic states, the Czech Republic, Hungary and Poland, all of which still had doubts about Russian intentions, particularly following the 2008 Russia-Georgia conflict. The second group also included France, whose nuclear forces are not formally committed to NATO but which did not wish to see the Alliance take any step that might call its nuclear position into question. Italy, Turkey, and the United Kingdom gravitated more toward the second view.[13] U.S. officials generally did not see a need to strengthen deterrence of Russia but were mindful of the need to assure the Central Europeans that their concerns would not be short-changed.

Nuclear burden-sharing emerged as a key consideration for many NATO allies. The fact that five European NATO members host U.S. nuclear weapons—Belgium, Germany, Italy, the Netherlands, and Turkey—and four provide dual-capable aircraft makes it easier politically for each of those governments.[14] Indeed, the desire to spread the nuclear burden is a prime reason why U.S. nuclear weapons are based in five countries (and used to be based in more). A decision by one or more of those European states to stop hosting nuclear weapons or providing dual-capable aircraft could raise political pressure on other European governments to follow.

The strategic concept adopted by NATO leaders at their Lisbon summit in November 2010 essentially incorporated Clinton's five principles from Tallinn. While stating that NATO had "the full range of capabilities necessary to deter and defend against any threat," it added that NATO leaders were "resolved to seek a safer world for all and to create the conditions for a world without nuclear weapons" and would "seek to create the conditions for further [nuclear] reductions in the future."[15] The differences among European allies over nuclear weapons, however, had not been fully resolved. NATO leaders thus announced that the Alliance would conduct a deterrence and defense posture review to define the "appropriate mix" of nuclear, conventional, and missile defense forces for the Alliance.

At their Chicago summit meeting in May 2012, NATO leaders approved the results of this review. The document noted that "nuclear weapons are a core component of NATO's overall capabilities for deterrence and defense" while conceding that the circumstances in which their use might be considered "are extremely remote." It stated NATO's readiness to "develop and exchange transparency and confidence-building ideas" with Russia and "to consider further reducing its requirement for nonstrategic nuclear weapons assigned to the Alliance in the context of reciprocal steps by Russia."[16]

The document appears to take a lowest common denominator approach, reflecting the premium that allies placed on maintaining a unified position. The deterrence and defense posture review does not change NATO's nuclear posture in any major way, that is, it contains no unilateral Alliance steps, as some had hoped. It does, however, open the door to possible change in the future. That change will depend on "reciprocal steps" that the Russians are prepared to take with regard to their nonstrategic nuclear weapons.

THE CURRENT STATUS OF NONSTRATEGIC NUCLEAR WEAPONS

Russia currently holds a significant numerical advantage over the United States in nonstrategic nuclear weapons. The U.S. arsenal currently consists of 500 B61 nuclear gravity bombs; 260 nuclear warheads for SLCMs have been retired from the inventory and placed in the queue for dismantlement. Russia, by contrast, is believed to possess a much larger and far more diverse stockpile, with some 2,000 weapons available for deployment on delivery vehicles and additional nonstrategic nuclear weapons in reserve or awaiting dismantlement (table 4-1).[17]

Although the Russian nonstrategic nuclear inventory is several times larger than the U.S. number, it has been reduced considerably since the end of the cold war. Estimates in 1991, before the Soviet Union collapsed, ran from 13,000 to 21,700. Following the collapse at the end of 1991, the Russians moved quickly to relocate all nonstrategic weapons in other former Soviet republics to Russia. It is believed that the vast majority, if not all, Russian nonstrategic nuclear warheads have been "demated"—or separated—from their delivery systems and have been placed in storage.

Of the 500 U.S. nuclear gravity bombs, some 200 are believed to be deployed at six air bases in Europe in hangars capable of housing delivery aircraft—two bases in Italy and one each in Belgium, Germany, the Netherlands, and Turkey. The nuclear weapons at one air base in Italy are designated for use by U.S. Air Force F-16s. The weapons at the other air bases are designated for use by Belgian and Dutch F-16s and by German and Italian Tornados. It is unclear whether the Turkish Air Force still maintains a nuclear role for its F-16 aircraft. There are no authoritative public breakdowns of the number of Russian nonstrategic nuclear weapons deployed in the

TABLE 4-1. U.S. and Russian Nonstrategic Nuclear Weapons, 2012

	United States	Russia
Gravity bombs and air-to-surface missiles	500	~730
Naval weapons (SLCMs, torpedoes, surface-to-surface missiles, depth charges)	0	~700
Land-based surface-to-surface missiles	0	~170
Air defense, ABM, and coastal defense missiles	0	~430
Total	500	~2,000

Source: The numbers in this table are drawn from Hans M. Kristensen, "Non-Strategic Nuclear Weapons," Special Report 3 (Washington: Federation of American Scientists, May 2012). See note 17 to this chapter for a full discussion of these figures.

European part of Russia as opposed to east of the Urals. None of the warheads are believed to be deployed in countries outside of Russia.

One looming issue that NATO faces over the coming decade is the need to replace its current generation of dual-capable aircraft. The United States is procuring the F-35 to replace its F-16s and F-15Es, and the Italians and Turks are also expected to buy the F-35 (beginning in about 2020, all F-35s are expected to be dual-capable). The Dutch government has long expressed interest in purchasing the F-35, but the Dutch parliament voted in June 2012 to withdraw from the F-35 program, and other allies are concerned about the plane's cost. The German Air Force is buying the Eurofighter—which is not nuclear-capable—to replace its Tornados. While the Germans plan to keep some Tornados flying until at least 2020, when these aircraft are retired, the German Air Force will no longer have a nuclear delivery capability. Given antinuclear sentiment in Germany, very few expect Berlin then to retain nuclear weapons on its soil. That could affect decisions by other allies, in particular the Netherlands and Belgium, about continuing a nuclear role. Some analysts believe there will be significant changes in NATO's dual-capable aircraft posture in the next seven to ten years and have suggested that the Alliance consider ways to strengthen non-nuclear means of assuring allies of NATO's commitment to their defense in anticipation of those changes.[18] The deterrence and defense posture review committed the Alliance to look into developing "concepts for how to ensure the broadest possible participation of allies concerned in their nuclear sharing arrangements, including in case NATO were to decide to reduce its reliance on nonstrategic nuclear weapons based in Europe."

The Alliance today views nuclear weapons almost solely in terms of their political utility. The military utility seems to have faded in importance; with the dramatic decline in Russian conventional force capabilities over the past two decades, NATO conventional forces would likely suffice to defeat a Russian attack. Moreover, given political changes since the end of the cold war, the prospect of a Russian conventional attack has also dropped significantly. When asked in April 2010 whether there was "a military mission performed by these aircraft-delivered weapons [B61 gravity bombs in Europe] that cannot be performed by either U.S. strategic forces or U.S. conventional forces," Vice Chairman of the Joint Chiefs of Staff James Cartwright answered simply, "No."[19] (A number of senior U.S. officials in the past have also seen the deployment of these weapons in Europe as providing little incremental military value and to be primarily of political and symbolic importance.)

The Russians appear to attach both military and political utility to their nonstrategic nuclear weapons, seeing them as contributing to deterrence of both nuclear and conventional attacks against Russia. Russia adopted a new military doctrine in 2010. The public version—there is a reportedly a classified annex about which little is known—reserves for Russia the right to use nuclear weapons in response to a conventional attack that puts at risk the very existence of Russia. The 2010 doctrine does not draw a distinction between strategic and nonstrategic nuclear weapons, although, compared with its 2000 predecessor, it does appear to envisage slightly narrower circumstances in which nuclear use might be contemplated. It does not offer any specific thoughts regarding nonstrategic nuclear arms control.[20]

The doctrine does not clarify why Russia maintains such a large number of nonstrategic nuclear weapons. The Russian military is institutionally conservative and has a greater say on nuclear weapons issues in Moscow than does the U.S. military in the Washington interagency process. The Russian military may value the weapons as representing one of the few categories where Russia maintains a clear advantage over the United States and NATO. While Moscow might claim a legitimate requirement for more nonstrategic weapons than the United States, given differences in the two countries' geostrategic positions—Canada and Mexico certainly do not pose the security challenges for the United States that China and NATO are seen to by Russia—the rationale for such a large inventory is still difficult to understand. Looking forward, some analysts expect the number of Russian nonstrategic nuclear weapons to continue to decline as older warheads age and are replaced at a less than one-for-one ratio.

THINKING ABOUT NONSTRATEGIC NUCLEAR WEAPONS ARMS CONTROL

The Obama administration went on record in 2010 as favoring inclusion of nonstrategic nuclear weapons in a new round of U.S.-Russian negotiations, a position that the Senate adopted as well. NATO supports this position, calling for inclusion of the weapons in the U.S.-Russian negotiating process and stating its readiness to consider reducing NATO's nonstrategic stockpile if Russia takes reciprocal steps.*

---

*A reelected Obama administration would likely continue to pursue negotiated reductions of these weapons with Russia. While a Romney administration might be skeptical of the need for, or value of, further reductions of strategic nuclear forces, it could be more open to measures regarding nonstrategic nuclear arms, including negotiations to reduce the disparity between the United States and Russia in the number. Romney himself criticized the New START Treaty for not limiting nonstrategic nuclear arms. In this, he echoed concerns expressed by others, including Republican senators during the ratification debate over New START. Assuming that the concern voiced about these weapons was not merely a pretext to oppose the New START Treaty, this kind of Republican concern might

The ability to get into a serious dialogue on nonstrategic nuclear arms will, of course, depend also on the attitude in Moscow. Since the signing of New START, the Russians have shown little enthusiasm for any further nuclear reductions—strategic or nonstrategic. Given Russian perceptions of their conventional force disadvantages compared to NATO and China, many in Moscow may see a need for greater reliance on nuclear weapons and thus not favor further nuclear reductions—at least until such time as force modernization significantly upgrades Russian conventional capabilities, if not indefinitely given NATO's far larger aggregate size, combined gross domestic product, and current as well as likely future defense budgets.

The Russians, moreover, have stated that all U.S. nonstrategic nuclear weapons must be withdrawn to U.S. national territory before Moscow would engage in any negotiation on such weapons. For the foreseeable future, the United States and NATO almost certainly will not agree to such a precondition. Getting the Russians to agree to put their nonstrategic nuclear weapons into a negotiation will not be an easy task and will require that the United States offer up something of interest to Moscow. As discussed later, there may be ways to bring the Russians around.

---

be a reason that a Romney administration would be interested in exploring some arms control measures on nonstrategic weapons and that it would have Republican support on the Hill for doing so.

A Romney administration, moreover, might find that it needed to pursue negotiations with Russia on these weapons for purposes of managing NATO. The Obama administration's interest in taking up nonstrategic nuclear arms in an arms control negotiation with the Russians undoubtedly has helped to contain sentiments to take unilateral national actions by those allies who no longer see a need for U.S. nuclear weapons in Europe. Keeping that group on board with Alliance policy could become more difficult if allies perceived that Washington was no longer interested in arms control regarding nonstrategic nuclear weapons. So, just as allied concerns led Ronald Reagan to agree to an early negotiation on intermediate-range nuclear weapons, a Romney administration might face a similar need to pursue nuclear arms control and reductions.

Should the United States and Russia begin a negotiation on nonstrategic nuclear weapons, several factors would likely shape how the sides approached those negotiations. First, the New START Treaty limits the numbers of deployed strategic warheads and deployed strategic delivery vehicles. However, Washington and Moscow would likely focus on limiting nonstrategic nuclear weapons themselves, and not the delivery systems, virtually all of which are dual-capable. Given their more likely and more important conventional roles, neither side will want to constrain these delivery vehicles. A negotiation on nonstrategic nuclear weapons thus would focus on the warheads, the vast majority of which are located in storage sites.

Second, these warheads are small and easily transportable, a factor that would argue for global numerical limits—any regional limitation could quickly be circumvented by moving in nuclear weapons from areas outside of the region. For example, it would not be technically difficult for the U.S. and Russian militaries to overcome limitations that applied only to Europe (including Russia up to the Ural Mountains) by transporting nonstrategic warheads from storage locations in the continental United States and the Asian part of Russia to locations in Europe. One could expect Japan and other Asian states to argue for a global limit and to object strongly to any regional approach that would have the effect of moving Russian nuclear weapons from European to Asian storage sites. Such considerations might not, however, preclude adoption of some transparency or confidence-building measures on a regional basis.

Third, any treaty limiting nonstrategic nuclear weapons would have to include equal de jure limits. Any agreement with unequal limits could not be ratified in the Senate. Persuading the Russians to give up their large numerical advantage and accept equal limits would not be easy.

Fourth, verification would be a very challenging issue. The problems surrounding monitoring of nonstrategic nuclear weapons would be similar to those of monitoring limits on nondeployed strategic warheads, discussed in chapter 3. The sides would have to negotiate provisions to allow inspections inside of storage facilities. And the sides likely would not be able to monitor limits on nuclear warheads in storage sites with the same degree of confidence as they can now monitor New START's limits on deployed strategic warheads on ICBMs and SLBMs.

The verification challenges are such that some nongovernmental Russian analysts have suggested that an agreement limit all nonstrategic nuclear weapons to declared storage sites but not seek to constrain the number. Under this approach, the sides would monitor the storage sites to ensure no removal, or no removal that had not been prenotified, of nonstrategic warheads.[21] The problem with such an approach, however, is that the nuclear weapons would exist, albeit in storage and separated from their delivery systems. They could be moved out of those storage sites and put on delivery systems in a matter of days, augmenting the deployed strategic warheads that the sides already have.

When looking at nonstrategic nuclear arms, three approaches for dealing with them are evident: transparency and confidence-building measures, unilateral steps (perhaps conducted by the sides in parallel), and negotiated limits. These categories are not necessarily mutually exclusive; the sides might agree to apply certain transparency measures while negotiating something more substantive.

TRANSPARENCY AND CONFIDENCE-BUILDING MEASURES

The first approach to addressing nonstrategic nuclear weapons includes transparency, codifying the separation of warheads from delivery systems (demating), relocation and consolidation of stored nuclear warheads, and measures to enhance warhead security.

Transparency

Neither the United States nor Russia has provided much public information on the numbers or locations of their nonstrategic nuclear weapons. NATO basing countries are not eager to talk about the nuclear arms on their territory. Transparency could prove useful in helping the sides shape proposals for a negotiation addressing these weapons. If the United States and Russia exchanged information on the numbers of their nonstrategic nuclear weapons, each could then check that information against the databases that they have built over the past decades regarding the other's nuclear forces, thus advancing work on what might become an agreed database for a formal treaty. Short of that, transparency could be used to check implementation of other confidence-building measures. One question that has bedeviled the 1991–92 presidential nuclear initiatives is concern that Russia has not implemented all of the measures it announced it would take. There is no way to confirm specific or even general compliance by either side with its announced unilateral undertakings.

NATO stressed transparency in its 2010 strategic concept and in the deterrence and defense posture review. Speaking at an arms control conference in March 2011, U.S. National Security Advisor Tom Donilon stated that reciprocal transparency "on the numbers, locations, and types of nonstrategic [nuclear] forces in Europe" should be the initial step toward a U.S.-Russian negotiation addressing these weapons.[22]

In an April 2011 letter to the NATO secretary general, ten heads of NATO missions transmitted a paper prepared by Germany, the Netherlands, Norway, and Poland on transparency and confidence-building measures regarding tactical nuclear weapons as a means of opening a path to reductions in those weapons. The paper agreed with Donilon on the need for transparency on the numbers, types, and locations of such weapons and also called for transparency on "command arrangements, operational status, and level of storage security." The paper further suggested that NATO and Russia agree on "a standard reporting formula" for information on their tactical nuclear inventories, notify one another of plans to move the weapons, and focus first on exchanging information to clarify how many nuclear weapons had been eliminated or placed into storage as a result of the 1991–92 presidential nuclear initiatives.[23]

Other analysts have also suggested an exchange of data regarding the numbers of weapons removed from the U.S. and Russian inventories and dismantled following the presidential nuclear initiatives. The exchange of this kind of historical data would be less sensitive but would still provide useful information that could be checked against the sides' own databases.

In the run-up to their May 2012 summit, NATO officials reportedly discussed a menu of eleven transparency and confidence-building measures that might be explored with the Russians. In the end, the Alliance decided not to publicize those ideas—the deterrence and defense posture review mentions transparency and confidence-building measures only in very general terms—in the belief that first engaging the Russians privately on the proposals might increase the likelihood that Moscow would take up some of them.

Confidence-building measures may have some resonance in Moscow. The Russians continued to observe the Organization on Security and Cooperation in Europe's "Vienna Document" on confidence-building measures as well as the "Open Skies" agreement, even after they suspended their participation in the Conventional Armed Forces in Europe Treaty in 2008.

Codifying Demating of Warheads

As a general rule, the U.S. Air Force does not keep nuclear weapons on board delivery aircraft, whether the weapons are strategic or nonstrategic. They are demated, although in the case of B61 gravity bombs deployed in Europe for use by U.S. and allied air forces, the weapons are kept in special storage vaults under the floors of hangars capable of accommodating the delivery aircraft.

On the Russian side, it is believed that most, if not all, of its nonstrategic nuclear weapons are separated from their delivery systems. While some warheads are stored at military bases where delivery systems are located, many are maintained at storage sites some distance away from the delivery systems.

One confidence-building measure thus might be to codify what already appears to be standard operational practice on both sides. The United States and Russia could each state that, as a matter of policy, it would not maintain nonstrategic nuclear warheads on delivery systems. Such a measure could have political value, although its practical impact might well be limited. If the sides observed the policy, it could at least marginally increase the time it would take to prepare to use the weapons.

A further possible benefit from codifying demating practices is that it would help establish a precedent that could extend beyond U.S.-Russia bilateral arms control to other possible accords in the future, including multilateral ones. More generally, it could also give a boost to the prospect of "de-alerting" efforts with super-power strategic forces.

If the United States and Russia agreed to a demating confidence-building measure, they might also consider a parallel measure to refrain from exercising their tactical aircraft to carry out nuclear strike missions. Such a measure might be expanded to include NATO aircraft as well, although it would have to be a topic of careful consultation with NATO allies, particularly those who see a need for the current nuclear posture.

Relocation and Consolidation of Warheads

Another possible confidence-building measure would be relocation of nonstrategic warheads away from the NATO-Russia border. Some Russian nuclear storage sites are quite close to the Baltic states and northern Norway (storage sites on the Kola Peninsula are believed to support Russian strategic as well as nonstrategic nuclear forces). The active NATO nuclear storage site closest to Russian territory is Incirlik Air Base in Turkey; it lies about 800 kilometers from Russia.

The Alliance earlier expressed considerable interest in such a step. The 2010 strategic concept stated that NATO should aim for Russian agreement to greater transparency and to "relocate these weapons away from the territory of NATO members." Relocation of Russian nuclear weapons would be a positive and welcome political gesture, although its practical impact would be quite limited, since the weapons could be removed from their storage sites, transported, and then remated with delivery systems in a matter of days.

Two other observations apply. First, any relocation of Russian nuclear weapons away from the NATO-Russia border should generally be to storage sites west of the Urals, that is, in the European part of Russia. Any U.S.-Russia or NATO-Russia agreement that relocated Russian weapons to Asia would undoubtedly raise concerns in Japan, China, and other Asian states.

Second, while relocation may look attractive when applied to Russian nuclear weapons, NATO might regard it as problematic if applied to U.S. nuclear weapons. Given the configuration of active U.S. nuclear weapons storage sites—six sites in five countries—relocating weapons out of any of the sites except one of the two in Italy would result in one less country hosting U.S. nuclear arms. That could raise political pressure on the other basing countries to withdraw as hosts. So the Alliance may be leery of this, especially if the agreement did not also reduce the overall Russian numerical advantage in nonstrategic nuclear weaponry.

The same considerations would apply to consolidation of nonstrategic nuclear weapons. NATO undoubtedly would welcome a Russian decision, as a confidence-building measure, to consolidate Russian nuclear weapons at a smaller number of storage sites, especially if those sites were located away from NATO territory and not collocated with delivery systems. NATO could find it difficult, however, to come up with a consolidation measure of its own that did not leave some European allies feeling that they were assuming a relatively larger share of the nuclear burden as other allies ended their nuclear hosting role.

Nuclear Warhead Security

Although both NATO and Russia are believed to apply serious security measures to protect all nuclear weapons, including nonstrategic ones, such warheads separated from their delivery systems are considered to be vulnerable to theft or unauthorized access. The United States and Russia supported UN Security Council Resolution 1540, which among other things called for tighter security standards for nuclear weapons and materials. They thus might establish a dialogue to exchange views on the possible threats to nuclear warheads in storage and on measures to upgrade their security. In such a dialogue, U.S. and Russian officials could draw on the experience that they have gained over the past two decades under the Nunn-Lugar Cooperative Threat Reduction program, which included work to upgrade the security at numerous sites where Russia stored nuclear arms and fissile material. Again, the benefits of such steps could be just as great beyond the U.S.-Russia or NATO-Russia domain, creating useful precedents that countries such as India and Pakistan as well as China might benefit from down the road.

UNILATERAL STEPS

A second category of possible actions includes unilateral steps that the United States and Russia could undertake, perhaps in parallel, to limit or reduce their nonstrategic nuclear weapons. This would look back to the experience of the 1991–92 presidential nuclear initiatives, which set in motion the elimination of many thousands of U.S. and Russian nonstrategic nuclear weapons.

No-Increase Commitment

One measure would be for Washington and Moscow to declare in parallel that, as a matter of policy, neither would increase the number of its nonstrategic nuclear weapons. Both sides could find it relatively easy to take this step. Such a commitment might have positive political impact, but its practical effect would be limited given that the two sides' arsenals would not be affected in any significant way (neither is expected to increase its stock of these weapons).

Some analysts have suggested that a no-increase commitment could be coupled with a commitment not to modernize the capabilities of nonstrategic nuclear weapons. A no-modernization commitment could be tricky. U.S. B61 nuclear bombs are due for a life extension program later this decade. Although the life extension program is expected to refurbish and reuse existing nuclear components, the bomb is scheduled to receive a new tailfin and other modifications designed to make it more accurate. Would that constitute modernization? The Russian practice is to dismantle old nuclear warheads and build new ones as replacements, an ongoing process that allows them to maintain an effective nuclear stockpile. How would it be possible to ensure that this process did not result in some modernization of Russian nonstrategic nuclear capabilities?

Unilateral Reductions

The sides might choose to pursue unilateral reductions. One option apparently ruled out by the deterrence and defense posture review would be a unilateral NATO decision to remove some or all U.S. nonstrategic nuclear weapons from their European bases back to the United States. The results of the review make clear that any actions regarding NATO nonstrategic nuclear weapons must take place in the context of reciprocal steps by the Russians. (While NATO allies agreed to this, in part for purposes of alliance unity, significant sentiment for unilateral reductions persists in some NATO capitals.)

The "reciprocal steps" criterion would be met if the United States and Russia were, as matters of national policy, to take unilateral steps in parallel to reduce the number of their nonstrategic nuclear weapons by a certain percentage. For example, the United States and Russia might each unilaterally reduce the number of nonstrategic nuclear warheads by 50 percent. Ideally, the reduction—or elimination—would be applied globally, with the understanding that the numbers of weapons deployed in Europe would also be cut in half.

Such a reduction would still leave Russia with a numerical advantage in nonstrategic weapons, both globally and in Europe, but it would prove attractive to many, if not most, NATO allies. Since NATO's nonstrategic nuclear weapons are seen now almost solely in political terms, there is nothing magical about the current level of some 200. A reduction to 100 weapons in Europe would still leave a politically significant number. Assuming an equal percentage reduction in the number of weapons in each basing country, such a reduction would still spread the nuclear burden. A 50 percent reduction would entail a significant cut in Russian weapons. And by allowing a sustained Russian advantage, albeit a declining one, in this area of nuclear weaponry, NATO might be able to soften Russia's objections to at least some types of missile defense systems where NATO capabilities already exceed, and will continue to outdistance, Moscow's.

Parallel reductions of 50 percent would be workable as parallel unilateral actions. It would likely be impossible, however, to incorporate such a scheme into a legally binding treaty, because of the political requirement for equal de jure limits. But parallel reductions like this might be salable to congressional skeptics if most NATO allies supported the move.

NEGOTIATED LIMITS

The third category of measures is legally binding limits negotiated between the United States and Russia. The sides could seek to limit nonstrategic nuclear weapons separately or as part of a broader limit covering all nuclear weapons.

Discrete Limit

The sides could decide to seek a treaty to reduce and limit only their nonstrategic nuclear warheads. Alternatively, nonstrategic nuclear weapons could be separately covered by different provisions in a broader agreement that also limited strategic forces (perhaps including nondeployed strategic warheads as well as deployed strategic warheads). In either case, a primary challenge facing the negotiators would be the disparity in numbers. Even when we use the most conservative estimate of the number of Russian weapons, Russia will have a fourfold advantage over the United States for the foreseeable future.

Stanford professor emeritus Sidney Drell and former senior U.S. government official James Goodby have proposed separate but parallel negotiations on strategic and nonstrategic nuclear weapons. They argue that the latter should receive priority, in part because their transportability could make them a target for terrorist seizure, and suggest that a separate limit on nonstrategic nuclear warheads be based on proportional reductions, with the end goal being elimination of all such weapons.[24]

Negotiating an equal de jure limit on nonstrategic nuclear weapons would likely prove more difficult than negotiating proportional reductions. Many possible equal limits would require reductions only on the Russian side. For example, if one assumed a Russian inventory of 2,000 nonstrategic nuclear warheads and a U.S. inventory of 500 (all B61 gravity bombs), an equal limit of 1,000 would require the Russians to cut their arsenal in half in return for no reductions on the U.S. side. Such an outcome would not be attractive to Moscow unless the United States was prepared to offer concessions elsewhere, for example, on its strategic forces or ballistic missile defense. And there might be objections in Washington that, since the United States has no plans to increase its nonstrategic nuclear weapons, such an outcome would codify a de facto Russian advantage.

A treaty limiting nonstrategic nuclear warheads would need to incorporate intrusive verification measures, such as inspections of warhead storage sites. Even with such measures, however, such a treaty could encounter questions, particularly in the Senate, about the level of confidence with which the other side's compliance could be monitored.

Combined Aggregate Limit

An alternative approach would be to negotiate, in a follow-on treaty to New START, a single aggregate limit that covered all U.S. and Russian nuclear warheads, strategic and nonstrategic, deployed and nondeployed. Such a treaty might include a sublimit on deployed strategic warheads, the warheads of greatest concern. The treaty could contain ancillary limits on deployed strategic delivery vehicles and on deployed and nondeployed strategic launchers and heavy bombers, but it would not limit delivery systems for nondeployed strategic warheads. (The sides would also have to agree on some regime to cover warheads that were out of the inventory and in the queue for dismantlement.)

For example, such a treaty might limit the United States and Russia each to no more than 2,000–2,500 total nuclear warheads (not counting those awaiting dismantlement); no more than 1,000 could be deployed strategic warheads. Ancillary limits would restrict each side to no more than 500 deployed strategic delivery vehicles and no more than 575–600 deployed and nondeployed strategic launchers and heavy bombers. No limits would be placed on delivery systems for nonstrategic nuclear weapons.

Under such a treaty, both sides presumably would maintain 1,000 deployed strategic warheads, down from the 1,550 limit in New START. Each would then be free to choose its mix of nondeployed strategic warheads and nonstrategic warheads to make up the remaining 1,000 or 1,500 weapons to reach its aggregate limit of 2,000 or 2,500. The United States might opt to maintain more nondeployed strategic warheads but would still have to reduce them compared with its current number; the Russians might choose to maintain more nonstrategic nuclear warheads, but they too would have to reduce that category compared with their current level. In effect, the single aggregate limit would serve as the mechanism to encapsulate a trade-off: a U.S. reduction of its advantage in nondeployed strategic nuclear warheads—which would also constrain U.S. upload capability—in return for a Russian reduction of its advantage in nonstrategic nuclear warheads.

The Obama administration has reportedly weighed an approach that would put all nuclear warheads under a single ceiling precisely because it would allow the sides to trade off between different types of nuclear warheads. A U.S. readiness to reduce the limit on deployed strategic warheads to below New START's 1,550 limit and to constrain nondeployed strategic warheads could create leverage that might be used to get Moscow to cut its nonstrategic nuclear warhead numbers.**

Of course, in such an agreement, the sides would still face the same challenges regarding verification of compliance with limits on nondeployed strategic nuclear warheads and nonstrategic nuclear warheads. As noted, there might be high confidence in the ability to monitor the limits on deployed strategic warheads and delivery vehicles, and on deployed and nondeployed strategic launchers and heavy bombers, but less confidence in the ability to monitor limits on nondeployed strategic warheads and nonstrategic warheads, which would be separate from their delivery systems.

Some NATO allies might welcome the single limit as treating all nuclear weapons equally. Others could worry, however, if a U.S. preference to hold nondeployed strategic warheads led to a significant de facto Russian advantage in nonstrategic weapons.

**It is less clear what a Romney administration might think of this kind of approach. To achieve reductions in Russian nonstrategic nuclear warheads, the United States might have to be prepared to further reduce its deployed strategic warhead level and put its nondeployed strategic warheads under constraint. A Romney administration might not be enthusiastic about the notion of further reductions in strategic nuclear forces.

Limit to National Territory

The New START Treaty requires that strategic delivery vehicles be based on national territory, with a proviso that heavy bombers may deploy temporarily outside of the United States or Russia. The Russians have consolidated all of their nonstrategic nuclear warheads on Russian territory and have called for the United States to withdraw its nonstrategic nuclear weapons from Europe. The 200 or so U.S. B61 gravity bombs currently deployed in Europe are the only nuclear weapons based outside the territory of a nuclear weapons state.

The Russian attempt to make withdrawal of U.S. nuclear weapons deployed in Europe a precondition for negotiations is plainly a nonstarter. NATO's deterrence and defense posture review underscored the Alliance's requirement for reciprocal steps from Russia. However, if the United States and Russia do negotiate a treaty that limits nonstrategic nuclear weapons, either separately or as part of a single aggregate limit covering all U.S. and Russian nuclear warheads, Moscow would almost certainly insist that the new treaty incorporate a requirement that all nuclear weapons be based on national territory. Whether in the end such a provision would be acceptable to the U.S. government and to NATO allies would depend on other terms of the treaty, in particular, how far the treaty would reduce the Russian nonstrategic nuclear stockpile. Some Obama administration officials indicated privately in 2011 that such a "base on national territory" provision might be acceptable depending on the impact of the overall treaty.

CONCLUSIONS AND RECOMMENDATIONS

It is in the U.S. interest to seek limits on nonstrategic nuclear weapons and to reduce the current disparity that favors Russia. Democrats and Republicans appear to agree on the value of reducing this disparity, although some of the latter harbor doubts about the wisdom of engaging in arms control to achieve that.

We believe the United States should seek to include nonstrategic nuclear weapons in the next round of negotiations with Russia. As steps to take before negotiations or while they are under way, we favor transparency regarding the numbers and locations of weapons and perhaps parallel unilateral reductions by an equal percentage. We would suggest caution about seeking withdrawals away from the NATO-Russia border and consolidation of weapons at fewer sites; while desirable on the Russian side, NATO would have a difficult time reciprocating.

In a negotiation with Russia, the United States should seek an aggregate limit that covers all nuclear weapons (except those in the dismantlement queue, which would be dealt with separately). The limit should be set at no more than 2,000–2,500, which would represent a reduction of about 50 percent for each side. Within that overall limit, deployed strategic warheads, the weapons of greatest concern, should be limited to no more than 1,000. The United States and Russia would be free to determine the mix of nondeployed strategic warheads and nonstrategic nuclear weapons to fill out the difference between the 1,000 sublimit and the overall cap of 2,000–2,500.

Limiting nonstrategic nuclear warheads would pose verification challenges similar to those posed by limits on nondeployed strategic nuclear warheads. The sides should consider a requirement that all such weapons be maintained at declared storage facilities that would be subject to inspection. We believe the United States could accept a lower degree of confidence for monitoring limits on nonstrategic nuclear weapons in the context of this overall agreement.

If the rest of the terms could be worked out satisfactorily, the United States should be prepared—in consultation with NATO—to accept what would be an almost certain Russian demand for a provision requiring that all nuclear weapons be based on national territory. That would require removal of U.S. nonstrategic nuclear weapons from Europe, but in conjunction with very significant Russian reductions and in a substantially improved political environment, and greater accord ideally over planned NATO missile defense systems for Europe (as discussed more in the next chapter).

Finally, in deciding its arms control policy on nonstrategic nuclear weapons, the U.S. government must be mindful of the continuing need for close consultation with NATO (and Asian) allies— and the fact that U.S. nuclear weapons remain deployed in Europe far more for reasons of assuring allies than for deterring outside aggression. Few things would undermine allied trust in the United States more quickly than a perception that Washington was taking decisions on issues affecting their security without involving them. On the other hand, a strong process of consultation—as occurred in the NATO Special Consultative Group during the INF negotiations in the 1980s and the discussions with allies in the run-up to the completion of the 2010 nuclear posture review—can strengthen alliance cohesion and confidence and bolster a U.S. negotiating approach with Moscow.

CHAPTER FIVE

MISSILE DEFENSE ISSUES

BOTH THE UNITED STATES and Russia have long been interested in missile defense. In 2013, missile defense and the interrelationship between strategic offense and strategic defense are likely to occupy a central spot on the agenda between Washington and Moscow, as they have done for much of the time since the 1960s. The Russians attach great importance to the interrelationship and assert that planned U.S. missile defense deployments in Europe could degrade their strategic missile force and undermine the strategic balance. Moscow thus has demanded a legally binding guarantee that U.S. missile defenses would not be directed against Russian strategic forces, a demand that has stalemated the prospects for establishing a cooperative NATO-Russia missile defense. U.S. officials argue that planned U.S. missile defenses pose no serious threat to Russian ballistic missiles, even theoretically, and that no legal document limiting missile defenses would be approved by the Senate.

The president in 2013 could face several questions regarding missile defense. One might be whether to reassess and perhaps alter or adjust the current program. A second question would be whether to continue to seek a cooperative NATO-Russia missile defense arrangement. A related question is how far the United States should extend itself to secure Russian assent to cooperation (by offering transparency regarding its missile defense plans, for example), and how explicitly should missile defense deployments be connected to the evolving threat. Yet another possible issue could be a legally binding treaty constraining missile defenses, although strong Senate opposition to such limits currently makes that a nonstarter.

We believe a cooperative NATO-Russia missile defense arrangement is in the U.S. interest. Access to Russian early warning and tracking data would provide for a better missile defense capability for Europe, and a cooperative arrangement would defuse missile defense as a difficult problem that might undermine the broader U.S.-Russia and NATO-Russia relationships. The president thus should reiterate the offer to the Russians of a political commitment that U.S. missile defenses would not be directed against Russian strategic missiles, combined with maximum transparency regarding U.S. missile defense programs and plans. NATO should be prepared to take account of Russian ideas that would not degrade NATO's ability to defend NATO members, and the United States should make clear that it could adjust its missile defense efforts if countries such as Iran did not develop long-range ballistic missiles. Washington and NATO should seek to make it as easy as possible for Moscow to agree to a cooperative arrangement.

Moscow's views on missile defense are complex. On the one hand, it seems preoccupied with an old strategic calculus based on hypothetical nuclear exchanges between the United States and Russia that appear entirely inconsonant with the current state of their political relations. In the process, it also tends to give U.S. missile defense technologies too much credit and the capabilities of its own strategic forces too little. On the other hand, in fairness to Moscow, some Americans also still think in traditional nuclear-balance terms, and some American analysts argue that proposed U.S. missile defenses could have a notable hypothetical capability against a fraction of the Russian nuclear arsenal.

A SHORT HISTORY OF MISSILE DEFENSE

Missile defense and the interrelationship between offense and defense have been topics of discussion between Washington and Moscow for almost fifty years. As the United States and Soviet Union each built up their intercontinental and submarine-launched ballistic missiles in the 1960s, both sides considered ways and developed missile defense systems to defend against ballistic missile attack.

By the mid-1960s, the Soviets had begun to develop an anti-ballistic missile system around Moscow, while the Johnson administration proposed the Sentinel system, the purpose of which was to defend U.S. cities against a Chinese ballistic missile attack or a small, unauthorized Soviet attack. The Nixon administration reconfigured the plan into the Safeguard system, which used the same interceptor missiles. Safeguard was intended to defend U.S. ICBM fields, rather than cities, against Soviet ballistic missile attack, thus contributing to maintaining a strong U.S. retaliatory capability.

Given the challenges of intercepting and destroying ballistic missile reentry vehicles (warheads) traveling at high speeds—ICBM warheads travel at a velocity of around 7 kilometers a second—the Russian (Galosh) and U.S. (Spartan and Sprint) interceptors all were armed with nuclear warheads. In the event of an attack, ground-based radars would guide the interceptors to points close to incoming warheads, where their warheads would be detonated, in theory destroying the enemy warheads.

As Washington began to consider the possibility of negotiations to limit strategic offensive forces, it also considered limits on ABM systems. The Nixon administration believed that tightly constrained ABM systems would have a positive effect on strategic stability. First, with limited numbers of ABM interceptors, neither side would be able to successfully defend itself against a retaliatory strike, which would reduce the incentives to strike first in a crisis. Second, since adding more ICBM and SLBM warheads was one way to try to overwhelm the other side's defense, capping ABM systems would ease that pressure for a strategic offensive arms buildup.

In June 1972, President Richard Nixon and General Secretary Leonid Brezhnev signed the Anti-Ballistic Missile Treaty, along with the Interim Offensive Arms Agreement as a result of the SALT I process.[1] The ABM Treaty banned the United States and Soviet Union from deploying a nationwide ABM defense. The sides were allowed to deploy no more than 100 ABM interceptor launchers at each of two sites, one near its national capital and the second near an ICBM field, reflecting each side's preferred ABM deployment plan.

The treaty also limited the battle management radars that guide ABM interceptors. It further required that the United States and Soviet Union deploy any new radars for early warning of a strategic ballistic missile attack "at locations along the periphery of its national territory and oriented outward," which limited their utility for guiding ABM interceptors. The treaty banned development, testing, or deployment of "sea-based, air-based, space-based, or mobile land-based" ABM systems.

Two years after the ABM Treaty entered into force in October 1972, President Gerald Ford and Brezhnev met in Vladivostok and signed a protocol to the treaty restricting each side to only one ABM deployment area with no more than 100 interceptor launchers. The Soviets maintained their ABM system around Moscow, which has been modernized and remains active to the present day. Shortly after the protocol was signed, Congress cut off funding for the ABM interceptor site at the Grand Forks ICBM base in North Dakota (the United States never built a system around Washington).

The Strategic Defense Initiative (SDI) launched by President Ronald Reagan in 1983 sought explicitly to end U.S. vulnerability to Soviet ballistic missile attack. The program funded exploration of a broad range of defensive technologies, including "hit-to-kill" technologies for ground-based interceptors whose kinetic kill vehicles would ram and destroy incoming warheads. The "Smart Rocks" program, which later became "Brilliant Pebbles," envisaged hit-to-kill technology on small interceptors, which would be carried on a large number of satellites in space. They would be launched from these satellites in near-Earth orbits to collide with strategic ballistic missiles in their boost phase, an attractive option because it offered the possibility of destroying a missile before it could release multiple warheads and penetration aids.

The initiative also examined more exotic technologies, such as directed-energy weapons. One proposal entailed using nuclear devices on satellites to power an X-ray laser. When the nuclear device detonated, it would produce a pulse of X-rays that could be directed against ballistic missiles in their boost phase or against individual warheads in the midcourse portion of their flight.

The SDI program raised a host of ABM Treaty compliance issues. For example, the treaty prohibited space-based ABM systems. Lasers fell into the category of ABM systems that were based on "other physical principles"; the treaty required that, should such systems be created, limitations on those systems would be a subject for discussion between the sides.

Initially, the SDI program provoked concern among Soviet military planners that a U.S. technological breakthrough might weaken their strategic offensive force capabilities. The Soviets raised those concerns in the Standing Consultative Commission, a body established by the ABM Treaty to discuss its operation. They also insisted that, when in 1985 the Strategic Arms Reduction Treaty (START) and Intermediate-Range Nuclear Forces (INF) negotiations resumed, there be a new forum—the Defense and Space Talks, which would include ABM issues. (In contrast to START and INF, this new negotiation failed to produce any kind of agreement.)

In the second half of the 1980s, Soviet concerns about SDI began to subside as experts such as Roald Sagdeyev, head of the Moscow Space Research Institute, explained the full difficulty of the task of defending against a large-scale ballistic missile attack and questioned the feasibility of mounting an effective defense against the missiles. General Secretary Mikhail Gorbachev went on to sign the INF and START treaties without new limitations on ABM systems.

Likewise, by the end of the 1980s, Washington came to realize that developing successful missile defense technologies would be far more difficult and expensive than originally thought. The George H. W. Bush administration downsized U.S. missile defense ambitions, adopting a system known as Global Protection against Limited Strikes (GPALS). The goal was to defend against a limited ballistic missile attack on the United States. While much more modest than SDI, GPALS, had it come to fruition, still would have encountered problems with the ABM Treaty, because it envisioned several hundred interceptors spread across a half dozen bases or so and a layer of space-based interceptors. The Clinton administration chose not to pursue the plan.

U.S. missile defense efforts in the early 1990s switched focus to theater missile defenses to protect U.S. forces against shorter-range ballistic missiles in the context of a theater conflict.[2] The difficulties caused by Iraqi Scuds during the 1991 Gulf War were a principal reason. Over the 1990s, the U.S. military developed several interceptors and supporting radars: the land-based Patriot Advanced Capability (PAC-3) system and Terminal High Altitude Area Defense (THAAD) system, and the Standard SM-2 interceptor to provide U.S. Navy warships with a terminal defense against shorter-range missiles.

The Russians questioned whether these interceptors would be capable of engaging reentry vehicles traveling at higher velocities, such as those on ICBMs and SLBMs. If so, the Russians argued, they would be captured by the ABM Treaty's limits. Washington expressed readiness to define a threshold that would divide missile interceptors that fell under the purview of the treaty from those that did not.

In 1997, U.S. and Russian negotiators concluded a set of agreed statements that were referred to as the demarcation agreement.

In essence, the statements defined any interceptor missile with a velocity of less than 3 kilometers a second and tested against a target whose speed was less than 5 kilometers a second and whose range was less than 3,500 kilometers as a tactical rather than a strategic missile defense interceptor. Such interceptors, which were too slow to engage ICBM or SBLM warheads and which could not be tested against targets that replicated the speed of strategic warheads, would not be subject to the ABM Treaty.

Meanwhile, concern grew in Congress about the threat posed by ballistic missile developments in countries such as North Korea and Iran. The Commission to Assess the Ballistic Missile Threat to the United States, chaired by Donald Rumsfeld, claimed that North Korea and Iran could construct, within five years of deciding to do so, an ICBM that could reach the United States. This concern spurred congressional passage of the Missile Defense Act of 1999, which stated that "it is the policy of the United States to deploy as soon as technologically possible an effective national missile defense system capable of defending against limited ballistic missile attack (whether accidental, unauthorized, or deliberate)."[3]

The Clinton administration explored developing ground-based interceptors that used hit-to-kill technology to destroy reentry vehicles in the midcourse portion of their flight, with a missile defense architecture entailing 100–250 interceptors that would be deployed in Alaska and possibly North Dakota. The number of interceptors was judged too low to blunt a major Russian missile attack, but any number of interceptors in excess of 100, and their deployment in Alaska, would have contradicted the terms of the ABM Treaty. U.S. officials in late 1999 and early 2000 discussed with Russian officials the possibility of amending the ABM Treaty to accommodate U.S. plans, but Moscow showed no interest. A failed test of the ground-based interceptor in 2000 delayed the program, saving Clinton from having to choose between defending the United States against limited ballistic missile attack and preserving the ABM Treaty together with good relations with Russia.

President George W. Bush opted for missile defense. In his first two years in office, he decided to withdraw from the ABM Treaty and instructed the Pentagon to move forward with deployment of a missile defense capability for a limited defense of the U.S. homeland. The Defense Department began deployment of ground-based interceptors (GBIs) in 2004—before completing the interceptor's test and development program. Currently twenty-six GBIs are deployed at Ft. Greeley, Alaska, and four are at Vandenberg Air Force Base, California. The Pentagon intends to complete silos to hold fourteen more GBIs at Ft. Greeley.

The three-stage GBI has had, at best, a mixed record in flight tests. It is designed to intercept ballistic missile warheads in space during the midcourse phase of flight and has the velocity and range to engage ICBM warheads. Once launched, the GBI receives initial guidance from a ground-based radar. The kinetic kill vehicle mounted on top of the GBI has an infrared seeker that picks out the warm incoming warhead and directs the kinetic kill vehicle to collide with and destroy it. It has failed to intercept its target in about half of its test flights. Moreover, as missile defense critics point out—and Defense Department officials acknowledge—the current seeker cannot discriminate between a warhead and realistic decoys. While rudimentary long-range missiles might carry only a warhead, as a country's program matures and becomes more sophisticated, it could master decoys, chaff, jammers, and other countermeasures.

GBI deployments in Alaska and California are well placed to intercept ICBMs coming out of North Korea and also can protect reasonably well against ICBMs launched from Iran, which would fly a polar route. To improve defense against an Iranian ICBM, the Bush administration decided to add a third interceptor site in Poland, which would host a two-stage variant of the GBI. In 2007–08, U.S. officials reached agreement with the Polish government on deploying ten GBIs in Poland and with the Czech government on deploying a supporting X-band tracking and discrimination radar in the Czech Republic.

The Russians objected vociferously. They argued that Iran had no ICBM and asserted that the Iranians were years away from acquiring such a capability; the planned Poland-based GBIs thus had to be intended for use against Russian ICBMs. Russian officials asserted that the number of interceptors could be increased beyond ten and that the planned radar could precisely track objects in space over Russia (which the Pentagon later acknowledged to be true).

In 2007, Russian President Vladimir Putin suggested a cooperative U.S.-Russian missile defense system and offered to contribute Russian early warning and tracking data from two radars that provided good coverage of Iran. He demanded, however, that in return the United States forgo deployment of GBIs in Poland, a price the Bush administration was not prepared to pay. Discussions on possible cooperation made little headway, and missile defense proved one of the most difficult issues on the U.S.-Russia agenda in 2007 and 2008.

THE EUROPEAN PHASED ADAPTIVE APPROACH

The Obama administration reviewed the missile defense policy that it inherited from the Bush administration and in September 2009 announced a reconfiguration of the plan to focus on missile defense of Europe. The White House said the change resulted from a revised assessment regarding Iran's ballistic missile capability: "The intelligence community now assesses that the threat from Iran's short- and medium-range ballistic missiles is developing more rapidly than previously projected, while the threat of potential Iranian intercontinental ballistic missile (ICBM) capabilities has been slower to develop than previously estimated."[4]

The current threat posed by Iranian ballistic missiles comes from short-range missiles, such as the Scud, and the medium-range Shabab-3 missile. The Shabab-3's estimated range of 1,000–1,600 kilometers allows it to hit Israel and Turkey. The Iranians are also developing the Sejjil-2, which, with a projected range of 2,200 kilometers, could reach southeastern Europe.

The Obama administration replaced the Bush plan with the European Phased Adaptive Approach (EPAA), which it said would allow earlier deployment of capabilities to defend U.S. forces in Europe and NATO allies against Iran's short- and medium-range ballistic missiles. Those capabilities could be increased in anticipation that the Iranians might develop longer-range ballistic missiles.

The Aegis system—which provides the core of the EPAA—combines an advanced SPY-1 radar capable of tracking multiple ballistic missile targets and providing guidance information to interceptors, the associated computer hardware and software, and the solid-fueled Standard SM-3 interceptor capable of destroying attacking ballistic missile warheads in midcourse, while they are still outside the atmosphere. The SPY-1 radar provides initial guidance and, as the Standard SM-3 nears the incoming warhead, its kinetic kill vehicle activates its infrared seeker, which steers the vehicle into a collision with the warhead. The EPAA currently comprises four phases:[5]

—Phase 1, which began in 2011, entails the U.S. Navy operating Aegis-capable warships with Standard SM-3 Block IA interceptor missiles in the eastern Mediterranean. This missile reportedly has a velocity of about 3 kilometers a second and can engage current Iranian short- and medium-range ballistic missile warheads (based on the testing record, the effectiveness appears reasonably high—as long as Iranian decoy technology is not advanced). The U.S. Navy presence in the Mediterranean is augmented by an AN/TPY-2 radar in Turkey to provide early warning and tracking information. In 2014 and 2015, the U.S. Navy plans to base four Aegis-class warships in Spain to eliminate the need for trans-Atlantic transit from and back to home ports on the U.S. East Coast.

—Phase 2, to begin in 2015, will deploy the Standard SM-3 Block IB interceptor missile on board U.S. Navy ships. This interceptor will use an improved infrared seeker to guide its kinetic kill vehicle. Twenty-four SM-3 interceptor launchers and a supporting

SPY-1 radar are also scheduled to be placed in an "Aegis-ashore" configuration in southern Romania.

—Phase 3, planned for 2018, involves deployment of the Standard SM-3 Block IIA interceptor on U.S. Navy warships and of twenty-four launchers and an SPY-1 radar in Poland. The SM-3 Block IIA, which is being codeveloped with Japan, will be larger than SM-3 Block I missiles. It is planned to have a velocity of about 4.5 kilometers a second, which should give it the capability to engage intermediate-range ballistic missile warheads. The Polish deployment site, near the Baltic coast, will extend missile defense protection to northern Europe.

—Phase 4 was originally scheduled to begin in 2020, but the date appears to be slipping. It will involve deployment of the Standard SM-3 Block IIB. Still on the drawing board, the SM-3 Block IIB is planned to have a velocity of 5 to 5.5 kilometers a second. The SM-3 Block IIB interceptor will enhance U.S. capability to engage medium- and intermediate-range ballistic missile warheads and provide some capability against Iranian ICBM warheads launched toward the United States. It is expected to be deployed at the Polish site. The Block IIB interceptor may carry some liquid fuel, in contrast to Blocks IA, IB, and IIA, which are all solid-fueled. That might raise a question about deployment at sea, since the U.S. Navy prefers to avoid liquid-fueled missiles on board its warships for fire safety reasons.

The Defense Department's fiscal year 2012 budget submission stated that 43 U.S. Navy warships would be capable of deploying SM-3 interceptors in fiscal year 2020, by which time the total planned buy of the missiles is projected to be 515. These will primarily be SM-3 Block IA and Block 1B missiles; only 29 Block IIA interceptors are scheduled for purchase by fiscal year 2020. The budget submission did not indicate the number of SM-3 Block IIB interceptors to be procured, but in a decade's time they will constitute only a small part of the total SM-3 missile buy, very probably less than 50. (It is worth bearing in mind that the Aegis/Standard program was well under way before the EPAA was conceptualized and that it has a multitude of other possible purposes globally, from the Persian Gulf to the Western Pacific.)

At their summit meeting in Lisbon in November 2010, NATO leaders endorsed the idea of adapting NATO's Active Layered Theater Ballistic Missile Defense (ALTBMD) system and combining it with the EPAA program to defend all of NATO Europe against a limited attack by ballistic missiles: "The aim of a NATO missile defense capability is to provide full coverage and protection for all NATO European populations, territory, and forces against the increasing threats posed by the proliferation of ballistic missiles."[6]

The Alliance, which had already allocated $800 million of common NATO funds to set up the command and control system for the ALTBMD system, agreed to spend an additional $200 million to adapt the command and control system for the Europe-wide defense mission. The U.S. EPAA is planned to operate under this system, as can missile defense contributions from other allies, such as the Patriot PAC-3 systems operated by the Dutch and German militaries. At their May 2012 summit meeting in Chicago, NATO leaders announced that the Alliance had achieved an "interim" operational capability for missile defense of a portion of NATO territory, meaning that the Alliance had the necessary capabilities, command and control procedures, and rules of engagement so that it could conduct territorial defense over southeastern Europe in a crisis. The U.S. AN/TPY-2 radar in Turkey was placed under NATO operational control, and the U.S. government indicated that, if necessary, its Aegis-capable warships could also be placed under NATO control. NATO's missile defense system aims to achieve initial operational capability in 2015, followed by full operational capability in 2018.[7]

Given concerns among U.S. allies and partners about North Korea, China, and Iran, the U.S. government is exploring regional missile defense architectures in the Western Pacific and the Persian

Gulf. U.S. sea-based SM-3 missiles supported by the SPY-1 radar could make a contribution to such regional arrangements; they were deployed in April 2012 in anticipation of a North Korean satellite launch, which failed shortly into its flight. These plans, however, are not nearly as developed as those for the EPAA and NATO's territorial missile defense capability.

NATO, RUSSIA, AND MISSILE DEFENSE

The Russian government at first appeared to welcome the Obama administration's decision to replace the planned ground-based interceptors in Poland and X-band radar in the Czech Republic with the EPAA, presumably because the SM-3 interceptor has a significantly lower velocity and range than the GBI. In November 2010, NATO leaders and President Dmitry Medvedev agreed to explore the possibilities for a cooperative NATO-Russia missile defense arrangement for protecting Europe. Medvedev suggested a sectoral approach, whereby NATO and Russia would each take responsibility for defending designated parts of Europe. NATO was cool to the idea, because some NATO member states would have found themselves in the Russian sector.

Meeting in the first part of 2011, experts from the U.S. Defense Department and the Russian Ministry of Defense reportedly found broad agreement on the outline of a cooperative NATO-Russia missile defense system. Both sides understood that NATO and Russia would each maintain independent control over a decision to launch its interceptors. The sides also agreed that each should maintain control over its sensors, including satellites and radars, that would provide launch warning and tracking data on a ballistic missile and its warheads. And they agreed that a cooperative missile defense should initially aim to defend Europe against threats coming out of the broader Middle East. Their views converged on the need for transparency regarding missile defense capabilities and the potential for joint missile defense exercises. They further discussed the possibility of two jointly staffed centers. A "data fusion center" would combine warning and tracking information from both sides to create a "common operational picture," which would be shared with the NATO and Russian missile defense command centers, where it would inform their (independent) decisions about launching an interceptor. A "planning and operations center" would provide the venue for conducting transparency exchanges; consulting on ballistic missile threats and possible attack scenarios against Europe; and discussing planned intercept operations, possible rules of engagement, and procedures for coordinating intercepts in areas of overlapping intercept capability.[8]

Several U.S.-Russian Track II dialogues—the Euro-Atlantic Security Initiative, the Albright-Talbott-Ivanov-Dynkin dialogue, and the PIR Center-Ploughshares Fund Sustainable Partnership with Russia dialogue—met in 2010 and 2011 and generated similar ideas for a cooperative missile defense arrangement.[9] Taking official and nonofficial discussions together, a full menu of ready ideas exists regarding the architecture and operation of a cooperative NATO-Russia missile defense.

In spring 2011, however, Russian officials began to insist that Russia required a legal guarantee that U.S. missile defenses would not be directed against Russian strategic missiles. Russian officials noted that such a guarantee should be accompanied by "objective criteria," which they defined as limits on the numbers, velocities, and locations of missile defense interceptors and the numbers, locations, and capabilities of supporting radars.[10] This demand seemed to reflect a desire to conclude a new ABM Treaty or something like it. The Obama administration offered to make a political commitment that the EPAA would not pose a threat to Russia's strategic nuclear deterrent but showed no interest in negotiating a legally binding treaty constraining U.S. missile defense capabilities. Among other things, it believed that any treaty that limited missile defense would have virtually no chance of approval by the Senate.

On the eve of the May 2011 Group of Eight summit in France, U.S. and Russian officials came close to an agreement on the principles of a political framework for a cooperative missile defense system but could not reach final closure.[11] Thereafter, Moscow's public attacks on U.S. missile defense plans intensified.

The Russian position—which blocked NATO-Russia progress toward creating a cooperative system—stemmed from a variety of motivations. Russian analysts do not appear concerned by the first and second phases of the EPAA but rather with Phase 4 and the alleged threat that the SM-3 Block IIB could pose to Russian ICBMs, given its projected velocity of 5 kilometers a second (in the 1997 demarcation agreement, the Russians were comfortable that interceptors with speeds below 5 kilometers a second were no threat to strategic ballistic missiles). U.S. officials have responded that SM-3 Block IIB missiles based in Poland would have to "chase" Russian ICBMs launched from European Russia and could not catch them, and that the number of warheads on Russian strategic ballistic missiles would easily overwhelm the small number of SM-3 Block IIB missiles, especially as those warheads could be augmented by advanced decoys and other countermeasures.

Russian officials nevertheless continued to express concern about the plan to deploy the SM-3 Block IIB in Poland. They may be more concerned about what could come after Phase 4. Russian Deputy Prime Minister Dmitry Rogozin—who served previously as Russia's ambassador to NATO and was deeply engaged in discussions on missile defense—observed in January 2012: "Do you really think they [the United States] will halt all their technologies after 2020? That's nonsense! They will go ahead with developing and boosting the technical parameters of their interceptor missiles and performance capabilities of their warning systems."[12]

A second reason for Russian reluctance may be the Ministry of Defense, which has never shown much enthusiasm for cooperation on missile defense. Officials in the ministry may calculate that, by portraying U.S. missile defenses as a threat to Russia's strategic deterrent, they can secure greater funding for modernization of Russian military forces, including more modern air and missile defense systems. A number of Russian military programs, such as testing of new ICBMs, already have been publicly justified as responses to U.S. missile defense, even when those programs were launched well before the September 2009 announcement of the EPAA.

Two other reasons for Russian opposition likely relate to NATO. Russian officials regularly make clear their unhappiness about the waves of NATO enlargement that followed the end of the cold war. Moscow particularly does not like the prospect of American military infrastructure and personnel on the territory of countries that joined NATO over the past fifteen years, even if the planned missile defense detachments in Romania and Poland are quite small.

Moscow may also hope that missile defense, absent Russian cooperation, could be turned into a divisive issue among the NATO allies. The Russians likely recognize that few allies worry about a missile attack from Iran but instead have other reasons for supporting the EPAA, such as an interest in U.S. military deployments on their territory or a belief that missile defense might assume some of the deterrence and defense burden from nuclear weapons and enable a reduction in the number of U.S. nonstrategic nuclear weapons deployed in Europe. Russian officials may conclude that this issue could be used to drive wedges among European allies or between the United States and Europe.

More generally, the Russians appeared to have gone into a holding pattern on missile defense until after the U.S. 2012 presidential election. They seemed to calculate that a Romney administration would pursue a different approach to missile defense, and perhaps to missile defense cooperation, than would a reelected Obama administration. Republicans had sharply criticized the September 2009 decision to reconfigure missile defense in Europe. Before revealing its bottom line on missile defense cooperation with NATO, Moscow may want to know what approach the United States will take on missile defense in 2013. (Obama's comment to Medvedev in Seoul in March 2012 to the effect that he would have greater flexibility after his reelection may well have encouraged Russia to wait and see.)

Ultimately, the Russian position will turn on Putin's decision and will be shaped in part by his view of how the issue plays in Russian domestic politics. During his presidential campaign in early 2012, Putin adopted a harsh line toward Washington, suggesting to some analysts that he may seek to portray the United States as an adversary to distract attention from domestic economic or political problems. As Russian strategic forces expert Pavel Podvig observed: "In terms of an actual impact on Russia's security, U.S. [missile] defense is largely irrelevant. The intensity of Russia's opposition to the missile defense plans owes more to its internal political circumstances than to anything else."[13] Although Putin has taken a negative tone on missile defense, a change in course should not be excluded. If the United States and NATO go forward with the current plans without Russia, Putin runs the risk of appearing impotent to affect the missile defense debate and NATO's planned deployments.

POSSIBLE APPROACHES TO MISSILE DEFENSE AND COOPERATION

The U.S. administration in 2013 will have several options for dealing with missile defense. One question is how it chooses to structure (or restructure) its missile defense efforts. Several recent reports have raised questions about the effectiveness of current U.S. missile defenses.[14] That said, the notion of missile defense has a significant degree of political support in Washington. Either a Democratic or Republican administration is likely to pursue missile defense, the latter almost certainly with greater intensity. A key unknown at this point, however, is how missile defense would fare if the defense budget is subject to further large-scale cuts and funding has to be weighed against funding for other pressing Pentagon needs.

Some argue for changes in the Obama administration's approach to missile defense. Republicans in Congress have expressed interest in building a third GBI site in the northeastern United States, and a recent National Research Council report appears to support that approach.[15] The Pentagon says that a third site is unneeded now and prefers to go forward with the EPAA as currently planned. Another option is to return to the Bush administration plan to deploy two-stage GBIs in Poland (which would protect the United States more than Europe). That is a possibility, but it would not seem likely. NATO has already endorsed the EPAA, and it is not clear how quickly the two-stage GBIs could be developed—certainly not faster than the 2015 date for the SM-3 Block IB interceptor deployment in Romania and possibly not sooner than the 2018 SM-3 Block IIA deployment in Poland.

Again reconfiguring the missile defense plan could prove disruptive to the consensus that has now formed within NATO around the EPAA as the U.S. contribution to NATO's European missile defense. It would raise a number of questions—such as whether the GBIs would be deployed in addition to or in place of the later SM-3 phases—that could cost allied support. Several allies, such as Germany, remain sensitive to Russian concerns. While Moscow has made clear that it is unhappy with the current U.S. missile defense plan for Europe, the higher velocity and significantly greater range of the GBIs would likely provoke an even greater outcry from Moscow.*

Another option would be to continue to pursue missile defense cooperation with Russia, as the Obama administration has sought to do. Republicans in general have expressed skepticism about Russia and Russian policies, however, and Republicans in Congress have made several attempts to block or hinder the exchange of sensitive or classified missile defense information with Russia, a stance that could severely inhibit any effort to build a cooperative NATO-Russia missile defense system. At a minimum, the United

---

*While a Romney administration would probably reassess U.S. missile defense plans, it might well decide to simply continue with the EPAA rather than risk undoing the NATO consensus that developed between 2009 and 2012.

States would have to be prepared to share U.S. early warning data if Washington and NATO expected to gain access to Russian detection and tracking data.

U.S. officials are interested in the data that could be provided to NATO missile defense operations by the new, large, phased-array radar at Armavir in southern Russia and the older Russian-operated phased-array radar at Gabala in Azerbaijan. These radars have excellent views of Iran. While the two radars cannot provide the precision tracking and discrimination information that the U.S. AN/TPY-2 radar in Turkey can, they could likely provide earlier warning of a ballistic missile launch coming out of Iran. Given the speed with which a decision about launching an interceptor would have to be made, an earlier warning, even one that is only a few seconds earlier, would help.

Washington thus has a practical reason to seek a cooperative arrangement with Russia. It also would have a political reason to do so. While NATO allies have expressed support for the EPAA and European territorial defense, several allies strongly desire a cooperative missile defense agreement with Russia. A decision in Washington not to pursue such cooperation could create problems with allies such as Germany and undermine NATO support for going forward with the European missile defense system. A more conservative U.S. administration might find that Alliance management required that it make a more intense effort to gain Russian agreement to missile defense cooperation than it would be inclined to make on its own.

The next administration has several options for advancing a cooperation agreement with Russia. It could reiterate the offer of a political commitment, in place of a legally binding guarantee, that U.S. missile defenses would not be directed against Russian strategic forces. NATO has already provided such language following the May 2012 summit: "Such concrete missile defense cooperation is the best means to provide Russia with the assurances it seeks regarding NATO's missile defense plans and capabilities. In this regard, we today reaffirm that the NATO missile defense in Europe will not undermine strategic stability. NATO missile defense is not directed against Russia and will not undermine Russia's strategic deterrence capabilities."[16]

Other steps include transparency. In 2011, Lieutenant General Patrick O'Reilly, director of the U.S. Missile Defense Agency, expressed a readiness to host visits by Russian experts to observe flight tests of the SM-3 interceptor. As he told the Atlantic Council in October 2011, "We have offered for them to participate in our flight testing. [So] they can measure it themselves with their own systems and verify [that] the performance . . . is effective against regional and limited missiles—long-range missiles—but not effective for the strategic threat that they're concerned about."[17] The U.S. government could reiterate this offer and make clear that it would include tests of the SM-3 Block IIA and Block IIB, the interceptors of greatest concern to Moscow. Such observations could confirm what U.S. officials have said—that the SM-3 interceptor lacks the velocity and range to pose a threat to Russian strategic missiles. Such an offer could cause concern among some members of Congress who are sensitive about sharing information with Russia and who might raise objections. But the SM-3 tests normally occur over international waters, so the Russians likely could position sensors to observe tests in any event, albeit with greater difficulty if they did not have advance notice of specific test events.

The U.S. government could also offer greater transparency regarding its future plans for missile defense programs. For example, the U.S. government might on an annual basis provide Russia with a notification, which would note for each major element of the U.S. missile defense system—GBIs, SM-3 missile interceptors (broken down by the four blocks), GBI silos, land-based SM-3 launchers, associated radars, and Aegis-capable warships—the number currently deployed and the number projected to be deployed each year for the coming ten years. The U.S. government could also commit to provide advance notification of any increases in the projected numbers of various missile defense elements. The advance notice would be substantial, given that it takes time from a decision to produce extra missile defense elements to contract, build, and actually deploy them.

This kind of transparency would provide the Russians with a relatively detailed and regularly updated picture of U.S. missile defense plans and capabilities, which could inform their assessments of whether a genuine threat to their strategic ballistic missiles existed. Much of this information is already publicly available from Defense Department documents and budget submissions. If U.S. officials could work out an arrangement whereby the Russians provided similar notifications, Washington would gain information about Russian missile defense plans that is not currently in the public domain.

The United States and NATO might consider two other steps to make it easier for Russia to agree to missile defense cooperation. First, the U.S.-NATO position to date has been that cooperation with Russia would not in any way change U.S. and NATO missile defense plans for Europe. That can hardly be expected to make the prospect of cooperation appealing to Moscow. NATO might instead state that it is prepared to consider and adopt Russian proposals, provided that they do not reduce the ability of NATO missile defense systems to provide coverage for Alliance members. That would leave room for accommodating Russian proposals while protecting the key requirement for NATO: that the ability of its missile defense system to protect NATO allies not be degraded. For example, one Russian nongovernmental expert suggested in 2011 that the SM-3 interceptor site in Poland be relocated to a military facility in southwestern Poland, which would move it away from possible Russian ICBM tracks toward the United States. Washington and NATO might leave open the possibility of considering such an idea—if the Russian government were to advance it—if the relocation would not degrade NATO's ability to defend NATO members.

Second, U.S. officials could indicate that the "adaptive" part of the EPAA envisages a possibility that the United States could delay development or deployment of the SM-3 Block IIB, should it become evident that the Iranians are not making substantial progress toward achieving an ICBM capability. This would require a change in emphasis from current U.S. policy—senior U.S. officials have voiced a commitment to deploying all four phases of the EPAA—and would likely be controversial with Republicans in Congress. But, if Iran does not get close to fielding an ICBM, what would be the purpose of deploying an interceptor to defend against it?

The U.S. administration in 2013 could bundle some or all of these measures in a package to increase the prospect that the Russians would agree to work with NATO on a cooperative missile defense system. At a minimum, extending such a package would position Washington to make the case to NATO allies that it had made a maximum effort to address legitimate Russian concerns and that the onus for any lack of agreement on missile defense cooperation rested solely in Moscow.

A different approach to missile defense would be to accept the Russian demand for a legally binding guarantee and agree to negotiate a treaty, perhaps of limited duration, constraining missile defense. For example, the United States might agree to a ten-year treaty that allowed each side no more than 125 missile interceptors with the velocity and range to engage ICBMs (with no constraint on where such interceptors might be deployed). That would capture the GBI and SM-3 Block IIB on the U.S. side and at least the Moscow ABM system interceptors on the Russian side. Such a constraint would permit the United States to deploy everything that it is likely to want and to be capable of deploying over the next decade to deal with ICBM threats from North Korea or Iran but still limit the number of U.S. interceptors to a level that would not seriously threaten the Russian strategic ballistic missile force.

Limiting the treaty to ten years' duration would allow the sides to reassess the prospects for future missile defense capabilities in the early 2020s and determine whether to continue to constrain these defenses. The Russians undoubtedly would reserve the right to reconsider adherence to nuclear arms reduction agreements in this case, but they would have the right in any event if the agreement contained the standard supreme national interests withdrawal clause.

Such a treaty would also defuse missile defense as an issue in New START's implementation and in a possible negotiation of a follow-on treaty. Even in the unlikely event that the administration would choose to negotiate such a treaty, however, there is virtually no chance of consent to ratification in the current or next likely Senate, where Republicans have made clear their antipathy toward anything that would constrain U.S. missile defense. Even if the agreement were limited to ten years, missile defense proponents would worry that, once the United States had reentered an ABM-type treaty regime, it could be difficult to leave should circumstances change.

Although the Russian concern about the SM-3's capabilities against Russian strategic ballistic missiles appears to be overblown, Moscow nonetheless has a legitimate concern regarding the broader point. If U.S. missile defenses continue to develop and expand beyond the EPAA and current ground-based interceptors, at some point the United States could field serious capabilities to engage Russian strategic missiles and affect the strategic offensive nuclear balance between the United States and Russia. Ideally, by the time such a situation became hypothetically feasible, the United States and Russia would have further improved their relationship to the point where nuclear competition between them had become anachronistic, if not simply nonsensical, and Moscow would not feel it had any reason to worry. If that were not the case, Moscow could decline to engage in further nuclear reductions or even exercise its right to withdraw from New START or a successor nuclear arms reduction treaty. The Russians could pose a stark choice: firm, legally binding limits on missile defenses or no further nuclear arms cuts. For those who are committed to missile defense—and perhaps skeptical of the value of nuclear arms reductions—this would not be a difficult decision. For a president who wished to continue reducing nuclear forces, it could pose a tough dilemma. But this is a dilemma for a time in the future.

CONCLUSIONS AND RECOMMENDATIONS

A cooperative NATO-Russia arrangement for territorial missile defense of Europe is in the U.S. interest. Access to early warning data from the Russian-owned or operated radars at Armavir and Gabala would usefully augment the data from NATO sensors, including by providing earlier radar warning and tracking of ballistic missile launches from Iran. A cooperative missile defense thus would offer a better defense of Europe than NATO alone could provide. Moreover, by engaging in missile defense cooperation, the sides could defuse a difficult issue that now appears likely to undermine the broader U.S.-Russia and NATO-Russia relationships. At a time when the West needs Moscow's help on questions such as pressuring Iran to abandon its nuclear weapons program and providing key supply lines to U.S. and NATO forces in Afghanistan, Washington should look for ways to minimize problems on the agenda with Russia. Finally, genuine NATO-Russia missile defense cooperation holds the potential to alter cold war stereotypes about the Alliance that linger in Russia. We thus believe that the U.S. government and NATO should consider ways to facilitate Russian agreement to a cooperative missile defense.

A legally binding U.S.-Russian agreement limiting missile defense is politically unattainable; in current circumstances, the Senate would not consent to its ratification. We believe the president should instead offer a political commitment not to direct U.S. missile defenses against Russian strategic forces, much along the line of the recent NATO assurances, and should offer to regularize and maximize transparency regarding U.S. missile defense programs and plans. This includes annual notifications of the number of key missile defense elements, both current and projected for each year over the next ten years, as well as an opportunity for Russian experts to observe SM-3 interceptor flight tests.

NATO might propose a time limit on the cooperative arrangement, say, four years. That would allow the Russians to "test drive" the arrangement and see if the enhanced transparency that would come from day-to-day missile defense cooperation eased their concerns. If not, they could walk away, and NATO would acknowledge that possibility up front. The timing should not be a problem. In his November 2011 statement on missile defense, Medvedev indicated that the crunch point for Moscow would not come for six to eight years.[18]

In our view, NATO should make clear that it would fully consider Russian proposals for a cooperative missile defense, including those that might alter NATO plans, provided that the proposals did not degrade the ability of NATO missile defenses to protect NATO members. Washington should state that "adaptive" envisages the possibility that development and deployment of the SM-3 Block IIB interceptor might be slowed if the Iranians do not appear to be making progress toward an ICBM capability.

The goal of all of this would be to encourage—and to make it as easy as possible for—Russia to agree to a cooperative missile defense arrangement. In the end, Moscow might not agree, for the reasons discussed. In that event, the United States and NATO would be positioned to argue that they had made every reasonable effort and that the Russians were responsible for the failure to cooperate on missile defense.

Finally, as to the dilemma that a president may someday face with regard to pursuing missile defense or further nuclear arms reductions: the interrelationship between strategic offense and strategic defense is a fact of life. The Russians attach great importance to the interrelationship, which has proved problematic in the Senate, where Republicans worry that the link could lead an administration to scale back U.S. missile defense efforts. Our inclination is to favor proceeding with further nuclear arms reductions while developing defenses to protect the United States and its allies from the threat of limited ballistic missile attack by nations such as Iran and North Korea. Reliable and affordable technologies that could protect the United States against anything like a full-scale Russian ballistic missile attack simply do not exist today and will not emerge over the next decade given current U.S. plans and available defense budget resources. While a breakthrough might come at some point in the more distant future, the history of the past fifty years suggests that highly effective missile defenses are more difficult to achieve than anticipated and that strategic offense can find ways to overcome defensive advances. Washington should show caution about pursuing missile defense courses that are not justified by the technology at hand and that could well trigger a Russian or Chinese strategic nuclear missile buildup, which would not be in the U.S. interest. The administration should engage Congress on the implications of these trade-offs.

CHAPTER SIX

THE COMPREHENSIVE TEST BAN TREATY AND STOCKPILE MAINTENANCE

ONE QUESTION THE PRESIDENT will need to consider in 2013 is what to do about the Comprehensive Nuclear Test Ban Treaty (CTBT). For fifteen years, an uneasy compromise has existed in American nuclear weapons policy. President Bill Clinton signed the treaty in 1996, but in 1999 the Senate refused to approve it for ratification. The Obama administration, according to its 2010 nuclear posture review, states as a matter of official policy that it intends to pursue ratification of the CTBT but has not indicated any specific plans for doing so.[1] Yet, the United States has not tested a nuclear weapon since 1992—even through the eight years of the George W. Bush administration. Neither have any of the other four original nuclear powers tested since the mid-1990s. And nuclear testing has not been an issue in the 2012 presidential campaign.

Why has this consensus not to test endured and in fact strengthened? Is this state of suspended animation a sufficient foundation for U.S. policy in the area of nuclear weapons testing and stewardship? If not, what should replace it, and when? How well can the U.S. nuclear weapons stockpile be maintained safely and reliably—indefinitely into the future—without testing? These are the questions addressed in this chapter.

The CTBT is not, of course, the only treaty ever proposed to limit nuclear testing. Spurred by growing appreciation of the dangers of fallout from atmospheric tests, enabled by improved verification methods, and further catalyzed by the fear associated with the Cuban Missile Crisis, President John Kennedy and Soviet Premier Nikita Khrushchev signed the Limited Test Ban Treaty in 1963. It banned tests in the atmosphere, in space, and underwater. The 1974 Threshold Test Ban Treaty and 1976 Peaceful Nuclear Explosions Treaty then limited even underground testing—although to a fairly high threshold of 150 kilotons, about ten times more than the yields of the bombs that had destroyed Hiroshima and Nagasaki. But the CTBT would, as its name connotes, be the first comprehensive ban on nuclear weapons tests of any significant yield at all.

As inherently unstable as it may seem and as unsatisfying as it may be to many, the current de facto policy toward nuclear testing and modernization is actually working reasonably well for the United States. The U.S. nuclear stockpile appears robust and dependable, now and for the foreseeable future; indeed, confidence in its safety and reliability appears to have grown in recent years, despite the absence of testing or production of different types of warheads. Meanwhile, the voluntary moratorium against nuclear testing by the major powers is effective in helping mobilize pressure against countries such as North Korea that do test regardless.

That said, the current situation is not ideal. The holding pattern that U.S. policy toward nuclear stockpile maintenance and the CTBT is in cannot last, unchanged, forever. The Obama administration believes ratification of the CTBT would be useful to codify and formalize a situation that, while temporarily stable, could change at any point. U.S. ratification could also pressure China, the only other formal nuclear power—that is, a nuclear weapons state as recognized by the Nuclear Non-Proliferation Treaty—that has not ratified, to do the same. U.S. ratification could also lock Russia into its position and make it harder for countries like Pakistan to test again.

Others believe that ratification is not in the U.S. interest. They argue that the United States should maintain an option to resume nuclear testing so that it can either check the reliability of existing warheads or develop new warheads; question whether the treaty can be effectively verified; and doubt that Senate approval would cause many other countries to follow suit. A Romney presidency likely would have doubts about the wisdom of ratifying the CTBT. That said, virtually no one appears to be arguing that the United States has an urgent need now to resume testing.

The testing moratorium and current stockpile stewardship efforts can likely endure for the next presidential term without the need for major change—and that status quo would be preferable to another failed Senate ratification effort. Issues concerning nuclear warhead maintenance and testing should be discussed, in part to ensure adequate resources for stewardship efforts and to test the waters for possible ratification efforts. But a major push to get sixty-seven votes in the Senate should be contingent on a high level of initial confidence that the effort would succeed. Ultimately, that will turn on the administration's ability to make the case that the reliability of the U.S. nuclear stockpile can be assured without testing and that any militarily significant cheating could be detected. Even if CTBT ratification cannot be accomplished through the necessary Senate vote (and then formalized by the president), whoever sits in the Oval Office come January 20, 2013, might declare that for the rest of his watch, there will be no American nuclear weapons testing—and no development of warheads with enhanced performance features either.

ENSURING STOCKPILE RELIABILITY
AND EFFECTIVENESS WITHOUT TESTING

Most agree that the United States needs a nuclear deterrent well into the foreseeable future. Some analysts believe that, at some future point, testing will be needed to ensure the arsenal's reliability. How can one go fifty or one hundred years without a single test and still be confident that the country's nuclear weapons will work? The U.S. military currently keeps at least one nondeployed (reserve) strategic nuclear warhead for every deployed one, as a hedge against geopolitical surprise or technological failure of a warhead type. Equally important, how can one be sure that other countries will be deterred by an American stockpile that at some point will be certified only by the experiments and tests of a generation of physicists long since retired or dead? Indeed, the day when no U.S. weapons scientist has any substantial experience in testing may only be a few years away.[2] This question is neither trivial nor easy. Even though the nuclear age is now nearly seventy years old, and even though the United States (like Russia) has tested nuclear weapons about a thousand times since its beginning, today's arsenal is so optimized for high performance and safety that its long-term dependability is not guaranteed.

From the nuclear arms control point of view, some might welcome any perception that the reliability of nuclear weapons is declining. Declining reliability might translate into declining likelihood of the weapons ever being used—especially in a first strike—and declining legitimacy for retention of a nuclear arsenal. If, however, the United States continues to rely on a nuclear deterrent, as a practical strategic and political matter, any test ban must allow the United States to ensure 100 percent confidence in its nuclear arsenal into the indefinite future. Even if some uncertainty over the functioning of a certain percentage of the arsenal is tolerable, doubt about whether *any* part of it would function effectively would disrupt the core logic of deterrence.

A reasonable confidence in the long-term viability of the U.S. nuclear arsenal should be possible without testing. To be sure, with time the reliability of a given warhead class may decline as its components age. High explosives can deteriorate; fissile materials can corrode; tritium (used to "boost" the yield of the primary or first stage of most weapons) can and will decay radioactively, and the effects might be greater than expected. In a worst case, it is conceivable that a category of warheads might become flawed without the U.S. military or Department of Energy knowing it; indeed, that has happened in the past, and testing has often been the way problems were discovered.[3] But at this point, the physics of warhead aging is much better understood. Through a combination of monitoring, testing, and remanufacturing the individual components and conducting sophisticated experiments (short of actual nuclear detonations) on integrated devices, the overall dependability of the American nuclear deterrent can probably remain very good indefinitely.

Notably, in today's U.S. arsenal, the so-called plutonium pits are holding up better than anticipated. These are the concentric shells of fissile material that make up the first stage, or primary, of most U.S. nuclear warheads, along with associated conventional explosives, detonation mechanisms, and other key technologies. The pits may remain dependable for up to a century without having to be remanufactured. As the so-called JASON advisory group wrote in 2006, "Most primary types have credible minimum lifetimes in excess of 100 years as regards aging of plutonium; those with assessed minimum lifetimes of 100 years or less have clear mitigation paths that are proposed and/or being implemented."[4] In other words, the longevity of these pits means that no near-term or even medium-term mechanism is needed to address any existing or expected problems.

That situation will not last forever, to be sure. Some argue that, before ratifying any CTBT of indefinite duration, the nation should know how it could respond decades down the road when today's pits are no longer so robust. Part of the solution could be, of course, to remake the pits. But that may not be a sufficient policy. Pits, and weapons primaries more broadly, are very sensitive devices with only small error tolerances in many of their components. If not remade very precisely, the weapon that they are intended to drive can fizzle. The first part of a thermonuclear weapon, the primary, depends mainly on the fission of uranium-235 or plutonium to generate a nuclear yield. That initial yield then heats and pressurizes the warhead's "secondary" to the point where thermonuclear combustion of its hydrogen fuel results, generating the warhead's main explosive power. The primary is usually the most sensitive part of the weapon.

U.S. nuclear weapons in the cold war were designed to be as light as possible to fit atop ballistic missiles and produce large yields, so warhead designers tried to make the primaries light—which in turn meant that they used less fissile material than would otherwise have been preferred, lowering margins for error in the actual detonation of the primary and the ignition of the secondary.[5] It was largely the need to lighten the primaries that drove nuclear weapons design and the roughly 1,000 U.S. tests generating nuclear yield between 1945 and 1992.[6] And it is the associated complexity of the weapons, and their relatively small margins for imprecision or error, that led observers such as Secretary of Defense Robert Gates in 2008 to say that the existing American nuclear stockpile could not be assumed to be dependable indefinitely.[7]

To understand the challenge, consider in somewhat more detail what happens within a nuclear warhead primary. As noted, a typical warhead has a shell of plutonium that is compressed by a synchronized detonation of conventional explosives that surround it. Making sure the explosion is synchronized along all parts of the explosive, so that the compression of the plutonium is symmetrical, is critical if the warhead is to work. Over time, wires can age, detonators can age, and so forth. But these types of components can be easily replaced and their proper functioning can be verified through simulations that make no use of nuclear material (and are thus allowable under a CTBT).

Things become a bit more complicated once the compression of the plutonium is considered. The interaction of the conventional explosive with the plutonium is a complex physical phenomenon that is highly dependent not just on the basic nature of the materials involved but also on their shapes and their surfaces and the chemical interactions that occur where they meet. Plutonium is not a static material; it is of course radioactive, and it ages in various ways. Conventional explosives age too, meaning that warhead performance can change with time.

As an alternate way to address the aging issues, one could in theory simply rebuild the conventional explosives and the plutonium shells to original specifications every few decades, avoiding the whole issue of monitoring the aging process by simply remanufacturing the key elements of the weapon every so often. In fact, one of the fathers of the hydrogen bomb, Richard Garwin, has recommended doing exactly that. Remanufacturing appears to be similar to the Russian practice. Russian nuclear warheads have a much shorter shelf life than their U.S. counterparts. As the older warheads are retired, the Russians build replacements (though it is not known whether the Russians simply build new versions of the older warheads or whether they modernize some components).

But others point out that previous processes used to cast plutonium and to manufacture chemical explosives have become outdated. For example, previous generations of plutonium pits were machined to achieve their final dimensions, a practice that produced a great deal of waste. The goal for the future has been to cast plutonium pits directly into their final shape instead (by heating the plutonium to molten form, forming it into proper shape, and then letting it cool). Doing so, however, would create a different type of surface for the pit that might interact slightly differently with the conventional explosive relative to the previous design. Even a slight difference might be enough to throw off the proper functioning of a very sensitive, high-performance, low-error-tolerance warhead. Similarly, the way high explosives are manufactured typically changes with time. Replacing one type with another has in the past greatly affected warhead performance, even when that might not have been easily predicted—again, the detailed chemical and physical interactions with the plutonium pit, among other such complex phenomena, are of critical importance.

Garwin has argued that, for relatively small and shrinking nuclear arsenals, it is worth the modest economic cost and environmental risk (which is quite small by the standards of cold war nuclear activities) to continue making plutonium pits and conventional explosives as they have always been made, even if the methods are outdated. That would in theory ensure reliability by keeping future warheads virtually identical to those of the past. Mimicking past manufacturing processes should not be beyond the capacities of today's scientists. But Garwin's argument has not carried the day, in part because of the widespread view among bomb designers that, at a minimum, small differences in how warheads are built from one era to another are inevitable even if attempts are made to avoid it.[8]

The Department of Energy has instead devoted large sums of money to its science-based stockpile stewardship program, to understand as well as possible what happens within aging warheads and to predict the performance of those warheads once modified with slightly different materials in the future. The department says that the stockpile stewardship program has yielded information about weapons performance that had not been learned in forty-seven years of testing. It is currently spending about $7 billion a year on the effort, and is expected to do so through 2030 in constant-dollar terms, with about $1 billion of that annual amount devoted to refurbishing actual warheads.[9] That is more, in inflation-adjusted terms, than the average spent on nuclear warhead activities in the cold war (even though bombs were being designed and tested then).[10] The science-based stockpile stewardship program is a sound program, even as elements of it naturally remain debatable. It is also more scientifically interesting—and thus more likely to attract good scientists into the weapons business in future years—than a program for stockpile maintenance that would do no more than rebuild weapons every few decades. It has helped ensure that, two full decades after the last test of an actual bomb, key validators like the heads of the major weapons laboratories and the authors of a major new National Academy of Sciences study believe that the American arsenal is still dependable and safe.[11]

But the stockpile stewardship program still gives some people unease as they look to the future. Specifically, bomb designers and other technical experts debate whether, over time, this program will suffice to ensure the long-term dependability of the arsenal, as former Los Alamos bomb designer Stephen Younger has argued (Younger himself is skeptical about the current stewardship program's long-term viability).[12] For example, a key part of the effort is using elegant three-dimensional computer models to predict what will happen inside a warhead modified to use a new type (or amount) of chemical explosive based on computational physics. The existing stewardship program seeks to perfect computer models of how a warhead behaves during implosion to determine whether a modified warhead primary would generate enough yield to heat and pressurize the secondary sufficiently to cause thermonuclear ignition. The models account, for example, for the rate at which a plutonium pit is compressed by high explosives, and the way tritium gas released into the primary can "boost" the process to generate more fission and thus more yield before the primary self-destructs. Experimental capabilities such as the Dual-Axis Radiographic Hydrodynamic Test Facility, operational since 1999, allow calibration and refinement of the models by highly precise observations of how materials behave in mock nuclear explosions.[13] In theory, knowing the components of a nuclear device that had aged or otherwise changed relative to original parameters, the model could confirm that it would still generate an adequate nuclear yield. Yet this method, while impressive, does not reassure all bomb designers, given its theoretical methodology.

Another way to ensure confidence in the arsenal is to design a new type of warhead, or perhaps use a variant of an old design that is not currently represented in the active U.S. nuclear arsenal but that has been tested before. This approach would seek to use "conservative designs" that allow for slight errors in warhead performance and still produce a robust nuclear yield. The conservative warhead could then take its place among other types of warheads in the arsenal, providing an added element of confidence. Taking this approach might lead to a somewhat heavier warhead (meaning the number that could be carried on a given ballistic missile or bomber would have to be reduced) or a lower-yield warhead (meaning that a hardened Russian missile silo might not be so easily destroyed, for example). The weight question may not be so crucial because most U.S. ICBMs and SLBMs now carry operational loads below their capacity.

For purposes of post-cold-war deterrence, this approach of using less lethal warheads is generally sound. Weapons designers tend to agree that very reliable warheads can be produced if performance criteria are relaxed. Indeed, for certain purposes, some designers actually favor a smaller warhead yield, of perhaps ten kilotons. Approaching the power of the Hiroshima and Nagasaki bombs, such a warhead would hardly be "small" or easily "usable," and thus should not raise fears that the nuclear threshold would be easily crossed as a result in a future conflict. But it could be a more credible deterrent (say, for attacks against isolated military airfields) than today's huge warheads. It could also lead to less use of toxic materials such as beryllium and to use of conventional explosives that are less prone to accidental detonation than is the case for some warheads in the current arsenal.[14]

POSSIBLE DIFFERENT WARHEAD DESIGNS

It is for some of these reasons that the George W. Bush administration was interested in a Reliable Replacement Warhead concept. This was only a research concept, and a controversial one at that, with Congress often unwilling to provide even research funding.[15] Support for the weapon might have been greater had it not been presented as a new warhead but a variant on an older one, even if that might have been something of a semantic stretch—any discussion of new nuclear warheads inevitably conjures up images of

TABLE 6-1. Current Active U.S. Strategic Nuclear Warhead Inventory

W78 warhead for Minuteman III ICBM	250
W87 warhead for Minuteman III ICBM	250
W76 warhead for Trident II SLBM	768
W88 warhead for Trident II SLBM	384
W80 warhead for air-launched cruise missiles	200
B61 and B83 bombs	100

Source: Hans M. Kristensen and Robert S. Norris, "U.S. Nuclear Forces, 2012," *Bulletin of the Atomic Scientists* 68, no. 3 (2012): 86-89 (http://bos.sagepub.com/content/68/3/84.full.pdf+html).

Note: The table does not include nearly 3,000 nondeployed (reserve) strategic warheads and nonstrategic nuclear weapons.

trying to create weapons that are somehow more usable because of their more localized, limited effects, or alternatively somehow more lethal. And indeed, the U.S. stockpile of seven main types of warheads (table 6-1) is itself being upgraded—mostly for safety and reliability purposes, to be sure, and without tampering with the "physics packages" of the bombs—but upgraded nonetheless. (The Obama administration's nuclear posture review stated that the United States would maintain the existing stockpile through reuse, refurbishment, and replacement of nuclear weapons components, with a preference for the first two means, but without creating new nuclear weapons capabilities.)

The concept of a simple, dependable design—using elements of weapons designs that have been tested and deployed in the past—does have a certain logic and should be defensible even in a world where the United States wants to reduce the role and numbers of nuclear weapons. Such a warhead would not constitute modernization, because it would not be intended to improve performance or yield. If not the Reliable Replacement Warhead itself, then a subsequent related program—with a different name, and a more clearly articulated purpose that could not be construed as modernization—could someday make sense. In fact, it might even obviate the need to consider Garwin's idea, since the United States clearly could deploy such a warhead with extremely high confidence in its reliability.[16] It could also facilitate retiring one or two types of existing warheads in the U.S. arsenal today, reducing the burden on the stockpile stewardship program (and thus its cost). If brought into the arsenal gradually, this warhead would not require development of a major new plutonium pit manufacturing facility either.

In sum, testing is probably not necessary to maintain a basic arsenal. Indeed, few seem to doubt that countries like Israel or France can maintain viable arsenals without testing, another reason to think it could be done by the United States too. But there is another argument to consider. Some have suggested that testing may be needed for new types of warheads to accomplish new missions. For example, in the 1980s, some missile defense proponents were interested in a space-based nuclear-pumped X-ray laser. That idea turned out to be not practical. But the idea of developing a nuclear weapon that could burrow underground *before* detonating—the Robust Nuclear Earth Penetrator—has gained appeal, not least because countries such as North Korea and Iran are responding to America's increasingly precise conventional weaponry by hiding key weapons programs well below the planet's surface. The George W. Bush administration sought to develop such a weapon but could not secure congressional funding.

One possible argument for developing such a warhead is to increase its overall destructive depth. In theory, the United States could modify the largest nuclear weapons in its stockpile to penetrate the earth. This approach would roughly double the destructive reach of the most powerful weapons in the current arsenal, according to physicist Michael Levi.[17] But if an adversary can avoid weapons in the current arsenal, it could avoid the more powerful bombs by digging deeper underground. Given the quality of modern drilling equipment, that is not an onerous task.

Could weapons that penetrate deeply into the ground at least reduce the nuclear fallout from an explosion? This idea was of some interest and appeal to the Bush administration, and a future president might also consider it. Such weapons could not prevent fallout; given limits on the hardness of materials and other basic physics, no useful nuclear weapon could penetrate the earth far enough to keep the radioactive effects of its blast entirely below ground. But such weapons could reduce fallout. Relative to a normal bomb, it is possible to reduce the yield of an earth-penetrating weapon tenfold while maintaining the same destructive capability against underground targets, reducing fallout by a factor of ten as well.[18] That would be a meaningful change. But is that change really enough to alter the basic usability of a nuclear device? Such a weapon would still produce a huge amount of fallout. Its use would still break the nuclear taboo. It would still be capable of destroying underground targets only if their locations were precisely known, in which case conventional weapons or special forces might be able to neutralize the site.

FURTHER STRENGTHENING MONITORING AND VERIFICATION

One challenge to the CTBT is whether it can be effectively verified. Many experts argue that a country is extremely unlikely to be able to test a nuclear weapon clandestinely and learn enough from the test to make meaningful improvements in its weapons capabilities. (A country would find it easier, if hardly easy, to get away with secretly enriching uranium or working on warhead design—nuclear explosions are very hard to hide.) Further improvements in monitoring capabilities are worth pursuing, with or without a test ban treaty in effect, but the overall monitoring situation today is very reassuring.

Large nuclear weapons detonations are easy to detect. Tests that occurred in the atmosphere (in violation of the Limited Test Ban Treaty) would be visible from satellites, and their characteristic radiation distribution would make them easy to identify. As a result, no country trying to keep its nuclear capabilities secret has tested in the atmosphere in the modern era (South Africa is the last country that may have done so, several decades ago, but its actions were detected, and monitoring methods have improved since then).

Underground detonations have been far more common, but they are still straightforward to identify, largely through seismic monitoring, and also by sampling the air downwind of a suspected detonation to search for radioactive residues. Any weapon of a kiloton power or above (the Hiroshima and Nagasaki bombs were in the 10–20 ton kiloton range) can be "heard" via seismic means. Indeed, even though the weapon either "fizzled" or was designed to have a small yield in the first place (with a yield of about 1 kiloton), the October 2006 North Korean test was detected and clearly identified as a nuclear burst.[19] In other words, any weapon with significant military potential tested at its full strength is very likely to be detected. U.S. seismic arrays are found throughout much of Eurasia's periphery, for example. The U.S. system is augmented by the globally distributed International Monitoring System. With some 85 participating countries and more than 300 monitoring sites—which will ultimately include 50 primary and 120 auxiliary seismic stations—the system can detect nuclear tests of 0.1 kiloton (that is, 100 tons of high-explosive equivalent) or even less.[20]

The existing U.S. and international seismic systems are not sensitive enough to detect "microtests" (sometimes called hydronuclear tests) that would produce a nuclear yield equivalent to, say, 100 kilograms of high explosive. Such testing by sophisticated nuclear weapons states such as Russia or China cannot currently be ruled out. The military utility of such tests, however, is not clear.

There are only two viable ways for a covert weapons tester to reduce the chances of detection. First, test a device well below its intended military yield, through some type of modification of the weapon's physics. (Doing that may make the device very different from the actual class of weapon it is designed to represent, necessitating sophisticated extrapolation to deduce how the actual weapon would behave based on the results of the detonation of the modified device). Second, dig out a very large underground cavity in which to place a weapon, thereby "decoupling" the blast from direct contact with the ground, and allowing the blast to weaken before it then reaches surrounding soil or rock and causes the ground to shake. This approach is arduous and could be detected if satellites observed a large amount of dirt being removed from a cave or drill site. Moreover, this approach simply changes the threshold yield at which it could be heard by American, Russian, and international seismic sensors. It *might be* possible to get away with a test of about a kiloton, if the test occurred in a large cavity underground, such as a giant space carved out of salt flats. But tests even one-tenth that size would in fact be detected in many, if not most, of the possible sites where this approach could be used. [21]

In summary, a country very sophisticated in nuclear technology might be able to test, undetected, a device that had its normal yield reduced through modifications to the basic physics of the weapon. For example, less plutonium or highly enriched uranium might be used. An advanced type of weapon might be modified to use less tritium. But achieving such engineering feats would probably not teach an established nuclear power a lot that it did not already know—and such sophisticated extrapolation techniques are probably beyond the means of a fledgling nuclear power. Scientists can learn some things from artificially small explosions caused by modified devices—but probably not enough to give them high confidence that the weapon they have developed is highly reliable at its intended yield. A country could probably build and deploy a single-stage nonboosted nuclear weapon (that is, one that does not rely on tritium to help ensure its yield) without testing. But it probably could not build a high-yield and reasonably light warhead optimized for delivery by a ballistic missile absent tests.

CONSIDERING U.S. RATIFICATION OF THE COMPREHENSIVE TEST BAN TREATY

We believe that ratification of the Comprehensive Test Ban Treaty by the United States and other established nuclear powers would be in the U.S. national interest. The case for the CTBT begins with our assessment that the United States does not need new, improved types of nuclear weapons and that it can ensure the dependability of a nuclear stockpile indefinitely without testing. In addition, it can, working with other countries, detect any nuclear weapons test even a fraction the size of the Hiroshima or Nagasaki bombs that occurs virtually anywhere on Earth. Moreover, it is not clear that a resumption of testing would be politically possible at the former Nevada Test Site, now known as the Nevada National Security Site. The site lies just north of Las Vegas, which now has nearly three times the population that it did in 1992, when the last U.S. test was conducted. Given how hard Nevada has fought the prospect of storing nuclear waste, one could expect strong opposition to a suggestion of resuming nuclear testing.

Still, what is the real importance of CTBT ratification? Currently, the international consensus that nuclear weapons testing is not only unnecessary but unwarranted and indeed illegitimate is holding strong, as it has for nearly two decades. No established nuclear power has tested since France and China (both in 1996). Nor does any major power appear to be considering a change to its own moratorium. The George W. Bush administration briefly considered "unsigning" the treaty, but ultimately chose not to do so—and never tested, either. There has been no string of proliferative activity in recent years to suggest that the failure of the CTBT to enter into force has weakened the global norm against proliferation or testing. In fact, quite the opposite seems true. Sanctions against India and Pakistan when they tested in 1998 were milder and shorter-lived than those against North Korea in 2009 or those aimed at Iran in recent times as it has sought nuclear weapons capabilities even in the absence of testing. And should it someday test, one would predict a fairly strong international response. This situation is important, because minimizing the number of tests, even by countries that have already tested one or more times in the past, limits their ability to develop reliable weapons that can be delivered by ballistic missile or even aircraft.

The problem is that any such informal consensus not to test is probably less durable than a legally binding treaty commitment. Consider how other countries might modify their policies in the years ahead. Russia, like Britain and France, has ratified the CTBT. But its national security policies rely more heavily on nuclear deterrence than do most other established nuclear powers, in light of its long land borders and the deterioration of Russian conventional military force capabilities over the past two decades. Indeed, it may even have an interest in new and possibly more usable types of nuclear weapons, such as low-yield warheads, to defend borders.[22]

China has not tested in years. But, like the United States, it has not ratified the CTBT, and some worry that Beijing might be tempted to try to vault into the ranks of the nuclear superpowers at some future date—or at least stay ahead of India and its nuclear modernization efforts (see table 6-2). Either motivation, or concerns about defeating a U.S. missile defense or further solidifying its second-strike capabilities, could lead Beijing to reconsider its current restrained approach. Indeed, in 2008 Secretary of Defense Gates asserted that both Moscow and Beijing were hedging; in his words, "China and Russia have embarked on an ambitious path to design and field new weapons."[23] Gates was perhaps referring primarily to nuclear delivery vehicles rather than warheads, but their efforts may someday lead them to want to test. India seems relatively unlikely to test again, out of the blue. But the dynamics of the India-Pakistan or India-China relationship could alter the situation.[24]

A treaty would not, by the force of its own moral suasion, prevent countries from testing nuclear weapons. But, in the aftermath of a nuclear test by a country like North Korea or Iran, the U.N. Security Council could be more inclined to react strongly against such a transgression if a binding international accord prohibited it. Knowing that in advance, countries like Iran and North Korea

TABLE 6-2. The Status of the Nuclear Weapons Testing Moratorium and the CTBT Ratification Process

Last Nuclear Tests

United States—September 23, 1992	France—January 28, 1996
Russia/USSR—October 24, 1990	China—July 29, 1996
United Kingdom—November 26, 1991	

Comprehensive Nuclear Test Ban Treaty Status

Signed: 182 of 196 countries	North Korea—not signed, not ratified
Ratified: 157 of 196 countries	Pakistan—not signed, not ratified
China—signed, not ratified	Russia—signed, ratified
France—signed, ratified	United Kingdom—signed, ratified
India—not signed, not ratified	United States—signed, not ratified
Israel—signed, not ratified	

Sources: "United States Nuclear Tests July 1945 through September 1992," U.S. Department of Energy Nevada Operations Office, December 2000, p. 88 (www.nv.doe.gov/library/publications/historical/DOENV_209_REV15.pdf); "Ending Nuclear Testing," United Nations (www.un.org/en/events/againstnucleartestsday/history.shtml); "BBC on This Day. 1996: France halts nuclear testing," (http://news.bbc.co.uk/onthisday/hi/dates/stories/january/29/newsid_4665000/4665676.stm); "China Conducts Nuclear Test, Vows It Is Last," Associated Press, July 29, 1996 (http://articles.latimes.com/1996-07-29/news/mn-29215_1_nuclear-test); and "Status of Signature and Ratification," CTBO Preparatory Commission, April 2, 2012 (www.ctbto.org/the-treaty/status-of-signature-and-ratification). The authors thank Ian Livingston for preparing this table.

might be even less inclined to test nuclear devices if the treaty were ratified than they are now. Or, consider the so-called "123" civil nuclear cooperation deal negotiated by the Bush administration with India, which allowed American nuclear cooperation with India provided that India's commercial reactors were put under International Atomic Energy Agency safeguards. Some have criticized the agreement as too lenient, since India remains outside the Nuclear Non-Proliferation Treaty regime. Had the CTBT been in effect when the accord was negotiated, it might have been easier to persuade Delhi to agree not to test weapons in the future. Perhaps the United States would have been able to persuade India also to put military reactors under safeguards and to sign the CTBT as a precondition for such nuclear energy cooperation.[25] The possibility of future U.S. and Chinese ratification could increase the odds that India would feel obliged to sign and ratify, too.

So in many ways the issue comes down to a pragmatic calculation about the prospects of gaining Senate consent to ratification. It is a daunting proposition. Three-fourths or more of all Americans, including a strong majority of Republicans, support a nuclear test ban. But that has been true since the 1960s and is thus not a great guide to predicting congressional action.[26] In October 1999, the Clinton administration tried and failed—although Clinton administration officials later conceded that they did not prepare the ground well. The final vote was fifty-one nays to forty-eight yeas—nineteen votes short of the sixty-seven needed for ratification. Numerous moderate or internationalist Republican senators voted against, including Dick Lugar of Indiana, John Warner of Virginia , Pete Domenici of New Mexico, John McCain of Arizona, Chuck Hagel of Nebraska, and Olympia Snowe and Susan Collins of Maine; among Republicans, only John Chafee of Rhode Island, Jim Jeffords of Vermont, Gordon Smith of Oregon, and Arlen Specter of Pennsylvania supported it.[27]

Some have argued that ratification might have been within reach in the early Obama years, when Democrats could still muster sixty votes in the Senate. The newfound support of former Republican secretaries of state George Shultz and Henry Kissinger lent credence to the argument at that time.[28] But those days are unlikely to return soon. Furthermore, a second Senate rejection of the CTBT would likely doom its chances of ever being ratified. And with a clear verdict rendered on it within the U.S. system, other countries might face growing domestic pressures to resume testing (although this is admittedly hard to predict). Partisan acrimony might grow in the United States too; rejection of a proposed treaty is no small deal and tends to have consequences at home and abroad. It may be wise here not to let the best be the enemy of the good. Seeking out a ratification debate and vote only makes sense if sixty-five or more votes appear within reach from the outset of the effort.

A de facto international moratorium that may not preclude all nuclear testing but that sharply limits the ability of countries to conduct tests has great benefits and should be preserved. To be sure, the moratorium does not prevent countries from proving that they can produce nuclear yields. But it complicates their efforts to do repeated tests of the type generally needed in the past to ensure that relatively small and light high-performance warheads of the type needed for ballistic missile delivery are dependable. It would be best to lock in this situation formally through treaty ratification, but the current state of affairs is reasonably good for the moment.

BUDGET ISSUES FOR THE ADMINISTRATION AND CONGRESS

How will nuclear testing and arsenal maintenance issues likely affect looming decisions on how to spend increasingly scarce defense dollars? These are formally Department of Energy (DOE) costs within the broader national defense account of the federal budget, since nuclear warhead activities are conducted and resourced in that department.

An explicit policy that would have the United States design and build a simpler warhead, if and when needed years or decades in the future, could actually relieve some of the upward budgetary pressure currently being placed on DOE weapons accounts. If a highly dependable warhead type were added to the arsenal, the logic requiring two full-bore weapons design laboratories would no longer be so compelling, which in turn would reduce pressure on the stockpile stewardship program. This approach would further reduce the argument for a new plutonium pit facility too, since the specter of a possible future crisis in plutonium pits that then necessitated a crash program to rebuild them would be far less worrisome.

As a condition for ratification of the New START Treaty in December 2010, the Obama administration pledged to increase spending on the broader nuclear weapons complex, including DOE facilities and activities, by $85 billion over ten years. To some, this seemed a reasonable bargain for treaty support from Senate skeptics, especially because a substantive case could be made for the increases. Viewed from another angle, especially in light of subsequent severe downward pressure on the defense budget in general, this pledge may merit new scrutiny. The nation does not have the money to easily increase spending on any area of national security activity in the coming years. And more economical ways of pursuing stewardship may become possible through a combination of building a simple warhead and further downsizing the arsenal in the years ahead. If a future U.S. president were to choose this course, it could be important politically to emphasize that the course would not mean an increase in U.S. nuclear weapons capabilities.

Specifically, it is worth investigating whether any or all of the following steps could be adopted, either now or in the event of another nuclear arms reduction treaty with Moscow of the type discussed earlier in this book:

—Cancellation of plans to build a new plutonium pit fabrication site (known as the Chemistry and Metallurgy Research Facility Replacement Complex, or CMRR), and reliance instead on Los Alamos's existing small capacity in this area. The current Los Alamos facility can produce up to ten pits a year and could probably be scaled up to produce forty annually without huge cost.[29] If pits are believed to last one hundred years, and if a future arsenal is likely to total 1,000 to 3,000 warheads in all, this capacity would likely be adequate. (The reductions in the arsenal would also obviate the need to produce more tritium in coming decades. Because tritium has a half-life of only twelve years, it needs to be frequently replenished, but retired warheads can be "harvested" for their remaining tritium, which can then be recycled into functional warheads.) The CMRR has already been deferred, so a decision to cancel it would not produce savings for a few years, but those later savings could be quite considerable.

—A change in the philosophy that has undergirded American nuclear weapons research since the dawn of the nuclear age— the idea that the nation needs two independent laboratories doing basic physics work on the functioning and design of nuclear weapons. Los Alamos and Lawrence Livermore Laboratories, in New Mexico and California respectively, have played that role to date, with important additional work being conducted at Sandia National Laboratories in Albuquerque and the Nevada National Security Site among other locations. But in an era when new warhead design is no longer as important as it once was, reorienting the core mission of one of the two main labs, perhaps to civilian energy research, makes eminent sense and should be considered in the years ahead.

Proposing to save money with a less expensive approach to stewardship would risk a political confrontation with the directors of the nation's main weapons labs. Their yearly letters to Congress certifying the dependability of the nation's nuclear stockpile have been contingent on ample funding for the stockpile stewardship program as it has been defined in the past. It was this dialogue with Congress that helped explain the administration's willingness to commit added budgetary resources to the nuclear mission in recent years. Realistically, the nation may have to evolve toward this policy, rather than adopt it overnight. But as noted, there are real scientific reasons to doubt whether lab directors will indefinitely certify their confidence in the reliability of today's arsenal as the years go by—and very good reasons to be confident that a simpler warhead design based on existing concepts could provide a highly dependable warhead even absent testing.

CONCLUSIONS AND RECOMMENDATIONS

The United States has settled into a prolonged period in which its stewardship and maintenance of its existing nuclear weapons portfolio—now consisting of some seven types of highly advanced warhead designs—is carried out without actual nuclear detonations to ensure the reliability of the weapons. And the nation remains ambivalent about the Comprehensive Nuclear Test Ban Treaty—its signature is still affixed to that accord, yet the Senate has rejected ratification once and appears unlikely to change that position in the near future.

The status quo amounts to an open-ended moratorium on American testing, juxtaposed with similar moratoriums observed by the other official nuclear powers although not by India, Pakistan, or North Korea. If anything, the degree of U.S. consensus behind this de facto moratorium has only grown with time—time that has built confidence that nuclear weapons inventories can be maintained even as the weapons themselves age and the men and women who designed and originally tested them retire.

We believe that the CTBT should be ratified and entered into force, to lock in the international norm against testing, thereby making it much harder for other countries to develop or modernize their arsenals without paying a major price for their decision. Testing is not needed to ensure the viability either of today's U.S. nuclear arsenal or of a future U.S. arsenal. Testing is also unnecessary for developing new and improved types of warheads, since the case for new capabilities is weak. In addition, U.S. nuclear verification capabilities have picked up the Indian, Pakistani, and North Korean nuclear tests—even the small, relatively unsuccessful ones—in the past decade and would be able to do so with high confidence for tests from those or other countries in the future. Verification capabilities are not perfect, but, on balance, their limitations are probably not solid grounds on which to oppose a test ban treaty. Together, these points make a good case that ratification of the Comprehensive Test Ban Treaty would not hurt American national security and might benefit it.

But the timing of CTBT ratification can and must be subject to the practicalities and the feasibility of the enterprise within the American political system. The status quo is preferable to another rejection of the treaty in the U.S. Senate.

CHAPTER SEVEN

FISSILE MATERIALS AND A PRODUCTION CUTOFF

AN ARMS CONTROL PROPOSAL that has been around for many years, but that has gained greater currency in recent times and will be on the agenda in 2013, is a ban on the further production of plutonium and highly enriched uranium-235 for military purposes. One of these two materials is present in all nuclear bombs. They are the fissile materials that are split into smaller atoms in the chain reactions that power all nuclear weapons, whether of the simple one-stage variety or the thermonuclear type. They are also difficult to isolate in weapons-usable form, making them the hardest materials to produce and therefore the most controllable elements of weapons. And because their half-lives are very long—tens of thousands of years for plutonium and millions of years for uranium-235—it is possible to imagine banning new production even as nuclear arsenals are retained indefinitely.

The origin of the proposal has less to do with U.S.-Russia arms control, since the two nuclear superpowers have such huge stocks of fissile materials already, and more to do with other countries. By preventing further production of these bomb-ready materials, the global nuclear nonproliferation agenda could be advanced. Someday, once U.S.-Russian stockpiles of fissile materials have been dramatically reduced, a treaty cutting off production of fissile material could add a layer of insurance against nuclear breakout by these two powers. But that would presumably not be its chief initial benefit.

Pakistan, which has sought to increase its nuclear arsenal dramatically in recent years, opposes the treaty. Without Pakistan and thus India aboard such an accord, its value would be limited, and so in recent years Islamabad has had an effective veto over any further progress toward an accord negotiated under UN auspices. Nor is it clear that all of the established nuclear powers would support a fissile material cutoff treaty now. Although a formal accord is admittedly a long shot in today's international setting, informal variants of such a concept may be workable. And by continuing to promote the goal of a cutoff, the United States and other like-minded powers could reaffirm their arms control credentials internationally while also preparing for the day when a formal universal agreement might in fact prove feasible.

FISSILE MATERIAL STOCKPILES, PRODUCTION, AND USAGE TODAY

Understanding the prospects of options for a fissile material production cutoff requires some familiarity with current and likely future patterns of nuclear weapons and nuclear energy usage worldwide. Today, there are nearly 20,000 nuclear weapons globally, including those waiting dismantlement. Most are in the hands of Russia and the United States. The world's seven other nuclear powers together possess about 1,000. Expressed in terms of fissile materials, roughly 1,440 tons of highly enriched uranium (HEU) and 495 tons of plutonium are present in existing weapons and stockpiles elsewhere. Some 98 percent of each material, including weapons and civilian stocks, is held by the nine nuclear weapons states. These total amounts are, in principle, enough to build more than 100,000 nuclear bombs, or five times the existing number worldwide.[1]

The stocks of HEU appear to be declining. The five original nuclear powers are not producing it any longer. India and Pakistan continue to enrich, but at a relatively modest pace. Iran's enrichment efforts and North Korea's possible activities are believed to be quite modest by historical standards too. On balance, because Russia is blending down HEU to less highly enriched versions of uranium for use as fuel for energy reactors, the world's stockpile of HEU is declining by more than 5 percent a year. (In addition, U.S. naval reactors consume the equivalent of about two tons a year to propel aircraft carriers and submarines.)[2] Net global stocks of plutonium continue to increase, however. The five original nuclear powers no longer separate plutonium for weapons, but they have not yet begun to dispose of it, and some separation still takes place for possible energy-related purposes. India, Pakistan, and perhaps Israel are still making weapons-grade plutonium. Japan's civilian reprocessing program is in limbo after the 2011 Fukushima disaster but could be revived.[3]

Worldwide, more than 100 research reactors and a comparable number of naval reactors driving ships are fueled with HEU. Some 180 reactors that used HEU have been shut down or converted to uranium fuel that is not as highly enriched. Altogether, HEU can still be found in more than thirty countries, although the number has been reduced by twenty as a result of the Global Threat Reduction Initiative and related efforts.[4] Several plutonium reprocessing facilities intended to support civilian nuclear energy installations are still found in China, France, India, Japan, Russia, and the United Kingdom. Security standards for such sites are being improved through accords such as the Convention on the Physical Protection of Nuclear Materials and the International Convention on the Suppression of Acts of Nuclear Terrorism, through the nuclear security summits in Washington and Seoul in recent years, and through UN Security Council resolutions 1540 and 1887—although additional effort is needed to include more countries in these pacts and to implement specific, rigorous security standards.[5]

Today's world also has some 435 nuclear power plants operating in thirty countries as well as Taiwan. They account for nearly 15 percent of global electricity production. The typical gigawatt plant uses around 200 tons of uranium a year.[6] That translates into nearly 2 tons of HEU equivalent, although these plants do not run on HEU. Almost all are in the United States, Europe including Russia, India, and the East Asian littoral, with a few from South Africa to Mexico to Brazil to Argentina. China, Russia, India, and a few other countries such as South Korea are still building new power plants. Currently, 60 reactors are being built in fourteen countries, plus Taiwan; another 150 are being planned, and twice that number are being proposed and considered.[7]

Some countries appear to be moving toward less reliance on nuclear energy. In the aftermath of the Fukushima disaster, Japan and Germany have taken dramatic steps to reduce their dependence on nuclear power.

In the United States, unfavorable economics have prevented the construction of new plants for many years, waste disposal efforts remain in limbo, and Fukushima has again called into question the basic safety of nuclear power facilities. Fracking for natural gas and oil in North America has changed the global energy market substantially. Renewables continue to become more economical, albeit gradually.

Still, nuclear energy will remain part of the landscape for the foreseeable future. A number of major economies plan to continue using existing nuclear plants for several more decades. Research reactors, medical isotope production facilities, and large warships and submarines continue to operate with nuclear power generated by HEU. Whatever the long-term future of nuclear energy, there is little doubt that it will play a substantial role in the world economy through mid-century and probably well beyond. So the world will need substantial amounts of uranium fuel for decades, including, quite likely, HEU for purposes other than nuclear weapons.

But there are thresholds in the future use of nuclear energy that may not have to be crossed. Most likely, the world will *not* need reprocessing of plutonium for reactor operations, given the ample supply of natural uranium (enough for at least a century at anticipated usage rates). Cost, safety, and nonproliferation issues also argue against plutonium reprocessing. And with luck, HEU will not be needed for research or even for naval reactors at some point in the coming years. For example, the next generation of naval submarines could possibly be designed to operate on uranium fuel with lower enrichment levels without any compromise to vessel design or operation.[8]

DESIGNING A FISSILE MATERIAL CUTOFF TREATY

Most forms of a possible fissile material cutoff treaty would, as suggested above, apply specifically to fissile materials intended for weapons. They would no longer be produced. Uranium enrichment and plutonium-reprocessing activities would be constrained and monitored.

Under such approaches, highly enriched uranium for naval reactors and certain types of research reactors, and plutonium for energy-producing reactors that can make use of this fuel, would not be banned. Verification of such a treaty would require ensuring that fissile material produced for non-weapons purposes was in fact used for those purposes. The material would thus have to be followed from locations like centrifuge cascades or reprocessing facilities to the reactors where it was consumed (and sites along the way where it might be stored).

This classic version of a fissile material cutoff accord is not the only possibility, however. Having a huge loophole that would allow fissile material to be produced for some purposes even as it was banned for others would lessen the treaty's effectiveness and greatly complicate the verification challenge. Thus, a second option would be a global ban on production of all fissile materials. A global ban would be the optimal accord from a nonproliferation and nuclear safety and arms control perspective. Under its terms, any reactor that currently required HEU would probably have to be converted in fairly timely fashion to use lower enrichment levels of uranium fuel. Signatories would also have to forgo development of any breeder-reactor energy system in which substantial amounts of plutonium fuel would be needed over time.[9]

Just as it is possible to imagine a more sweeping fissile material cutoff treaty, it is also possible to imagine a more narrow one, as a third option. For example, Pakistan has held up efforts to negotiate a global accord at the Conference on Disarmament. A bilateral U.S.-Russian treaty that prevented further production of bomb-grade HEU and plutonium for weapons purposes by those two countries would help codify what is already a reality—neither nuclear superpower produces such materials today—while legitimating and practicing certain verification techniques. A bilateral treaty might later be broadened to more countries and to non-weapons-related stocks of fissile materials. Some critics would argue that a bilateral treaty would be of minimal immediate benefit. That is true, but it would also be low cost. And it could at least modestly improve the bargaining position of the superpowers as they seek to persuade other countries to halt their production of fissile materials and respect broader nonproliferation norms. As a way to set the stage for such an accord, the United States and Russia could volunteer to have some facilities monitored soon, by each other or an international body, as suggested by Scott Sagan and others.[10]

Finally, a fourth concept worth considering would be a global moratorium—rather than a formal treaty—on the production of fissile materials. This approach would retain the option to reconsider the policy at some specified future date, perhaps in one to two decades. It would have the advantage of not prejudging decisions about future naval reactors and the future economics of reactors burning plutonium as a fuel. It could also take the pressure off decisionmakers who, given the complexity of the subject, might not realistically feel comfortable anytime soon committing to a permanent accord banning the production of all HEU and separated plutonium. But it could create a norm that would help pressure countries such as Pakistan that have reserved the right to keep producing more fissile material for bombs, and help lock China into an arsenal that would not grow over time.

It is not clear that Russia would go along with such a treaty. Along with India and China, Russia is building reactors designed to use plutonium. (Japan and France have commercial plutonium-reprocessing facilities too.) Yet there is a chance that Russia would agree. It has such large stocks of plutonium that it might be able to fuel its reactors by burning excess plutonium from its weapons programs rather than by separating more plutonium.[11] And, if the United States and Russia agree on further nuclear arms reductions, Russia would be able to recover additional stocks of plutonium from dismantled nuclear warheads. Variants on a fissile material cutoff accord are worth discussing not only with Moscow but also with other key parties during the next American presidential term.

COMPLEMENTS TO A FISSILE MATERIAL CUTOFF ACCORD

Whatever type of fissile production cutoff might be negotiated, it is also worth examining additional constraints that might be placed on the spread of nuclear production technologies around the world. A number of possibilities could be considered:[12]

—Requiring significant constraints on any new uranium enrichment facilities. (Currently, uranium enrichment facilities are found in Argentina, Brazil, China, France, Germany, India, Iran, Japan, the Netherlands, North Korea, Pakistan, Russia, the United Kingdom, and the United States.)[13] In particular, Mohamed ElBaradei, former director of the International Atomic Energy Agency (IAEA), has suggested requiring multinational ownership for any new facility. That could increase the difficulty of illicitly and clandestinely converting such a facility to weapons-related purposes on short order and provide a greater likelihood of early warning if such a change were attempted. None of the owners of such a new facility would presumably be from countries that have been in recent violation of IAEA stipulations (such as Iran and North Korea).

—Banning any new plutonium-reprocessing facilities worldwide. The economic argument for using plutonium in reactors was never strong and has only weakened with time.[14] (With the exception of Germany, Iran, and the Netherlands, all the countries that have uranium enrichment facilities also reprocess plutonium. Britain, France, Japan, and Russia currently have or recently had particularly important reprocessing programs.)[15]

These constraints could be pursued as explicit parts of a fissile material cutoff treaty. However, they might not need to await such an accord—or might be pursued subsequently and separately, if it is more practical to proceed that way. For example, the United States could consider leading an international discussion to reinterpret Article IV of the Nuclear Non-Proliferation Treaty. Currently, that article is construed as guaranteeing access to all nuclear-related technologies as long as their usage does not lead to nuclear weapons capabilities. But if plutonium-reprocessing technologies were seen as inconsistent with scientific, commercial, and other energy-related purposes, and thus no longer a legitimate form of commerce, Article IV could be interpreted as no longer protecting them. And if low-enriched uranium could be made available to countries needing it for reactors through an international fuel bank, the case for ensuring access to enrichment technology could also be weakened.

THE VERIFICATION CHALLENGE

Formal verification of any fissile material cutoff treaty would pose a challenge, if a rigorous system capable of providing high confidence of compliance is deemed necessary. Verification concepts for fissile material cutoff treaties typically focus on large production facilities. Currently, uranium enrichment generally involves either large diffusion plants, which are conspicuous in their size and power requirements, or centrifuge facilities, which require large numbers of identical well-machined rotors. Plutonium production requires nuclear reactors that give off large heat signatures.

Finding these facilities is not guaranteed. For example, Iran's nuclear enrichment plant at Natanz was revealed by dissident groups—human intelligence, in 2002—not by satellite or other remote means.[16] The kinds of electromagnetic isotope separation ("calutron") technology used in Iraq in the 1980s, inefficient and small-scale as it might have been, is nonetheless capable of enriching uranium and hard to detect as well.[17] Future enrichment technologies such as laser isotope enrichment facilities may be even harder to locate from a distance. But for the most part, industrial-scale facilities for production of HEU and plutonium are hard to hide and feasible to monitor.

So the greater challenge is in finding or tracking materials. Finding fissile materials themselves is a daunting proposition. One can try to find the distinctive and visible "signatures" or emissions, spontaneous or induced, of these elements. However, the particles given off by plutonium or uranium through natural radioactive decay are few and far between—and fairly easily shielded by materials such as lead. Most of the recent innovations in detection technology work only when they are in very close proximity to the nuclear materials, and that will likely remain true with the next generation of detectors.[18] These technologies can be used at entry points to a country, where containers may be imported; at monitored production and storage facilities (or nuclear power plants), to detect any hidden nuclear materials being moved in or out; and at other sensitive locations worthy of extra layers of protection. But they are severely constrained in other settings.

Passive detectors that look for the signatures emitted naturally by radioactive materials may find unshielded plutonium or uranium at distances of several meters. Active detectors that fire one type of radiation or another at a suspicious object for telltale responses indicating the presence of fissile materials can work at somewhat greater distances. But they are unable to detect materials at a distance of a kilometer or even hundreds of meters. Even if muon radiography and other technologies are able to improve detection in coming decades, finding nuclear facilities deep within a country's territory, where facilities could be tens of kilometers away from even low-altitude orbiting satellites, will remain very difficult.[19]

What this means, for possible fissile material accords, is that monitoring the actual production or reprocessing of fissile materials is far easier than tracking them once they have been produced. This basic fact actually makes a broader, more comprehensive fissile cutoff accord *easier* to monitor than a more limited one targeted just on stopping production of plutonium or uranium-235 for weapons purposes. Because countries that use HEU or plutonium for civilian purposes could convert these fuels into weapons-grade materials relatively easily and quickly, a limited cutoff would be difficult to verify.

The International Panel on Fissile Materials summarized well the challenges posed by the nuclear energy industry:

> If countries are allowed to separate plutonium from spent power-reactor fuel—as it is done today in France, India, Japan, Russia and the United Kingdom—they could use this plutonium to make nuclear weapons within weeks. Countries with large national enrichment plants could similarly quickly begin to make large quantities of HEU for weapons. . . . The breakout times would be longer in a world without reprocessing and where states lacked national enrichment plants. But a state with nuclear reactors still could build a 'quick and dirty' reprocessing plant and recover plutonium from spent power reactor fuel within six months to a year.[20]

In addition to the difficulties of detecting new sources of illicit nuclear materials, any nuclear disarmament regime would face nontrivial tasks in verifying the dismantlement of existing warheads and the transformation or irretrievable elimination of existing stocks of fissile materials. U.S. and Russian officials in the early 1990s addressed some of these issues when discussing ways to make nuclear weapons reductions irreversible. A good deal of excellent work has already gone into understanding this task in the nongovernmental sphere, as reflected, for example, in George Perkovich and James Acton's recent publications. But this work also underscores the degree of the challenge. Perkovich and Acton write that "substantial uncertainties in [existing] fissile material inventories are unavoidable. Even with blameless intentions and honest accounting, such uncertainties would be on the order of a few percent of production." These uncertainties arise because the existing weapons states have destroyed material through testing, have not always accurately measured the amount of fissile material lost in waste streams, and have otherwise failed to maintain rigorous monitoring and accounting. As a result, nuclear powers today do not themselves know exactly how much usable fissile material they possess.[21] Russia and the United States in particular have had enough problems with their bookkeeping efforts over the years that it may never be possible to account accurately for about 1 percent of the world's current fissile materials—enough for 1,000 bombs.[22]

CONCLUSION AND RECOMMENDATIONS

A fissile material cutoff treaty has great appeal for slowing nuclear proliferation by helping to cap the arsenals of existing powers while further complicating any efforts by new powers to pursue the bomb. But for those very reasons, and because of the intended uses of highly enriched uranium and plutonium in some types of research, naval, and power reactors, it will also likely continue to prove difficult to negotiate.

At least four main types of fissile cutoff regimes can be imagined:

—A global ban on production of HEU and separated plutonium for weapons-specific purposes.

—A bilateral U.S.-Russia ban on production of these materials for weapons-specific purposes, designed to catalyze a process that could gradually include more states.

—A sweeping global ban on all production of HEU and separated plutonium for *all* purposes, with research and naval reactors gradually converted to use low-enriched uranium and any plutonium-consuming power reactors limited in number to a quantity that can be fueled by existing stocks of excess plutonium.

—A global moratorium on all production of HEU and separated plutonium, without the permanence or formality of a treaty but with the expectation that in ten or twenty years the moratorium would be reassessed in light of issues such as the potential need for breeder reactors to handle future global energy needs.

Beyond these kinds of measures, complementary limits on the spread of enrichment and reprocessing technologies could be considered, to reinforce the fissile material cutoff and hinder the efforts of those who might seek a way around it. For example, to improve transparency, any new enrichment facilities in countries not currently possessing them, and perhaps even in countries that do possess them, could be obliged to have multinational ownership. In addition, plutonium-reprocessing facilities could be strongly discouraged or prohibited, across the board and everywhere.

We believe that both of these latter measures plus a comprehensive global ban on the production of all fissile materials would be the optimal approach—the most likely to stem proliferation, cap arsenals, gain broad legitimacy, and enhance verifiability. There is no strong case against such a comprehensive accord, partly because there is no good economic argument for plutonium breeder reactors, which are dangerous from the proliferation standpoint in any event. In addition, research and naval reactors can almost certainly be switched to low-enriched uranium over time, and, in principle, there is ample HEU around to fuel existing naval vessels for decades if need be.

We see considerable appeal as well, should the above prove impossible, in two more limited measures—a near-term U.S.-Russian formal ban on production of fissile materials for weapons purposes,

173

combined with an informal global moratorium on the production of all fissile materials with the possibility of revisiting the accord down the road. This latter concept would pick up on a theme that appears elsewhere in our analysis—the desirability of using informal or temporary understandings rather than formal and permanent treaties when the latter prove infeasible in the short term.

CHAPTER EIGHT

MULTILATERALIZING THE PROCESS— AND ASPIRING TO ZERO?

ONE ISSUE REMAINS to be discussed—the multilateralization of the nuclear arms reduction process. Although securing the participation of other countries in this process may take some time, the U.S. government should be thinking now about steps that could encourage other countries besides Russia to begin to reduce their nuclear arsenals and perhaps even move toward total elimination of nuclear weapons. This objective has been advocated by important voices ever since the dawn of the nuclear age. In the modern era, Ronald Reagan was the first to articulate the goal forcefully, and Barack Obama reiterated it in his Prague speech of April 2009. It remains official U.S. policy as it has been for decades—and, in fact, as is technically required by the terms of the Nuclear Non-Proliferation Treaty (NPT). When signing that treaty some four decades ago, other countries around the world agreed not to pursue their own nuclear arsenals only on the condition that the existing nuclear weapons states—the United States, Soviet Union (now Russia), Britain, France, and China—promise to eliminate their own. By large majorities, publics around the world also favor the goal as well.[1]

Of course, nuclear zero is an extremely ambitious and long-term goal. Done too soon, or done wrong, it could be counterproductive, weakening deterrence and even encouraging proliferation.

Some ideas, such as the so-called nonaligned movement's official proposal for a denuclearized world by 2025, would be both impractical and dangerous if taken literally and pursued rigidly. President Obama embraced the goal while making clear that it might not be achieved in his lifetime and noting that, as long as nuclear weapons exist, the United States would maintain a safe, secure, and effective nuclear deterrent. The 2012 GOP contender, Mitt Romney, has taken a highly skeptical approach even to traditional arms control (although he is running for president under the banner of the same party as Ronald Reagan, who favored nuclear zero in principle; it may be difficult to predict where his views on this subject may go over time).

Surely, whoever wins the American presidential race in November, many members of the Senate will continue to have a skeptical view on disarmament—and their votes will be needed for any treaty ratification. Members of both houses of Congress will have a say, through their control of the defense budget, in what nuclear forces are maintained by the United States in the years ahead as well. As such, the views of skeptics must be fully recognized and accounted for, even if a proponent of a denuclearized world again sits in the White House come January.

Nuclear zero may or may not be the right goal. But to paraphrase Sam Nunn, former senator and nuclear-zero proponent, if we are currently at the bottom of a mountain, with the summit representing a world without nuclear weapons, we need to reach base camp before we can aim for the top. The smart approach is to take modest steps toward the goal of a world free of nuclear weapons that may help determine whether, in a few years or more likely a few decades, a real attempt at the mountain top—complete nuclear disarmament—is possible. Viewing the path ahead in these terms also constitutes a perfectly reasonable reply to those non-nuclear states that demand to see compliance with the NPT's call for eliminating all nuclear weapons—and that reiterate the demand every five years when the NPT is reviewed formally by its adherents. Such a goal must be pursued carefully, responsibly, and incrementally if it is to be attempted at all.

Putting matters in these terms suggests an agenda for the next American president. We believe that even a skeptic of the goal of nuclear disarmament like Romney should consider elements of such an agenda. There are near-term and practical benefits to that agenda, beyond the possible role it could play on the long path to global zero. It could enhance the near-term cause of nuclear safety, better securing nuclear materials around the world. It could also help shore up international consensus around the NPT. In fact, the Obama administration's perceived commitment to arms control and possible disarmament helped produce a 2010 review document for the NPT that sustained international support for nuclear nonproliferation, as well as furthering greater cooperation at the 2010 and 2012 nuclear security summits. Taking steps toward nuclear disarmament, without yet committing to the end goal, might also help discourage China from pursuing the status of a nuclear superpower even as Russia and the United States draw down their capabilities.

Much of the agenda has already been discussed in this book. A U.S.-Russia understanding on missile defense transparency and cooperation would help reestablish discussion of defensive technologies within the broader arms control process, as must happen in any pursuit of a nuclear-zero world. Placing caps on nondeployed strategic as well as nonstrategic nuclear warheads in a future U.S.-Russia arms reduction treaty would mean that all U.S. and Russian nuclear weapons would be limited—an important point when many third-country nuclear weapons are short range as well. Such a future treaty could also begin to develop the verification tools on the locations and certain key characteristics of the warheads themselves that would be needed in any future global disarmament accord. A ban on production of fissile materials, or at least a moratorium, would further improve controls and monitoring of more sensitive nuclear sites, not only enhancing arms control but also security considerations. A comprehensive nuclear test ban, if possible to ratify in the United States and China, and ideally India and Pakistan, would help reinforce the norm that nuclear deterrence is for very limited purposes only, at most.

Several other steps, some of them specific to nuclear arms control and others broader, should be considered in the interests of moving toward a smaller role for nuclear weapons in future global affairs. They include efforts by the medium nuclear powers to join the nuclear arms control process, more careful accounting of past production of fissile materials to obtain a more accurate handle on existing stocks, progress on biological weapons arms control, and changes in current nuclear targeting doctrine. These steps should also include discussion of what the various aspects of a nuclear-zero treaty might look like, including ways that the capacity for reconstitution could be preserved in extremis, and a clearer sense of what progress in great-power relations would be needed as a prerequisite for negotiating such a multilateral accord.

MULTILATERALIZING NUCLEAR ARMS CONTROL

If, as advocated in this book, the United States and Russia each reduced their deployed strategic nuclear inventories to 1,000 warheads and their inventories of nondeployed strategic and nonstrategic nuclear warheads to another 1,000–1,500, they would retain a clear numerical dominance over the medium nuclear powers. But the disparity in numbers would no longer exceed a factor of ten, and the trend lines on warhead totals would appear to begin converging. Given the potential for a future buildup by China or another power, the situation would no longer allow for the two nuclear superpowers to ignore the rest of the world as they cut their own forces. Russia, in particular, is unlikely to consider reductions below 1,000 deployed strategic warheads without third countries—at least, Britain, France, and China—assuming some arms control obligations.

Currently, France is believed to have just under 300 nuclear war-heads, mostly deployed on ballistic-missile submarines, although the number could be higher (it was around 500 recently but has been headed downward). China is estimated to have about 240 nuclear warheads; about 55–65 of them are on long-range missiles able to reach the United States. The Chinese arsenal has remained roughly the same size for three decades, though it is moving toward a more mobile and survivable force. Britain has perhaps 225 war-heads (like France having peaked at just over 500 warheads in earlier years), about two-thirds on longer-range systems, and is believed to be reducing its number. India is believed to have 80 to 100 warheads and Pakistan 90 to 110; both countries are seeking to put some of those warheads on medium-range missiles (India has recently tested the Agni 5 missile, capable in theory of reaching eastern Chinese cities). Israel's arsenal ranges between an estimated 100 and 200 warheads.[2] North Korea has perhaps 6 to 8.

Some critics would argue that it is unfair of Russia and the United States to have more nuclear warheads than other countries and that any path to zero must require as an interim step that those two countries relinquish their nuclear superiority. That is unrealistic. Russia depends on nuclear deterrence to compensate for its weak conventional forces and long borders, and it sees nuclear weapons as important for status purposes—they are the central reason justifying Russia's continuing claim to global superpower status. The United States maintains defense commitments to dozens of countries around the world, a number of which face possible nuclear threats from other countries. Developing a process by which superpower drawdowns create uncertainty as to who holds the nuclear trump cards in any crisis could well lead to the possibility of more crises—and more dangerous crises. It makes little sense to radically revise the existing global nuclear architecture which, at least in great-power terms, appears relatively stable and stabilizing.

Any nuclear drawdowns thus would need to preserve *some* level of advantage for Moscow and Washington, at least for a time.

But, of course, this conclusion has been reached by two Americans and may not seem so obvious to strategists and leaders of other countries. To gain their support and participation in future nuclear restraint regimes, the two superpowers would presumably have to forgo some of their current margin of superiority.

These considerations, taken together, suggest perhaps a four-step process toward multilateralization of arms control. Even if the process takes ten or twenty years, the logic of the approach needs to be conceptualized and explained fairly soon, to avoid creating uncertainty over the direction and goals of future arms control in ways that could be destabilizing and encourage proliferation. Specifically, we propose the following:

—The medium nuclear powers—Britain, France, and China—should ideally, in association with, or soon after, the next U.S.-Russia nuclear arms reduction treaty, make political commitments not to exceed their current nuclear warhead holdings. Ideally, India and Pakistan should be encouraged to do so too. Since these would all be unilateral statements, they would not imply any formal recognition of new nuclear weapons states by the rest of the international community. However, if need be, this first step could be undertaken without India and Pakistan (or Israel or North Korea). There would be a certain logic, and perhaps greater simplicity in negotiations, in beginning with the five original and official NPT nuclear weapons states.

—In a second step, each nuclear state could commit to the same proportionate cut in total nuclear warhead holdings in the future, say, by 10 percent to 20 percent. This step could be undertaken as a political accord (rather than a treaty) to save time and to ease the process. In the general spirit of reducing reliance on nuclear weapons, the two superpowers might further reduce the alert levels of their nuclear weapons as part of this process if they had not done so already. That could include exploring and adopting ways to be sure that ICBMs and SLBMs could not be quickly launched, thus reducing the chances of accident or unauthorized attack. Perhaps at this stage, a comprehensive monitoring and safety regime could be instituted—as universally as possible—to complement whatever other verification mechanisms existed by then; former senior U.S. government officials Richard Burt and Jan Lodal have offered some useful proposals along these lines (such as a fissile material cutoff regime, if not already in place). Such a regime could ensure that all fissile materials globally were under international supervision.[3]

—Once the principle of proportional reductions (or some modest variant) is established, a formal multilateral arms treaty could be considered next. Plausible levels of additional reductions might range from 10 to 50 percent, notionally.

—A second round of formal cuts—or perhaps more—would probably be needed before there could be any serious consideration of nuclear zero. These cuts would develop further confidence in the negotiation process, allow any disagreements over verification and compliance to be addressed before the stakes became even higher (as they would in pursuit of complete nuclear disarmament), and provide time for the various parties to internalize in their nuclear establishments the major changes in doctrine and targeting that would accompany very deep cuts before they had to take the even greater leap to zero.

Over the past two years, the United States, Russia, Britain, France, and China have held UN Security Council Permanent Five discussions on nuclear weapons and related arms control issues. Initially these talks have been focused on issues such as terminology, but this process could later expand its mandate and might offer a venue for addressing multilateral nuclear reductions.

MONITORING AND ARCHIVING EXISTING FISSILE MATERIAL STOCKPILES

Another problem that will need to be resolved before countries can be comfortable in reaching for nuclear zero is the amount of fissile material currently in existence. Today there is considerable uncertainty about how much fissile material exists in the world—

particularly in the United States and Russia. Even the ambitious arms control accords outlined in this book would not eliminate that uncertainty.

Reducing the uncertainty as much as possible is important, not only for future arms control but for nuclear safety and security. A good deal of excellent work has already gone into understanding this task, some of it described and summarized in chapter 7. But this work also underscores the degree of the challenge. U.S.-Russian consultations were held in the early 1990s on ways to make nuclear reductions transparent and irreversible, but the Russian side ultimately stopped the exchanges. Russia and the United States have had enough problems with their bookkeeping efforts over the years that it may never be possible to account accurately for about 1 percent of the world's current fissile materials—enough for 1,000 bombs.[4]

Whether verification methods will *ever* be good enough to account for all the fissile material produced to date is hard to predict. This reality may greatly complicate pursuit of nuclear zero—or at least affect the way a nuclear disarmament treaty is ultimately structured. But in the spirit of reaching Sam Nunn's base camp, it makes sense to begin to make accounting and monitoring of surplus fissile materials more rigorous right away—and thus to better understand or "archive" what has been produced in the past—not least because doing so could also further reduce the dangers of nuclear theft or other unintended diversion of fissile materials to unauthorized parties.

NUCLEAR DOCTRINE IN THE NEAR TERM

In near-term nuclear doctrine decisions, the United States should also clarify that only in extremely rare circumstances would it ever use nuclear weapons for any purpose other than deterring nuclear use by others. This is sound policy in the short term and would ultimately be a necessary prerequisite to a nuclear-free world as well. The Obama administration—with its declaration that the fundamental purpose of nuclear weapons is to deter nuclear attack and its goal of creating conditions in which the sole purpose of nuclear weapons would be to deter nuclear attack—is moving in the direction of trying to limit and make more transparent the circumstances under which the United States would resort to using nuclear weapons.

Historically, the United States has maintained a number of options for how it might use nuclear weapons. That was true in the cold war, when large Warsaw Pact armies made Western leaders feel the need for a nuclear deterrent against possible conventional aggression. It remained true when the George W. Bush administration expanded the possible role of nuclear weapons in the post-9/11 world. It was true in between as well. The administration of George H. W. Bush maintained numerous possible uses for nuclear weapons even after the collapse of the Warsaw Pact and the Soviet Union itself. In 1992, for example, its national military strategy discussed the possibility of using nuclear weapons "as a hedge against the emergence of an overwhelming conventional threat," should one again present itself. The strategy document also spoke of deterring an adversary's use of weapons of mass destruction in general, not just nuclear weapons specifically, as a role for U.S. nuclear forces.[5] The Clinton administration maintained ambiguity on the matter as well. Most of its policy documents kept to a narrow rhetorical role for nuclear weapons, emphasizing that American nuclear capabilities were designed to deter the use of nuclear weapons by others.[6] However, the Clinton administration rejected the proposal of some NATO countries, such as Germany and Canada, to consider a nuclear no-first-use doctrine; it ultimately preserved flexibility on the matter.[7]

As argued below, in theory, biological weapons could someday become every bit as devastating, indiscriminate, and lethal as nuclear weapons. As the 2010 nuclear posture review states, at some future point, Washington may find it necessary to remind possible adversaries that a decision on their part to develop and deploy—or to use—an advanced pathogen that was highly contagious, highly lethal, and very difficult to inoculate against or treat could lead to an American nuclear response.

But that day is not near. The United States therefore can and should be more willing to circumscribe the conditions under which it might use nuclear weapons. As a matter of state policy today, the United States should declare that it would *not* use nuclear weapons in response to contemporary chemical and biological arms that enemies might use against the United States, U.S. allies, or U.S. military forces. The Obama administration's nuclear posture review moved in the right direction in this regard. However, it unnecessarily preserved explicit nuclear exemptions for dealing with North Korea and Iran in the near future, even if those states themselves do not use nuclear weapons in an attack. In such an event, U.S. conventional striking power is capable of inflicting massive punishment, as the national posture review also noted in another context.

THE BIOLOGICAL THREAT AND NUCLEAR ZERO

Nuclear abolitionists often argue that not all weapons of mass destruction are created equal. And even though the term seems to imply otherwise, they are surely right. Biological and chemical weapons are cruel and potent killers. But they are relatively hard to deliver in most kinds of situations.

Chemical weapons are indeed terrible, and the world has witnessed even in modern times what they can do, particularly to unprotected troops or civilians. One need only recall the Iran-Iraq war and Saddam Hussein's pogroms against his own Kurdish population. To have major effects, however, chemical weapons typically need to be delivered in substantial quantity; the harm they can do, moreover, can be significantly mitigated by proper battlefield protection for troops. And of course they do not self-replicate. While terrible killers, they are not in the same league as nuclear weapons.

Although the notion of biological weapons conjures up horrible images of incurable and fatal diseases that create slow, painful death, their actual use to date has been so restricted that the perceived potency of the threat has diminished in the eyes of many. In addition, given their typically slow incubation times and indiscriminate effects, their utility in affecting battlefield operations is dubious, and they often have been seen, rightly, as instruments of terror rather than of purposeful state violence. In short, existing biological agents could be extremely lethal, but only if they can be disseminated extremely effectively and in a manner not yet witnessed. That highly contagious agents have not yet been combined with highly lethal ones further constrains the magnitude of the existing threat. That does not mean the world can safely forget about biological weapons, but it arguably does refute the notion that nuclear weapons would be an appropriate deterrent to their near-term use against the United States or its friends and allies.

The United States has at times recognized this reality. During the cold war and for some years afterward, the United States publicly committed not to use nuclear weapons against non-nuclear weapons states (unless the latter were allied with nuclear powers in wartime operations). It did that, for example, during the 1995 NPT review conference. Yet the policy has not been consistent. Even while making such commitments, the United States has also wanted to retain nuclear weapons as an explicit deterrent against other, non-nuclear forms of weapons of mass destruction as a matter of targeting policy and nuclear weapons doctrine.[8] The Obama administration's nuclear posture review reduces the contradiction but does not eliminate it, because nuclear weapons could in theory be used in response to chemical or biological attack by countries violating their NPT obligations or, someday, against countries that had developed more advanced biological pathogens than are currently available.

In the future, however, biological weapons could become much more potent or be dispersed far more efficiently than has been the case so far for either known biological pathogens or chemical arms. Biological knowledge is advancing rapidly. To take one metric, the number of genetic sequences on file, a measure of knowledge of genetic codes (short or long) for various organisms, grew from well under 5 million in the early 1990s to 80 million by 2006.[9] The number of countries involved in biological research is growing rapidly too. For Americans, who long led the way in biology, it is sobering to note that today at least half of all important biological research is being done abroad. For a movement focused on the future, many nuclear abolitionists have not squarely faced the challenge of biological weapons as they could evolve and improve in coming decades.

One can naturally hope that better monitoring and verification concepts will be developed for biological and chemical weapons—just as they must clearly be improved in the nuclear realm if abolition is ever to be feasible. But these will be very hard to devise and probably rather imperfect in their ability to provide timely warning. Various forms of direct and indirect monitoring can be tried—the latter including looking for mismatches between the numbers of trained scientists in a given country and the professional positions available to them there, or a mismatch between the numbers of relevant scientists and associated publications.[10] Big disparities could suggest hidden weapons programs. One can also build up disease surveillance systems and create rapid-response biological weapons investigation teams to look into any suspected development of illicit pathogens or any outbreak of associated disease. But luck would likely still be needed to discover most biological weapons programs. Microbiological research often takes place in small facilities that are hard, if not impossible, to identify from remote sensing.[11] In short, no inspection regime can confidently thwart the actions of a sophisticated state actor bent on developing advanced pathogens secretly.

For such reasons, it is eminently possible that a future aggressor state could secretly develop an advanced "bug"—perhaps an influenza-borne derivative of smallpox resilient to currently available treatments, for example. This bug could combine the contagious qualities of the flu with the lethality of very severe diseases.[12] Such a prospect led arms control expert John Steinbruner to note that "one can imagine killing more people with an advanced pathogen than with the current nuclear weapons arsenals."[13] The state developing this bug might simultaneously develop a vaccine or new antibiotic to protect its own people against the new disease; that would be difficult but perhaps not impossible.

Would there really be a definitive moral argument against the use of a nuclear weapon in retaliation for a biological weapons attack that killed hundreds of thousands—or even millions—of innocent Americans? What if the United States thought a biological attack by an aggressor imminent? What if it had already suffered one such attack, and others, against other parts of the country, seemed possible? Would there really be no potential value to, and no moral justification for, a nuclear threat against the belligerent state, warning that any future biological attacks might produce a nuclear response?[14]

In his classic book on just and unjust war, Michael Walzer asserts that "nuclear war is and will remain morally unacceptable, and there is no case for its rehabilitation." He also argues that "nuclear weapons explode the theory of just war. They are the first of mankind's technological innovations that are simply not encompassable within the familiar moral world." This would seem to argue (since biological weapons of certain types predated nuclear technologies) that in fact nuclear threats could never be justifiable against a biological attack. However, the logic of Walzer's overall case against nuclear weapons is based explicitly on their indiscriminate and extreme effects—characteristics that advanced biological pathogens, which did not truly exist when he wrote these words, could share.[15]

As this discussion implies, the prospect of a nuclear-free world will be more realistic if and when possible biological weapons can be better monitored. This discussion also suggests that, even if a nuclear-free world is achieved, there may be a need to retain reconstitution capacities, not only against nuclear treaty violators but against foes developing particularly lethal advanced biological pathogens.

GEOPOLITICS AND TIMING

Many proponents of a nuclear disarmament accord want to move rapidly to a treaty. Some aspire to a time line in which negotiations on a treaty would begin within ten years, with the global elimination of nuclear weapons ideally to occur by 2030 or 2035. On the other side of the coin, many foreign policy pragmatists and traditionalists are content to imagine a nuclear-free world as a worthy goal but see no possible way to reach it at this moment in history. In fact, a middle ground between these positions makes the most sense. Moving to nuclear disarmament now, by trying to write a treaty in the next few years, is too fast, but waiting for the distant future is too slow.

Trying to abolish nuclear weapons too soon could undercut U.S. allies who worry about how they would ensure their security in a dangerous world. That could weaken deterrent arrangements that are working today but might become fragile. And it could encourage extremist states to build up nuclear arsenals as existing nuclear powers build down. Such a move would also lack credibility when even some responsible countries have no interest in denuclearizing anytime soon. Absent a serious process for moving toward zero, declaration of ambitious but arbitrary and unattainable deadlines for action is more likely to discredit the nuclear disarmament agenda than to advance it.

Putting off the nuclear disarmament agenda creates its own substantial problems, however. It leaves existing nuclear powers in a weak position to pressure would-be proliferators to abstain from the pursuit of nuclear weapons by perpetuating the perception of a permanent double standard regarding who gets to own the bomb. It risks damaging the global political consensus in support of the

NPT and other nuclear safety and security efforts. It also fosters a false sense of complacency about the supposed safety of living with the bomb.

Where does this leave things? The timing of a nuclear disarmament agenda should not be set to a calendar. Rather, beyond progress in arms control for both nuclear and biological weapons, as discussed in this book, the right time horizon for seriously pushing a new nuclear accord is after most of the world's half dozen or so major territorial and existential issues involving major powers are resolved.[16] These issues include the status of Taiwan, a comprehensive Middle East peace, and the issue of Kashmir. (Nuclear crises involving Iran and North Korea also need to be addressed, although the beginnings of a move toward nuclear disarmament might not have to await their complete resolution.) Once these contentious matters are largely resolved, the plausibility of great-power war over any imaginable issue that one can identify today would be very low. That in turn would make the basic structure and functioning of the international political system stable enough to take the risk of moving toward a nuclear-free world—a process that would be so radical as to be inherently destabilizing in some sense and thus prudent to pursue only when the great powers are in a cooperative mode and undivided by irredentist territorial issues. With luck, most of those issues could be successfully addressed in the next couple of decades. But we cannot know that yet.

Why should negotiation of a global nuclear disarmament treaty await improvement of great-power relations and resolution of most of the main potential causes of crisis or war among them? The answer: because the process of moving toward zero would be disruptive to deterrent relationships that are currently working rather well. Fundamentally altering these dynamics should not be done carelessly or prematurely. This of course does not preclude making more limited progress on nuclear reductions.

Consider several specific cases, starting with Taiwan scenarios that could in theory pit the United States against China in a war. Generally, such crises have been handled fairly cautiously in recent decades. But the Taiwan crises of the 1950s involved nuclear threats, and future ones could, too. Indeed, some Chinese scholars and officials have raised the possibility, albeit somewhat tangentially, that China might use nuclear weapons during a Taiwan conflict.[17] Those risks could increase in a world in which the gap between U.S. nuclear force levels and those of China narrowed. Under such circumstances, China, thinking it already had several advantages (geographic proximity, greater interest in Taiwan than the United States might feel) and having a reduced sense of clear American nuclear dominance, might feel emboldened to take more assertive action with conventional forces and perhaps to make more forceful nuclear threats.

Matters that involve smaller regional powers may themselves be enough to impede any realistic path to nuclear disarmament. These include, notably, the Kashmir dispute between India and Pakistan. Perhaps it is possible to imagine a future world in which conventional military deterrence proves adequate to manage any major regional tensions that occur. Given current political realities, however, pursuing complete nuclear disarmament is too much, and imperfect verification methods reinforce the problem.

The chances that Iran or North Korea would go along with any verification regime seem slight. The chances that either would make a sincere commitment to forgo nuclear weapons seem low as well. The United States could respond to a possible nuclear threat by either state with U.S. conventional military forces, which could inflict considerable punishment. But the difficulty of making that threat credible and effective is greater than many realize. And there is the worry, small but real, that such states might transfer nuclear weapons to terrorists. Defense Secretary Robert Gates took this threat seriously enough in October 2008 to suggest a possible broadening of the United States' nuclear deterrence doctrine, pledging to hold "fully accountable" any country or group that helped terrorists obtain or employ weapons of mass destruction.[18] For these and other reasons, the likelihood of a serious move toward nuclear disarmament being welcomed today by American allies in the neighborhood of Iran or North Korea is low. And the potential for perverse, counterproductive effects that could actually *encourage* U.S. allies to seek their own nuclear arsenals is great indeed. Perhaps a nuclear zero accord could be partially negotiated while North Korea or Iran still had nuclear weapons, but it probably could not be implemented until such rogue states also could be pressured or cajoled into disarming.

DESIGNING A NUCLEAR ZERO TREATY AND THE ISSUE OF RECONSTITUTION

Even if now is not yet the time to start negotiating a nuclear disarmament treaty, it may be the time to start thinking about one. The prospect of such an accord can help existing nuclear powers rebut claims by the likes of Iran and North Korea that they are hypocritical. Tehran, Pyongyang, and others implicitly or explicitly argue that the established nuclear powers have no business denying others the full range of nuclear options when they insist on holding onto nuclear weapons themselves. Extremist regimes will find other ways to complain, of course, and they will not be impressed by the global move toward denuclearization. But they will lose a key excuse in the eyes of many other states about why they are supposedly within their rights in pursuing the bomb or dual-use technologies such as uranium enrichment centrifuges that could facilitate acquisition of the bomb if the established nuclear powers have set nuclear zero as a goal.

In addition, the nuclear disarmament issue is now squarely on the international agenda, thanks to the efforts of key nuclear disarmament advocates such as former secretaries of state Henry Kissinger and George Shultz, former defense secretary William Perry, and Sam Nunn, not to mention President Obama. That means the vision of a nuclear-free world can already be a force for good. Alas, if misunderstood, it can breed anxiety among peaceful states, or a sense of opportunity among aggressive ones, and do harm to the international security order.

One key question that a nuclear zero accord would have to address is the issue of reconstitution—that is, allowing for the possibility of rebuilding an arsenal for a specific (and probably temporary) purpose even after weapons have been eliminated. The capacity to make nuclear weapons is a permanent attribute of modern human civilization. No treaty can change it. Especially in a world with widespread use of nuclear energy, the materials needed for making bombs as well as the knowledge needed to fashion them into explosive devices will always be readily and widely available. The capacity for reconstitution, even after the complete elimination of nuclear weapons, is therefore a fact of life that will not change. For these and other reasons, nuclear abolition is unrealistic and probably impossible, if the term *abolition* is taken to mean the absolute, verifiable, and permanent elimination of nuclear weapons with complete confidence that they could never return. It is important to get this message out, loud and clear, early in discussions of a possible future nuclear-weapons free world—lest misunderstandings produce perverse effects (such as countries pursuing the bomb out of fear that U.S. extended nuclear deterrence will disappear in the near future).

One hopes, of course, that reconstitution would never be necessary. Ideally, once eliminated, nuclear weapons would no longer seem to have any place in world politics, and the state of the international system would continue to stabilize so that severe future challenges would be unlikely—especially from state-on-state violence. In that world, what is designed as a reversible measure might evolve into a de facto permanent reality. But that will be for future generations to decide.

Various questions must be considered in any strategy for reconstitution that would be motivated by detection of cheating (or other horrendous action) by a key party to the nuclear disarmament treaty. One question is what international body would justify and legitimate any decision to rebuild a small arsenal? In the end, we would argue that, as a matter of core national security, while the United States would never want to take such a measure lightly and would prefer not to do it unilaterally, it would have to retain the option of reconstituting a future nuclear arsenal without U.N. Security Council approval. This question merits extensive discussion; we do not provide it here but do suggest that the conversation should begin in earnest many years before a treaty negotiation process might be undertaken.

A second matter concerns the types of physical preparations that should be made to allow for the possibility of reconstitution, should it someday be necessary. The goal would be principally to deter treaty violations by making sure any would-be cheater knew that its actions would be detected and would not go unanswered—and also to persuade friends of the United States that have in the past counted on its extended nuclear deterrent that they need not build their own nuclear arsenals under a future nuclear zero accord.

Bomb-ready fissile materials should not be retained under a nuclear zero accord, if it is to have any real meaning. When writing about nuclear disarmament in the early 1980s, Jonathan Schell proposed dismantling weapons but keeping a stock of fissile material ready just in case—deterrence without weapons.[19] This idea goes a step beyond Bruce Blair's well-known and persuasive campaign, joined by many others over the years, for de-alerting nuclear forces.[20] But neither de-alerted nuclear weapons nor bomb-ready fissile materials should be retained under a genuine nuclear disarmament regime. A world without nuclear weapons but full of fissile materials only steps away from being assembled into bombs would seem oxymoronic—and perhaps not worth the trouble to create.

Fissile materials are also the most difficult components of nuclear weapons to develop or create, so a nuclear disarmament regime designed to be verifiable and to give adequate warning of any violations should not allow their existence. Stockpiles of fissile materials, at least as much as advanced, assembled bombs mated to delivery vehicles, represent the world's greatest collective threat in the age of terrorism. They are hard to make, easy to hide, dangerous if lost, and not particularly difficult to fashion into weapons. There is no reason they need exist under a nuclear disarmament regime, even for purposes of retaining a latent reconstitution capability.

It does make sense, however, to keep track of other latent capabilities for reconstitution. These include lists of people—the scientists and technicians who would be needed in a bomb program. Other items to track include hardware, materials, and infrastructure—uranium enrichment facilities, sophisticated machine shops where bombs might be built, and laboratories for making conventional explosives. Such reconstitution plans should include substantial amounts of redundancy as a hedge against sabotage or preemptive attack. An issue could arise as to how transparent a country should be regarding reconstitution plans and capabilities.

Getting rid of the weapons and fissile materials but keeping "warm" the lists of people who can regenerate them as well as the facilities needed to do so strikes the right balance in a nuclear disarmament regime. Eliminating weapons, some weapons delivery vehicles, fissile materials, and plutonium-reprocessing capabilities, these steps are verifiable—if not perfectly, at least to a degree. Erasing the knowledge of how to make the bomb, along with the understanding of nuclear physics among a country's technical classes, is neither feasible nor verifiable. Moreover, confirming that another country has no secret list of scientists, technologies, and facilities that would be needed to rebuild a nuclear arsenal would also be difficult. There is thus no reason to try to ban such latent lists and plans; it is too hard to do.[21] And there is no reason for the United States to abstain from maintaining such lists itself, as a hedge against unforeseen developments; in fact, the United States should do so. With this approach, it could rebuild some nuclear inventory, not overnight but within a number of months.

That is a good time frame for purposes of a nuclear disarmament treaty. If states could rebuild arsenals in just weeks, there would be little time to deliberate if suspected violations were uncovered, and the world might always be on the verge of rearming fast. If, however, years were required to rebuild nuclear arms, a great deal of havoc could be caused in the meantime by an aggressive state, depending on the scenario. The offending state might invade a neighbor with conventional forces and threaten to use nuclear forces against any state coming to the victim's aid, for example. In that event, a country like the United States might be deterred so long that the conquest of the victim state could begin to seem like a fait accompli. The American people might lose heart and choose not to support an extended period of rebuilding a nuclear arsenal while also preparing conventional forces for a possible counterinvasion. But if rearmament could be accomplished over a period of months, as would surely be the case for any world with significant ongoing use of nuclear power, the type of resolve that the United States maintained after the Iraqi invasion of Kuwait in August of 1990 until Operation Desert Storm was launched the following January, or in the one to two years after September 11, 2001, could likely be created and sustained.

Would the United States and other countries really be able to afford a several-month delay in response to an aggression? Certainly a Soviet-scale arsenal in the hands of an aggressor could be used to threaten all known concentrations of nuclear physics research and of nuclear physicists in the country—potentially "disarming" the United States in the process. But to be credible, this threat would require literally dozens of bombs, at a minimum, given the number of major physics research facilities, locations of fissile material concentrations, and machining facilities in the country—today the list would include half a dozen Department of Energy laboratories, about a hundred nuclear reactors, at least several dozen major metals processing centers, and another several dozen major university physics laboratories.[22] Several dozen airfields hosting major commercial and civilian aircraft would also likely have to be targeted to eliminate top candidates for delivery vehicles of any weapons used for retaliation. To make retaliation impractical in short order, therefore, at a bare minimum several hundred sites would need to be destroyed or severely damaged.

Even if in theory a cold-war-vintage Soviet (or American) arsenal might have been up to the task on paper, a country breaking out from a nuclear disarmament regime and needing to make hundreds of nuclear weapons would be extremely hard pressed to attempt it given the constraints imposed by the regime's verification system. The far more likely cheating scenario would be a state developing and revealing—or being discovered to have—a small nuclear arsenal, which would not give it the capability to destroy all the U.S. reconstitution sites. (Fewer warheads, however, could pose a mortal threat to a smaller state such as Israel. Thus, in a nuclear disarmament regime, the U.S. obligation to deter nuclear threats or attacks against other countries would grow in some ways. Such countries could be expected to give up or forgo their own arsenals only if they were confident that another country would help ensure their security.)

Some have argued that, with time, nuclear expertise would atrophy so much that any country would find it very difficult to build or rebuild the bomb.[23] That seems incorrect. To be sure, fluency with the details of the bomb would be lost as those who have actually worked with nuclear devices retired in the decades to come. But the basics of nuclear physics are not so easy to forget. Rebuilding a large arsenal might be harder with the nuclear weapons novices of, say, the twenty-second century. But their command of nuclear physics, of precision machining methods, and of the basic understanding of what goes into any device creating a self-sustaining chain reaction is unlikely to be lost. That may mean that mankind has to live, for centuries to come, with the fact that scientists will be capable of again building nuclear weapons fairly quickly if and when they have a national-scale effort to back them up. That may be sobering at one level, but it is also reassuring, for it means that if world events evolve in a direction that makes reconstitution seem desirable, rearming will in fact be quite feasible indefinitely into the future.

CONCLUSIONS AND RECOMMENDATIONS

We believe the United States should prepare the ground, using venues such as the UN Security Council Permanent Five discussions on nuclear disarmament and nonproliferation and the 2015 NPT review conference, for broadening the nuclear arms reduction process to include other countries. While one more U.S.-Russia nuclear arms accord should be possible, after that, third countries—including at least Britain, France, and China, and perhaps India and Pakistan as well—will need to begin taking on some nuclear obligations. Achievement of a follow-on treaty to New START—or substantial progress toward such an agreement—by early 2015 would position Washington and Moscow to press the case at the NPT review conference for multilateral nuclear arms reductions.

Looking to the longer term, a nuclear-weapons-free world is not attainable today, and a premature pursuit of such a world—as opposed to the more modest goal of multilateral nuclear reductions—would do more harm than good in the short term by encouraging proliferation and weakening deterrence. Whether it could become a good idea in the future remains to be seen.

Among the chief prerequisites to comprehensive nuclear disarmament are progress on various aspects of nuclear monitoring and verification; better monitoring of biological technologies; and resolution of key territorial disputes that could put nuclear-armed countries at war with each other, notably those over Kashmir, Taiwan, and the future of Israel. Even once a possible treaty was signed and implemented, it would have to include means for timely (if temporary) reconstitution of arsenals by one or more countries (or group of countries) to deal with possible violations.

We believe that nuclear zero makes sense as a long-term political goal, even if the United States is not certain how to achieve it. It is too soon to know if the summit of nuclear disarmament can ever be reached, but it makes good sense to pursue further nuclear reductions in a step-by-step manner and move to a possible way station on that path, from which Washington could then reassess the situation in the decades ahead. This course of action is particularly sensible because the various ideas and policies that it implies make sense in their own right for reducing nuclear danger in the short term. The more difficult theological debates can and should wait.

CHAPTER NINE

LOOKING FORWARD

IN THE PRECEDING CHAPTERS, we have offered ideas for further reducing nuclear arms that the president could pursue in 2013 and beyond. They include engaging in bilateral U.S.-Russian efforts to cut strategic nuclear weapons below the levels of New START, bringing nondeployed strategic and nonstrategic nuclear weapons into the arms control mix, and addressing missile defense in a way that would remove the issue as an impediment to further nuclear reductions and irritant in the broader U.S.-Russia and NATO-Russia relationships. We have also suggested that the United States could ratify the Comprehensive Test Ban Treaty and press to conclude a fissile material cutoff treaty—though with the caveat that political practicality must be a consideration, and that, in the arms control realm, "perfect" should not be made the enemy of the good (for example, a failed Senate effort to approve the CTBT would do more harm than good). Finally, we have offered ideas on steps that would begin to multilateralize the nuclear arms reduction process and move incrementally and provisionally toward a world free of nuclear weapons, even though it cannot now be known whether such an objective might be attainable.

What might adoption of these proposals mean for nuclear security at the end of Barack Obama's second term or Mitt Romney's first in January 2017? Given equal measures of political will; presidential attention; bureaucratic courage; and flexibility, reasonableness, and willingness to listen to the other side, plus a fair measure of luck, the nuclear arms control landscape in 2017 could look like the following:

The New START II Treaty, having been signed in fall 2015 and entered into force in 2016, would be in its first year of implementation. The United States and Russia would each be in the process of reducing to limits of no more than 2,000–2,500 total nuclear warheads, with a sublimit of no more than 1,000 deployed strategic warheads; no more than 500 deployed strategic delivery vehicles (ICBMs, SLBMs, and heavy bombers); and no more than 575–600 deployed and nondeployed strategic ballistic missile launchers and heavy bombers. The treaty would last for ten years, with the possibility of up to a five-year extension, and would require that all reductions be implemented by 2021.

As part of New START II, the United States would have accepted a requirement that, from 2021, all nuclear weapons must be based on national territory. The greater transparency and reductions in Russian nonstrategic nuclear weapons mandated by the treaty, an overall improvement in NATO-Russia relations (to which the treaty and NATO-Russia missile defense cooperation had contributed), and NATO's use of exercises and other non-nuclear means to bolster the confidence of allies in Central Europe would have led to NATO agreement on the withdrawal of U.S. B61 bombs from Europe in conformance with the treaty. By that point, the vestiges of cold war competition would have been nearly excised from the U.S.-Russia and more general NATO-Russia relationships.

The United States and Russia would have high confidence in their ability to monitor New START II's limits on deployed strategic warheads and strategic delivery vehicles. They would have less confidence in their ability to monitor the numbers of nondeployed strategic warheads and nonstrategic weapons, which would be restricted to declared storage sites that would be subject to inspections. But they would be gaining valuable experience that could generate new inspection procedures that would raise the monitoring confidence level in the future. And even if imperfect, their knowledge of each other's nonstrategic arsenals would greatly exceed what it is today, a worthy goal that could also provide the basis for extending such monitoring concepts to other nuclear weapons states in the future.

New START II's limits would allow the U.S. military to continue to maintain a triad of ICBMs, SLBMs, and heavy bombers if it wished. The reduced numbers permitted by the treaty would result in some budget savings, with the Defense Department planning to build perhaps ten, instead of twelve, new ballistic missile submarines (or new Trident SSBNs with fewer launch tubes) and fewer ICBMs than would have been the case under New START I limits. Savings could also be generated in the Department of Energy, which would have to support a smaller arsenal of nuclear warheads. Some of the budget pressure on the science-based stockpile stewardship program also might be eased through a decision to add a different type of warhead to the arsenal, one that was based on conservative, time-tested design principles intended to ensure reliability and safety, but that provided no new nuclear weapons capabilities. For their part, the Russians would have concluded that their existing ballistic missile programs could sustain the New START II levels with no need for a new heavy ICBM.

As for missile defense, NATO and Russia would in 2017 be in their fourth year of a cooperative missile defense arrangement for Europe, based principally on the operation of a data fusion center in Brussels and a planning and operations center in Moscow, both jointly staffed by NATO and Russian military officers. The day-to-day operations of these centers, the annual notifications of the current and projected numbers of key elements of U.S. missile defenses, and the ability to observe U.S. SM-3 flight tests would be providing the Russian military with a full picture of U.S. and NATO missile defense efforts, from which the Russians could assess whether a serious theoretical threat to their strategic ballistic missiles existed.

When signing the New START II Treaty in fall 2015, the Russian side issued a unilateral statement to the effect that quantitative and qualitative increases in U.S. missile defense capabilities could undermine the U.S.-Russian strategic offensive balance and lead Russia to exercise its right to withdraw from the treaty. Issuing their own unilateral statement and using language similar to the political commitment made by NATO in 2012 and the president in 2013, U.S. negotiators noted that U.S. missile defenses were not directed against Russia. In effect, Washington and Moscow called a temporary truce over missile defense, while both recognized that the issue could come back if missile defense technologies made significant advances in the 2020s and if their relationship still was imperfect enough that such issues caused meaningful angst in one or both capitals.

At the spring 2015 Non-Proliferation Treaty review conference, the U.S. and Russian delegations cited the progress that they had made on the almost finished New START II Treaty to press to expand the nuclear arms reduction process to include all nuclear weapons states, and two years later preliminary multilateral discussions would be under way. Ideally, in 2017, all the major nuclear weapons states had continued to observe the moratorium on nuclear testing, and the United States had ratified the Comprehensive Test Ban Treaty. While the CTBT might not yet have come into force, China had followed the U.S. example and ratified, and pressure would be mounting on other countries whose ratification was necessary to bring the treaty into effect. In any event, the U.S. and Chinese ratifications, following the earlier ratifications by France, Russia, and the United Kingdom, raised the political costs of any nuclear test by a third country. A fissile material cutoff treaty had not yet been negotiated by 2017, but the United States, Russia, and several other nuclear weapons states had adopted a moratorium on the production of fissile materials for weapons purposes. Moreover, multilateral discussions would be making slow progress toward a negotiating mandate for a treaty.

Is this an optimistic picture? Yes, but not impossible.

Some critics will say this vision goes too far. They would worry that a New START II Treaty further limiting the United States to 2,000-2,500 nuclear weapons would weaken U.S. security and would not suffice to deter the full spectrum of potential threats to the United States and its allies. But if America's nearest nuclear peer competitor, Russia, reduces to the same limits and no other nuclear weapons state has more than 300 nuclear weapons, the United States would be able to deter any rational adversary. We would put the burden on critics to say who would *not* be deterred by this force. To be sure, there may be irrational opponents who would not be deterred from certain actions, but 5,000 or 10,000 nuclear weapons probably would not deter them either.

The same critics would be uneasy about the less than high confidence level in the ability to monitor limits on Russian nondeployed strategic and nonstrategic nuclear weapons. Covert maintenance of an additional 200–300 nuclear weapons at an undisclosed site in the Ural Mountains would be a huge political problem, one that could derail the arms control process for years, but would it dramatically affect the strategic balance? Remember that the Russians today can maintain nonstrategic nuclear weapons (and nondeployed strategic warheads) without limit.

Critics might also worry about the denuclearization of the U.S. commitment to NATO. But the nuclear commitment would remain, sustained by U.S. strategic nuclear forces, just as those forces today provide a nuclear umbrella over U.S. allies in Asia. Critics might doubt that the CTBT would be compatible with long-term U.S. nuclear deterrent capabilities. But the proposed policy would allow, if necessary, building of warheads based on a conservative design—one incorporating previously tested warhead concepts, not new principles—that would address any uncertainties that emerged about the reliability and safety of the existing American arsenal. Any steps taken toward nuclear zero would have been modest, not prejudging any outcomes but rather undertaken in the spirit of exploring whether the goal endorsed by U.S. presidents from Nixon to Reagan to Obama was one the United States could seriously consider pursuing in coming decades.

Others will criticize our vision as being too modest, as not going far enough in reducing nuclear weaponry. While our proposal for a New START II treaty would reduce deployed strategic warheads only by one-third, it would bring all U.S. and Russian nuclear weapons under constraints for the first time ever. It would roughly halve the number of all nuclear weapons on the U.S. side and make a comparable cut on the Russian side—hardly insignificant reductions. And by bringing all nuclear weapons into the agreement, it would strengthen the U.S. and Russian position to expand the nuclear reductions process to the other nuclear weapons states, half of which have only nonstrategic nuclear arms. Importantly, it would not accelerate the arms reduction process so dramatically that China would be encouraged to seek to maneuver its way into the top tier of nuclear powers, building up while Russia and the United States built down.

Moreover, looking out over the next five years, we see no possibility that Russia would be prepared in a bilateral negotiation to go below the limits we have suggested. Even getting Moscow to go that far will prove a Herculean task. But we see value in attempting one more round of U.S.-Russia reductions. Once Washington and Moscow broaden the process to include other nuclear powers, the negotiations will become a far more complex proposition. The two nuclear superpowers can certainly take one more step without calling into doubt their substantial lead over other nuclear states today.

The kind of vision that we have described for 2017 would be one in which U.S. national security would be strengthened compared with current circumstances. The nuclear threat to America would be reduced. The United States would still have a secure, robust, and effective nuclear deterrent second to none, would be proceeding to refurbish that deterrent, and would be deploying a defense against a limited ballistic missile attack. The demonstrated U.S. commitment to nuclear reductions would bolster American credibility in building coalitions to raise the bar higher against nuclear proliferation and enhance U.S. diplomacy's ability to maximize pressure on those states that might contemplate trying to acquire or test nuclear weapons. Americans would be safer and more secure, and Washington would be positioned for the next step—negotiating a multilateral arrangement that would impose limits, and eventually reductions, on all nuclear weapons states.

NUCLEAR ARMS CONTROL TREATIES

SALT

The first U.S.-Soviet strategic arms negotiations, the Strategic Arms Limitation Treaty negotiations, began in 1969. They covered both strategic offensive systems and antiballistic missile defenses. Following seven rounds, the negotiations produced the Interim Offensive Arms Agreement and Anti-Ballistic Missile Treaty, which President Richard Nixon and General Secretary Leonid Brezhnev signed on May 26, 1972.

Often referred to as SALT I, the Interim Offensive Arms Agreement limited U.S. and Soviet intercontinental ballistic missile (ICBM) launchers—underground silos—to the number deployed as of July 1, 1972, and submarine-launched ballistic missile (SLBM) launchers—launch tubes on submarines—to the number deployed or under construction as of May 26, 1972. The agreement applied limits to launchers rather than missiles because the sides' national technical means of verification, such as reconnaissance satellites, could monitor ICBM silos and SLBM launch tubes but not actual missiles. The sides set a duration of five years for the agreement, expecting that U.S. and Soviet negotiators would shortly replace SALT I with a new treaty.[1]

Under the terms of SALT I, the Soviet Union had a numerical advantage in both ICBM and SLBM launchers (see table 2-1 in chapter 2). From the Nixon administration's perspective, that advantage was more than offset by the U.S. lead in heavy bombers—which the agreement did not constrain—and U.S. deployment of multiple independently targeted reentry vehicles (MIRVs) on its strategic missiles, which began in 1970.

The SALT II negotiations got under way in late 1972. The primary American concern—then and for the next two decades—centered on Soviet heavy ICBMs. As the Soviets mastered the MIRV technology, U.S. officials increasingly worried that large ICBMs carrying powerful MIRVs would pose a threat to U.S. ICBMs in their silos. Indeed, over the course of the 1970s, the Soviets replaced their heavy SS-9 ICBM, which carried a single warhead, with the heavy SS-18 ICBM, which could carry up to ten warheads.

In November 1974, President Gerald Ford and Brezhnev met in Vladivostok and agreed that SALT II would limit each side to no more than 2,400 strategic nuclear delivery vehicles—ICBM launchers, SLBM launchers, and heavy bombers—of which no more than 1,320 on each side could be MIRVed missile launchers. But they could not finalize the treaty before Ford finished his term.

Taking office in January 1977, President Jimmy Carter decided to try to limit U.S. and Soviet nuclear forces to lower levels, proposing to cap each side at 1,800–2,000 strategic nuclear delivery vehicles instead of 2,400. The Soviets insisted on maintaining the Vladivostok framework, but over the next two years, U.S. negotiators succeeded in bringing down the numbers somewhat. Carter and Brezhnev in July 1979 signed the SALT II Treaty.[2] It limited each side to no more than

—2,250 strategic nuclear delivery vehicles (ICBM launchers, SLBM launchers, and heavy bombers).

—1,320 MIRVed ICBM and MIRVed SLBM launchers plus heavy bombers that could carry air-launched cruise missiles.

—1,200 MIRVed ICBM and MIRVed SLBM launchers.

—820 MIRVed ICBM launchers.

SALT II required the United States and Soviet Union to make minor reductions in their strategic nuclear delivery vehicle numbers, but the treaty did not directly constrain warheads. As both countries continued to MIRV their ICBMs and SLBMs, and as the U.S. Air Force—followed later by Soviet Long-Range Aviation—deployed air-launched cruise missiles on its heavy bombers, the numbers of strategic nuclear warheads on both sides continued to climb.

SALT II never entered into force. Treaty opponents expressed particular concern about the threat that large, MIRVed Soviet ICBMs posed to U.S. ICBM silos. Moreover, the Soviet invasion of Afghanistan at the end of 1979 fueled a broader deterioration in U.S.-Soviet relations, reflected in declining Senate support for SALT II, so that consent to its ratification became increasingly uncertain, even unlikely. As a result, Carter asked the Senate to postpone the ratification process. He nevertheless indicated that the United States intended to observe the treaty as long as the Soviets did.

START AND INF

President Ronald Reagan took office in January 1981. He believed that the Soviets had achieved significant strategic advantages in the late 1970s and had criticized SALT II as "fatally flawed" throughout the 1980 presidential campaign. The threat to U.S. ICBMs in their silos carried particular weight with Reagan administration officials. Despite his opposition to SALT II ratification, Reagan nevertheless stated that, at least for the time being, the United States would not undercut the treaty's limits if the Soviets took a similar approach, a policy that Washington observed until 1986.

One of Reagan's critiques of SALT II was that it did not reduce nuclear weapons. By the end of 1981, Reagan had tabled the "zero-zero" proposal to eliminate all U.S. and Soviet intermediate-range nuclear force (INF) missiles; the United States would forgo deployment of its planned ground-launched cruise missiles (GLCMs) and Pershing II ballistic missiles if the Soviets agreed to eliminate all of their SS-20, SS-4, and SS-5 ballistic missiles. "Zero-zero" received an enthusiastic welcome from European publics, but Moscow rejected the proposal out of hand. Accepting the proposal in 1981 would have required that the Soviets scrap some 600 missiles carrying 1,100 warheads in return for the United States cancelling programs that were only in the test and development stages. The Soviets instead offered counterproposals that would have frozen a large numerical advantage.

In May 1982, Reagan proposed that SALT be replaced by the Strategic Arms Reduction Treaty (START) negotiations, and that the United States and Soviet Union each cut their ICBMs and SLBMs to no more than 850, capable of carrying no more than 5,000 warheads. The Soviets criticized Reagan's proposals as one-sided, but he succeeded in shifting the focus to reductions.

Many analysts believed that Moscow was unready for a serious give-and-take on INF missiles, in part out of a hope that the deployment track would collapse due to public opposition in Europe. In November 1983, following the arrival of the first GLCM and Pershing II missiles in Britain and Germany, the Soviets broke off the INF and START negotiations, neither of which had made serious headway.[3]

To the surprise of many, including official Washington, antinuclear sentiment in Europe declined in 1984. Once the Soviets had walked away from the negotiating table, the INF issue fell off the front pages, the public demonstrations that had in earlier years wracked Belgium, Britain, Germany, and the Netherlands subsided, and GLCM and Pershing II deployments proceeded apace.

In early 1985, the Soviets agreed to return to both the INF and START negotiations. That reflected Moscow's recognition that the walkout had failed to provoke a public outcry. It also reflected the view of the new Soviet general secretary, Mikhail Gorbachev. He saw little value in the Soviet Union piling up more nuclear arms and was prepared to negotiate serious reductions, in part to relieve the stress that the defense budget had placed on the rest of the Soviet economy.

The negotiations picked up steam following Reagan's summit meeting with Gorbachev in November 1985. In his second term, Reagan showed greater interest in arms control, and Gorbachev's desire to cut defense spending made him more willing than his predecessors to consider nuclear reductions.

Reagan and Gorbachev met again in Reykjavik in October 1986 for one of the most momentous arms control exchanges ever. The two leaders and their negotiating teams recorded major strides in defining limits for strategic nuclear weapons, agreeing that START should limit each side to no more than 1,600 strategic nuclear delivery vehicles and 6,000 strategic warheads. Gorbachev was prepared to ban all INF missiles from Europe, although the Soviets still wanted to maintain some SS-20 systems in Asia. On the last day of the summit, Reagan offered a ban on all nuclear-armed ballistic missiles, while Gorbachev proposed eliminating all nuclear weapons, a position that Reagan appeared to accept, at least in principle. However, differences over limits on the development and testing of missile defenses under the Strategic Defense Initiative proved too big a stumbling block.

The summit ended in apparent failure, but the negotiators returned to Geneva and incorporated most of the work that had been done in Reykjavik. By the end of 1987, Reagan and Gorbachev had signed a treaty banning all INF missiles. The INF Treaty was a landmark for arms reduction efforts. It banned all U.S. and Soviet land-based ballistic and cruise missiles with ranges between 500 and 5,500 kilometers. It included what were at the time the most intrusive verification measures ever recorded in an arms control agreement, including detailed data exchanges on INF missiles and launchers and a variety of on-site inspections.[4]

The INF Treaty entered into force in June 1988, and baseline inspections to establish the accuracy of the initial data exchange began the following month, with inspection teams fanning out to visit INF bases and facilities in the Soviet Union, Europe, and the United States. Preparations began for U.S. inspectors to take up continuous station at a missile factory outside of Votkinsk in the Ural Mountains, where the terms of the treaty allowed them to inspect railway cars departing the factory to confirm that SS-20 missiles were no longer being produced (the Votkinsk plant continued—and continues to this day—to produce a variety of other missiles not covered by the INF Treaty). All INF missiles on both sides were eliminated by June 1991.

Finalizing the details of the START I Treaty took longer, but it eventually was completed. In July 1991, President George H. W. Bush and Gorbachev signed the treaty, which limited each side to no more than

—1,600 strategic nuclear delivery vehicles (ICBM launchers, SLBM launchers, and heavy bombers).

—6,000 total attributed warheads.

—4,900 attributed warheads on ICBM and SLBM launchers.

—1,540 attributed warheads on heavy ICBM launchers.

—1,100 attributed warheads on mobile ICBM launchers.

The treaty did not count warheads directly but attributed a certain number of warheads to each type of ICBM, SLBM, and heavy bomber. For ballistic missiles, the number of warheads (or reentry vehicles) was generally the maximum number of reentry vehicles with which the missile had been tested. The attribution rules gave preferential treatment to heavy bombers in that they discounted the number of warheads attributed to those aircraft. Bombers equipped with air-launched cruise missiles (ACLMs) counted at one-half their capacity; other bombers not equipped to carry ALCMs were counted as one warhead. The discount rule reflected the U.S. position that bombers—primarily because they would take so much longer than ballistic missiles to reach their targets—posed far less of a first-strike threat to strategic stability.

START I had a duration of fifteen years and contained verification measures that went well beyond those negotiated in the SALT agreements. START I provided for an extensive data exchange, regular data updates, on-site inspections, and a requirement for access to telemetry, the information that a missile system broadcasts during a test flight to report on its performance.

In contrast to the SALT agreements, START I provided for genuine reductions in strategic offensive forces. It required the sides to reduce their strategic nuclear delivery vehicles by 30–35 percent to reach the 1,600 limit. Moreover, in the first data exchange conducted in 1990, each side declared more than 10,000 warheads attributed to its strategic missile launchers and bombers, so the treaty required a 40 percent reduction in attributed warheads.

As part of the presidential nuclear initiatives announced by Bush in September 1991, the United States immediately stood down from alert status all heavy bombers and all ICBMs scheduled to be removed under START I. Gorbachev responded shortly thereafter by removing Russian strategic bombers and 503 ICBMs from alert status and said that Russia would reduce to no more than 5,000 warheads over the course of START I. In January 1992, Bush announced further steps, including an end to production of the B-2 bomber, MX ICBM, and new warheads for the Trident II D5 SLBM.[5]

Just months after START I's signature—and before it could be ratified and brought into force—the Soviet Union collapsed, leaving Soviet strategic nuclear forces on the territories of the now independent states of Russia, Belarus, Kazakhstan, and Ukraine. The four states and the United States concluded the Lisbon Protocol to START I in May 1992, under which the post-Soviet states agreed to assume the Soviet Union's START I obligations. Belarus, Kazakhstan, and Ukraine further agreed to eliminate all strategic nuclear weapons on their territory. It took time and a trilateral U.S.-Ukraine-Russia negotiation to finalize the terms under which

Ukraine would eliminate the strategic weapons on its territory, but the START I Treaty entered into force in December 1994.

U.S.-Russian negotiations produced a follow-on treaty, START II, which was signed by Bush and Russian President Boris Yeltsin in January 1993. START II cut the overall strategic warhead limit to 3,000–3,500. Moreover, it resolved the long-standing U.S. concern about MIRVed ICBMs by banning all heavy ICBMs and all ICBMs with multiple warheads. It allowed some MIRVed ICBMs to be "downloaded"—to have some warheads removed—so that they carried just a single warhead. Analysts welcomed START II as a major advance for strategic stability: in a crisis, the incentives to strike the other side's ICBM silos when they contained single-warhead missiles would be significantly less than when the silos held multiple-warhead missiles.

START II was approved by the U.S. Senate in January 1996, but ratification on the Russian side became entangled with concerns expressed by the Duma (the Russian parliament) over issues such as NATO's decision to enlarge, the Alliance's 1999 conflict with Serbia, and U.S. interest in a national missile defense system. Moreover, some in Russia questioned the wisdom of giving up all MIRVed and heavy ICBMs, which had been the backbone of Soviet and then Russian strategic forces. In 1997, President Bill Clinton and Yeltsin agreed that START III should reduce the strategic warhead limit to 2,000-2,500. The sides never completed the treaty, however, and in the end, START II never entered into force.

SORT

President George W. Bush assumed office in January 2001. His administration did not favor negotiated limits on strategic weapons, considering such agreements no longer necessary with the cold war already ten years in the past. Rather than having limits on and predictability about Russian strategic forces, Bush administration officials preferred to maintain flexibility regarding U.S. strategic force choices.

When the administration's 2001 nuclear posture review concluded that the United States should maintain 1,700–2,200 operational strategic warheads, Bush suggested to Russian President Vladimir Putin that Washington and Moscow simply issue parallel statements regarding their intended strategic force levels. Putin pushed back, stressing his desire for a legally binding treaty, and Bush acceded to his direct request.

In May 2002, Bush and Putin signed the Strategic Offensive Reductions Treaty (SORT). The treaty limited each side to 1,700–2,200 operationally deployed strategic warheads, with the limits to take full effect on December 31, 2012, the day the treaty would expire. The two-page treaty contained no agreed definitions, counting rules, or verification measures. Bush administration officials said the verification provisions of the START I Treaty, which would be in force until December 2009, could help monitor implementation of SORT, but those provisions could not monitor operational warhead loadings.

With SORT concluded, the Bush administration paid relatively little attention to strategic arms control until 2008, when START I's expiration neared. U.S. and Russian officials consulted over the course of a year on what might replace START I. The Bush administration wished to limit only deployed strategic warheads, while the Russians wanted also to constrain strategic nuclear delivery vehicles. One Russian official described Moscow's concern about the U.S. position: a limit on deployed strategic warheads but no limits on strategic delivery vehicles or on nondeployed strategic warheads left open the possibility that the United States could put additional warheads on its (unlimited) strategic delivery vehicles— a breakout capability that was unacceptable to the Russians.[6] The sides could not reach agreement before the end of the Bush administration's term in office.

ABBREVIATIONS

ABM	antiballistic missile
ALCM	air-launched cruise missile
ALTBMD	Active Layered Theater Ballistic Missile Defense
CMRR	Chemistry and Metallurgy Research Facility Replacement Complex
CTBT	Comprehensive Nuclear Test Ban Treaty
DOE	Department of Energy
EPAA	European Phased Adaptive Approach
GBI	ground-based interceptor
GLCM	ground-launched cruise missile
HEU	highly enriched uranium
IAEA	International Atomic Energy Agency
ICBM	intercontinental ballistic missile
INF	intermediate-range nuclear forces
MAD	mutual assured destruction
MIRV	multiple, independently targetable reentry vehicle
NATO	North Atlantic Treaty Organization (the Alliance)
NPT	Nuclear Non-Proliferation Treaty
PAC-3	Patriot Advanced Capability-3
SALT	Strategic Arms Limitation Treaty
SDI	Strategic Defense Initiative

SIOP	Single Integrated Operational Plan
SLBM	submarine-launched ballistic missile
SLCM	submarine-launched cruise missile
SORT	Strategic Offensive Reductions Treaty
SSBN	ballistic missile submarine
SSBN(X)	ballistic missile submarine, new class
START	Strategic Arms Reduction Treaty
THAAD	Theater High Altitude Area Defense
UN	United Nations
WMD	weapons of mass destruction

NOTES

CHAPTER 2

1. Lawrence Freedman, *The Evolution of Nuclear Strategy* (New York: St. Martin's Press, 1983), p. 87.

2. Robert S. Norris, "United States Nuclear Weapons Deployments Abroad, 1950–1977," History of the Nuclear Age Dinner Series (Washington: Carnegie Endowment for International Peace, November 19, 1999).

3. Freedman, *The Evolution of Nuclear Strategy*, p. 246.

4. Harlan Cleveland, *NATO: The Transatlantic Bargain* (New York: Harper & Row, 1970), p. 82.

5. Richard M. Nixon, "U.S. Foreign Policy for the 1970s," Report to Congress, February 18, 1970.

6. Freedman, *The Evolution of Nuclear Strategy*, p. 378.

7. See Elbridge A. Colby, "The United States and Discriminate Nuclear Options in the Cold War," in *Limited Nuclear War in the 21st Century,* edited by Jeffrey A. Larsen and Kerry M. Kartcher (Stanford University Press, forthcoming) for a more detailed discussion of efforts in the 1960s, 1970s, and 1980s to incorporate discriminating nuclear strike options into U.S. nuclear war plans.

8. U.S. Strategic Air Command, *History of the Strategic Air Command, July–December 1968,* vol. 1 (February 1969, partially declassified and released under the Freedom of Information Act).

9. Secretary of Defense, "Policy Guidance for the Employment of Nuclear Weapons" (April 3, 1974, declassified and reproduced at the National Archives).

10. The terms "warheads" and "reentry vehicles" are often used interchangeably with regard to the weapons carried by strategic ballistic missiles. However, "warheads" can also be used more broadly to include gravity bombs and air-launched cruise missiles carried by heavy bombers as well as warheads—or reentry vehicles—on ICBMs and SLBMs, as was the case in the START I and New START treaties.

11. Ronald Reagan, "Address to the Nation on Defense and National Security, March 23, 1983," Reagan Presidential Library (www.reagan.utexas.edu/archives/speeches/1983/32383d.htm).

12. Department of Defense, "Increasing Transparency in the U.S. Nuclear Weapons Stockpile," Fact Sheet, May 3, 2010. The nuclear stockpile refers to active warheads, which are operational and ready for use, and inactive warheads, which are maintained at storage depots in nonoperational status (for example, the tritium bottles—tritium boosts nuclear fission—have been removed). The stockpile number does not include retired warheads that are in the queue for dismantlement.

13. Federation of American Scientists, "Nuclear Posture Review, Extract from the 1995 Annual Defense Report" (www.fas.org/nuke/guide/usa/doctrine/dod/95_npr.htm).

14. "Nuclear Posture Review Report," foreword by Donald H. Rumsfeld, Secretary of Defense, 2002 (www.defense.gov/news/jan2002/d20020109npr.pdf).

15. Department of Defense, "Increasing Transparency in the U.S. Nuclear Weapons Stockpile."

16. Letter from Secretary Samuel W. Bodman to Senator Dianne Feinstein, March 4, 2005.

17. The White House, Office of the Press Secretary, "Remarks by President Barack Obama, Hradcany Square, Prague, Czech Republic," April 5, 2009.

18. Robert S. Norris and Hans M. Kristensen, "U.S. Nuclear Forces, 2010," *Bulletin of the Atomic Scientists* 66, no. 3 (2010): 60–61.

19. The following discussion is drawn from the Department of Defense, *Nuclear Posture Review Report* (Washington, April 2010).

20. Hans M. Kristensen and Robert S. Norris, "Reviewing Nuclear Guidance: Putting Obama's Words into Action," *Arms Control Today* 41, no. 9 (2011): 14–17.

21. Phil Stewart and David Alexander, "Pentagon Chiefs Grilled over Possible Nuclear Cuts," Reuters, February 15, 2012 (www.reuters.com/article/2012/02/15/us-usa-nuclear-pentagon-idUSTRE81E28X20120215).

22. For an overview of the questions that need to be addressed when considering the stability implications of lower nuclear force levels, see Jeffrey Larsen and Polly Holdorf, "Strategic Stability at Low Numbers of Nuclear Weapons, Excerpts of the 10th Strategic Concepts Roundtable," Defense Threat Reduction Agency, Washington, November 2010.

23. The White House, Office of the Press Secretary, "Remarks by President Obama at Hankuk University, Seoul, Republic of Korea," March 26, 2012.

24. "Statement of the Honorable Madelyn R. Creedon, Assistant Secretary of Defense, Global Strategic Affairs, Office of the Under Secretary of Defense for Policy on the Fiscal Year 2013 Budget Request for Atomic Energy Defense Activities and Nuclear Forces Programs," before the House Armed Services Strategic Forces Subcommittee, April 17, 2012.

25. "The Military Doctrine of the Russian Federation," approved by Russian Presidential Edict on February 5, 2010 (carnegieendowment.org/files/2010_russian_military_doctrine.pdf).

26. Hans M. Kristensen and Robert S. Norris, "Russian Nuclear Forces, 2012," *Bulletin of the Atomic Scientists* 68, no. 2 (2012): 87–97.

27. Department of Defense, "Annual Report to Congress: Military and Security Developments Involving the People's Republic of China, 2011" (Washington: 2011), p. 34.

28. This discussion of strategic force modernization draws heavily on Amy F. Woolf, "Modernizing the Triad on a Tight Budget," *Arms Control Today* 42, no. 1 (2012): 8–13, and on Hans M. Kristensen and Robert S. Norris, "U.S. Nuclear Forces, 2012," *Bulletin of the Atomic Scientists* 68, no. 3 (2012): 84–91.

29. Inside Defense News, "Lynn: DOD Eying Cost-Cutting Options That Would Maintain Nuclear Triad," October 5, 2011 (http://defensenewsstand.com/ pdf/201110052378115/Inside-Defense-Daily-News/DefenseAlert/lynn-dod-eying-cost-cutting-options-that-would-maintain-nuclear-triad/menu-id-1.pdf).

CHAPTER 3

1. The White House, Office of the Press Secretary, "Joint Statement by President Dmitry A. Medvedev of the Russian Federation and President Barack Obama of the United States of America," London, April 1, 2009.

2. The White House, Office of the Press Secretary, "Joint Statement by Dmitry A. Medvedev, President of the Russian Federation, and Barack Obama, President of the United States of America, Regarding Negotiations on Further Reductions in Strategic Offensive Arms," London, April 1, 2009.

3. Much of the following discussion regarding the New START negotiations draws on conversations with U.S. officials, 2009–10.

4. See the White House, Office of the Press Secretary, "Joint Understanding," July 8, 2009, for the full set of parameters agreed by the presidents for the negotiation on New START.

5. Hans M. Kristensen and Robert S. Norris, "U.S. Nuclear Forces, 2012," *Bulletin of the Atomic Scientists* 68, no. 3 (2012): 84–91.

6. Department of State, Bureau of Arms Control, Verification and Compliance, "New START Treaty Implementation Update," Fact Sheet, May 17, 2012.

7. Alexei Arbatov, "Gambit or End Game? The New State of Arms Control" (Washington: Carnegie Endowment for International Peace, March 2011), pp. 14–15.

8. Ministry of Foreign Affairs of the Russian Federation, Information and Press Department, "Statement by H. E. Mr. Sergey Lavrov, Minister of Foreign Affairs of the Russian Federation, at the Plenary Meeting of the Conference on Disarmament, Geneva, 1 March 2011" (www.In.mid.ru/bdomp/brp_4.nsf/e78a48070f128a7b432 56999005bcbb3/2de66a92e764dbb8c3257846004dfd44!OpenDocument).

9. Conversations with senior Russian diplomats, May and August 2011.

10. Amy F. Woolf, "U.S. Strategic Nuclear Forces: Background, Developments and Issues" (Washington: Congressional Research Service, February 22, 2012), pp. 11–12.

11. Madeleine Albright and Igor Ivanov, "Moving Ahead on Reducing Nuclear Arms," *International Herald Tribune*, April 6, 2011.

12. Phil Stewart and David Alexander, "Pentagon Chiefs Grilled over Possible Nuclear Cuts," Reuters, February 15, 2012 (www.reuters.com/article/2012/02/15/ us-usa-nuclear-pentagon-idUSTRE81E28X20120215).

13. Sidney D. Drell and James E. Goodby, "Nuclear Deterrence in a Changed World," *Arms Control Today* 42, no. 5 (2012): 8–13.

14. Global Zero, "Global Zero U.S. Nuclear Policy Commission Report: Modernizing U.S. Nuclear Strategy, Force Structure, and Posture" (Washington: May 2012).

15. U.S. Navy Fact File, "Tomahawk Cruise Missile," updated April 23, 2010 (www.navy.mil/navydata/fact_display.asp?cid=2200&tid=1300&ct=2).

16. Bruce Blair, "Conventional Forces for Extended Deterrence," technical report (Washington: Global Zero, forthcoming).

17. Conversations with U.S. Strategic Command officers, August 2010.

18. Robert S. Norris and Hans M. Kristensen, "Nuclear Notebook: Worldwide Deployments of Nuclear Weapons, 2009," *Bulletin of the Atomic Scientists* 65, no. 6 (2009): 86–98.

CHAPTER 4

1. Article 5 of the Washington Treaty, which established NATO in 1949, reads in part: "The Parties agree that an armed attack against one or more of them in Europe or North America shall be considered an attack against them all and consequently they agree that, if such an armed attack occurs, each of them, in exercise of the right of individual or collective self-defense recognized by Article 51 of the Charter of the United Nations, will assist the Party or Parties so attacked. . . ." Article 5 has been invoked only once in NATO's sixty-three-year history: following the September 11, 2001, terrorist attacks on the United States.

2. These and other numbers for U.S. nuclear weapons in Europe through 1977 are drawn from Robert S. Norris, "United States Nuclear Weapons Deployments Abroad, 1950–1977," History of the Nuclear Age Dinner Series (Washington: Carnegie Endowment for International Peace, November 19, 1999).

3. For an excellent discussion of the origins of the flexible response doctrine, see David N. Schwartz, *NATO's Nuclear Dilemmas* (Washington: Brookings, 1983), pp. 136–92.

4. Federation of American Scientists, "Intermediate-Range Nuclear Forces (INF)" (www.fas.org/nuke/control/inf/index.html).

5. Hans M. Kristensen, "Non-Strategic Nuclear Weapons," Special Report 3 (Washington: Federation of American Scientists, May 2012), pp. 14–22.

6. NATO, "The Alliance's New Strategic Concept, agreed by the Heads of State and Government participating in the meeting of the North Atlantic Council," November 7–8, 1991 (hwww.nato.int/cps/en/natolive/official_texts_23847.htm).

7. NATO, "The Alliance's Strategic Concept, approved by the Heads of State and Government participating in the meeting of the North Atlantic Council in Washington, D.C.," April 24, 1999 (www.nato.int/cps/en/natolive/official_texts_27433.htm).

8. NATO, "NATO's Nuclear Forces in the New Security Environment," p. 4 (www.nato.int/issues/nuclear/sec-environment.html).

9. Robert S. Norris, William M. Arkin, and William Burr, "Where They Were," *Bulletin of the Atomic Scientists* (November/December 1999): 26–35.

10. Elbridge A. Colby, "U.S. Nuclear Weapons Policy and Policymaking: The Asian Experience," in *Tactical Nuclear Weapons and NATO,* edited by Tom Nichols, Douglas Stuart, and Jeffrey D. McCausland (Carlisle, Pa.: Strategic Studies Institute, 2012), pp. 75–105.

11. Department of Defense, *Nuclear Posture Review Report* (Washington: April 2012), pp. 32–35.

12. Arms Control Association, "NATO Clings to Its Cold War Relics," Issue Brief 1, no. 1 (April 27, 2010) (www.armscontrol.org/issuebriefs/NATORelics).

13. Conversations with diplomats from eight NATO missions and a NATO international staff official, November 2010.

14. Kristensen, "Non-Strategic Nuclear Weapons."

15. NATO, "Active Engagement, Modern Defense: Strategic Concept for the Defense and Security of Members of the North Atlantic Treaty Organization, adopted by Heads of State and Government in Lisbon," November 19, 2010 (www. nato.int/cps/en/natolive/official_texts_68580.htm).

16. NATO, "Deterrence and Defense Posture Review," May 20, 2012 (www. nato.int/cps/en/natolive/official_texts_87597.htm?mode=pressrelease).

17. These numbers, the numbers in table 4-1, and the following breakdowns are drawn from Kristensen, "Non-Strategic Nuclear Weapons." While the United States has not publicly disclosed the number of its nonstrategic nuclear weapons, the total of 500 seems broadly consistent with the figure of 5,113 total nuclear weapons in the U.S. inventory as of September 2009 (as disclosed by the Defense Department in May 2010). In its January 2010 report to Congress on implementation of the 2002 Strategic Offensive Reductions Treaty, the State Department advised that the United States maintained 1,968 operationally deployed strategic warheads, and the U.S. military is believed to maintain at least one nondeployed strategic warhead for each deployed warhead. There is a significant range in the estimates of the current Russian nonstrategic nuclear stockpile about which there is even less transparency.

18. For more detailed discussion, see George Perkovich and others, "Looking beyond the Chicago Summit: Nuclear Weapons and the Future of NATO," Carnegie Papers (Washington: Carnegie Endowment for International Peace, April 2012).

19. Council on Foreign Relations, "Nuclear Posture Review" (Washington: April 8, 2010) (www.defense.gov/npr/docs/Council_on_Foreign_Relations.pdf).

20. "The Military Doctrine of the Russian Federation," approved by Russian Presidential Edict on February 5, 2010 (carnegieendowment.org/files/2010_russian_military_doctrine.pdf).

21. Alexei Arbatov, "Gambit or Endgame: The New State of Arms Control" (Washington: Carnegie Endowment for International Peace, March 2011), pp. 31–33.

22. The White House, Remarks as Prepared for Delivery by Tom Donilon, National Security Advisor to the President, "The Prague Agenda: The Road Ahead," Carnegie International Nuclear Policy Conference, Washington, March 29, 2011.

23. Letter of the ambassadors of Poland, Norway, Germany, the Netherlands, Belgium, the Czech Republic, Hungary, Iceland, and Luxembourg and chargé d'affaires of Slovenia to Secretary General Anders Fogh Rasmussen, April 15, 2011.

24. Sidney D. Drell and James E. Goodby, "Nuclear Deterrence in a Changed World," *Arms Control Today* 42, no. 5 (2012) 8–13.

CHAPTER 5

1. For a history of the SALT I negotiations, see John Newhouse, *Cold Dawn: The Story of SALT* (New York: Holt, Rinehart and Winston, 1973).

2. The ranges for ballistic missiles break down as follows: short-range—up to 1,000 kilometers; medium-range—1,000–3,000 kilometers, intermediate-range—3,000–5,500 kilometers, and ICBMs—5,500 kilometers or greater. The INF Treaty had a different definition, categorizing all ground-based missiles with ranges between 500 and 5,500 kilometers as intermediate-range.

3. U.S. Congress, "National Missile Defense Act of 1999."

4. The White House, "Fact Sheet on U.S. Missile Defense Policy: A 'Phased Adaptive Approach' for Missile Defense in Europe," September 17, 2009.

5. The following information draws on U.S. Department of Defense, "Ballistic Missile Defense Review Report, February 2010"; Ronald O'Rourke, "Navy Aegis Ballistic Missile Defense (BMD) Program: Background and Issues for Congress" (Congressional Research Service, December 22, 2011); and Arms Control Association, "The Phased Adaptive Approach at a Glance" (Washington) (www.armscontrol.org/factsheets/Phasedadaptiveapproach).

6. NATO, "Lisbon Summit Declaration: Issued by the Heads of State and Government participating in the meeting of the North Atlantic Council in Lisbon," November 20, 2010.

7. Conversation with a U.S. government official, May 2012; White House, Office of the Press Secretary, "Fact Sheet: Chicago Summit—NATO Capabilities," May 20, 2012.

8. Conversations with U.S. officials, 2011 and 2012.

9. For further information on the Track II discussions, see Euro-Atlantic Security Initiative, Working Group on Missile Defense, "Missile Defense: Toward a New Paradigm" (Washington: Carnegie Endowment for International Peace, February 2012); Brookings and Institute for World Economy and International Relations, "Next Steps on U.S.-Russian Nuclear Negotiations and Nuclear Non-Proliferation: Recommendations from the June 23 Meeting of Madeleine Albright, Strobe Talbott, Igor Ivanov, and Alexander Dynkin" (Washington: October 2010); and PIR Center (Russian Center for Policy Studies), "Recommendations of the Sustainable Partnership with Russia (SuPR) Group" (Moscow: March 2011).

10. Conversations with U.S. and Russian officials, April, May, and July 2012.

11. Conversations with U.S. and Russian officials, May 2011.

12. RIA Novosti, "U.S., NATO Have Some 1,000 Interceptors—Rogozin," January 20, 2012 (http://en.rian.ru/world/20120120/170856516.html).

13. Pavel Podvig, "Point of Distraction," *Bulletin of the Atomic Scientists* web edition, June 1, 2012 (www.thebulletin.org/web-edition/columnists/pavel-podvig/point-of-distraction).

14. See, for example, U.S. Government Accountability Office, "Missile Defense: Opportunity Exists to Strengthen Acquisitions by Reducing Concurrency" (April 2012); and Defense Science Board Task Force, Office of the Secretary of Defense, "Science and Technology Issues of Early Intercept Ballistic Missile Defense Feasibility" (September 2011).

15. Letter from L. David Montague and Walter B. Slocombe to Representatives Michael R. Turner and Loretta Sanchez regarding questions on missile defense, April 30, 2012. Montague and Slocombe cochaired a committee that prepared a recently completed National Research Council report entitled "Making Sense of Ballistic Missile Defense: An Assessment of Concepts and Systems for U.S. Boost-Phase Missile Defense in Comparison to Other Alternatives." The final unclassified report is awaiting declassification review by the Missile Defense Agency.

16. NATO, "Chicago Summit Declaration Issued by the Heads of State and Government participating in the meeting of the North Atlantic Council in Chicago on 20 May 2012" (www.nato.int/cps/en/natolive/official_texts_87593.htm?mode=pressrelease).

17. Atlantic Council, "Transatlantic Missile Defense Conference," transcript (Washington: October 18, 2011) (www.acus.org/event/transatlantic-missile-defense-phase-ii-and-lead-nato-chicago-summit/transcript/1).

18. President of Russia, "Statement in Connection with the Situation Concerning the NATO Countries' Missile Defense System in Europe" (November 23, 2011) (http://eng.news.kremlin.ru/news/3115).

CHAPTER 6

1. Department of Defense, *Nuclear Posture Review Report* (2010), p. 38.

2. Kate Brannen, "Nuke Expert Pool Shrinking," *Defense News,* April 16, 2012, p. 6.

3. Steve Fetter, *Toward a Comprehensive Test Ban* (Cambridge, Mass.: Ballinger Publishing, 1988), pp. 72–78.

4. R. J. Hemley and others, "Pit Lifetime," JSR-06-335 (McLean, Va.: Mitre Corp., January 2007) (www.fas.org/irp/agency/dod/jason/pit.pdf); Matthew L. Wald, "U.S. Has No Need to Test Atomic Arsenal, Report Says," *New York Times,* March 31, 2012 (www.nytimes.com/2012/03/31/science/earth/us-tests-of-atomic-weapons-not-needed-report-says.html?scp=1&sq=nuclear%20test%20ban&st=cse).

5. National Research Council, *The Comprehensive Nuclear Test Ban Treaty— Technical Issues for the United States* (Washington: National Academy of Sciences, 2012), p. 16 (www.nap.edu/catalog.php?record_id=12849).

6. U.S. Nuclear Weapons Cost Study Project, "Fifty Facts about Nuclear Weapons" (Brookings Institution, 1998) (www.brookings.edu/projects/archive/nucweapons/50.aspx).

7. Secretary of Defense Robert Gates, "Gates: Nuclear Weapons and Deterrence in the 21st Century," Speech at the Carnegie Endowment for International Peace, Washington, D.C., October 28, 2008 (www.carnegieendowment.org/files/1028_transcrip_gates_checked.pdf).

8. Jonathan Medalia, "The Reliable Replacement Warhead Program: Background and Current Developments," *CRS Report for Congress,* RL32929 (Congressional Research Service, July 2007), pp. 4–9.

9. Nick Roth, "Fact Sheet: DOE Stockpile Stewardship and Management Plan" (Washington: Union of Concerned Scientists, July 2010) (www.ucsusa.org/

nuclear_weapons_and_global_security/nuclear_weapons/policy_issues/stockpile-backgrounder.html).

10. Congressional Budget Office, *The Bomb's Custodians* (July 1994), pp. 2–9; Stephen I. Schwartz, ed., *Atomic Audit: The Costs and Consequences of U.S. Nuclear Weapons since 1940* (Brookings, 1998), pp. 562–63.

11. National Research Council, *The Comprehensive Nuclear Test Ban Treaty—Technical Issues for the United States* (Washington, D.C.: 2012).

12. Stephen M. Younger, *The Bomb: A New History* (New York: Harper-Collins, 2009), pp. 178–88.

13. National Research Council, *The Comprehensive Nuclear Test Ban Treaty—Technical Issues for the United States*, p. 23.

14. National Nuclear Security Administration, "Reliable Replacement Warhead Program" (Washington: March 2007) (www.nnsa.doe.gov/docs/factsheets/2007/NA-07-FS-02.pdf).

15. Walter Pincus, "New Nuclear Warhead's Funding Eliminated," *Washington Post*, May 24, 2007, p. A6.

16. John R. Harvey, "Nonproliferation's New Soldier," *Bulletin of the Atomic Scientists* (July/August 2007): 32–33; Jonathan Medalia, "The Reliable Replacement Warhead Program: Background and Current Developments."

17. Michael A. Levi and Michael E. O'Hanlon, *The Future of Arms Control* (Brookings, 2005), p. 28.

18. Michael A. Levi, "Dreaming of Clean Nukes," *Nature* 428 (April 29, 2004): 892.

19. Zhang Hui, "Revisiting North Korea's Nuclear Test," *China Security* 3, no. 3 (2007): 119–30.

20. Damien J. LaVera, "Looking Back: The U.S. Senate Vote on the Comprehensive Test Ban," *Arms Control Today* (October 2004) (www.armscontrol.org/epublish/1/v34n8). (www.armscontrol.org/act/2004_10/LookingBack_CTBT).

21. National Research Council, *The Comprehensive Test Ban Treaty—Technical Issues for the United States*, pp. 100–112.

22. Stephen J. Blank, "Russia and Nuclear Weapons," in *Russian Nuclear Weapons: Past, Present, and Future*, edited by Stephen J. Blank (Carlisle, Pa.: Strategic Studies Institute, U.S. Army War College, 2011), pp. 315, 347–48.

23. Gates, "Gates: Nuclear Weapons and Deterrence in the 21st Century."

24. Bruce Riedel, *Deadly Embrace: Pakistan, America, and the Future of the Global Jihad* (Brookings, 2011), p. 116; A. Vinod Kumar, "India and the CTBT: The Debate in New Delhi," *Bulletin of the Atomic Scientists* (November 4, 2009) (www.thebulletin.org/print/web-edition/features/india-and-the-ctbt-the-debate-new-delhi).

25. For a riveting discussion of how the 1999 Senate vote affected U.S.-India deliberations on nuclear matters, see Strobe Talbott, *Engaging India: Diplomacy, Democracy, and the Bomb*, rev. ed. (Brookings, 2006), pp. 179–85.

26. Jeff Lindemyer, "Potential U.S. Ratification of the Comprehensive Nuclear Test Ban Treaty (CTBT) Fact Sheet" (Washington: Center for Arms Control and Non-Proliferation, April 15, 2008) (www.armscontrolcenter.org/policy/nuclear-weapons/articles); Nuclear Age Peace Foundation, "Public Support for a Nuclear Test Ban Treaty Remains High," *NuclearFiles.org*, July 20, 1999 (www.nuclearfiles.org/menu/library/opinion-polls/test-ban/test-ban-treaty-support-remains-high.htm).

27. Terry L. Deibel, "The Death of a Treaty," *Foreign Affairs* 81, no. 5 (2002) (www.foreignaffairs.com/articles/58251/terry-l-deibel/the-death-of-a-treaty); Helen Dewar, "Senate Rejects Test Ban Treaty; Nuclear Pact Falls 51 to 48 as GOP Deals Clinton Major Defeat," *Washington Post,* October 14, 1999, p. A1.

28. George P. Shultz, and others, "A World Free of Nuclear Weapons," *Wall Street Journal,* January 4, 2007, p. A15.

29. National Research Council, *The Comprehensive Nuclear Test Ban Treaty—Technical Issues for the United States.*

CHAPTER 7

1. International Panel on Fissile Materials, *Global Fissile Material Report 2011: Nuclear Weapon and Fissile Material Stockpiles and Production* (Program on Science and Global Security, Princeton University, January 2012), pp. 2–3 (www.fissilematerials.org).

2. Chunyan Ma and Frank von Hippel, "Ending the Production of Highly Enriched Uranium for Naval Reactors," *Nonproliferation Review* (Spring 2001): 92.

3. International Panel on Fissile Materials, *Global Fissile Material Report 2011*, pp. 2–3.

4. Matthew Bunn and Eben Harrell, "Consolidation: Thwarting Nuclear Theft," Project on Managing the Atom (Belfer Center, Harvard University, March 2012), p. v (www.managingtheatom.org).

5. Matthew Bunn, Eben Harrell, and Martin B. Malin, "Progress on Securing Nuclear Weapons and Materials: The Four-Year Effort and Beyond," Project on Managing the Atom (Belfer Center, Harvard University, March 2012), pp. 16–19 (www.managingtheatom.org).

6. Frank von Hippel, "Overview: The Rise and Fall of Plutonium Breeder Reactors," in International Panel on Fissile Materials, *Fast Breeder Reactor Programs: History and Status* (Program on Science and Global Security, Princeton University, February 2010), p. 5 (www.fissilematerials.org).

7. World Nuclear Association, "Plans for New Reactors Worldwide" (London, February 2012) (www.world-nuclear.org/info/inf17.html).

8. Ma and von Hippel, "Ending the Production of Highly Enriched Uranium for Naval Reactors," pp. 93–96.

9. Bunn and Harrell, "Consolidation: Thwarting Nuclear Theft," pp. vi–vii.

10. David Cortright and Raimo Vayrynen, *Towards Nuclear Zero* (London: International Institute for Strategic Studies, 2010), pp. 131–32.

11. Frank von Hippel and others, "The Uncertain Future of Nuclear Energy," Research Report 9, (International Panel on Fissile Materials, Princeton University, September 2010), p. 38 (www.fissilematerials.org).

12. For more on this, see Michael A. Levi and Michael E. O'Hanlon, *The Future of Arms Control* (Brookings, 2005), pp. 58–63.

13. World Information Service on Energy Uranium Project, "World Nuclear Fuel Facilities," Amsterdam February 29, 2012 (www.wise-uranium.org/efac.html).

14. John P. Holdren and others, *The Economics of Reprocessing versus Direct Disposal of Spent Nuclear Fuel* (Harvard University Press, 2003).

15. World Information Service on Energy Uranium Project, "World Nuclear Fuel Facilities."

16. David E. Sanger and William J. Broad, "U.S. and Allies Warn Iran over 'Nuclear Deception,'" *New York Times*, September 26, 2009, p. 1.

17. See, for example, Hans Blix, *Disarming Iraq* (New York: Pantheon Books, 2004), pp. 23–24.

18. Katie Walter, "The Hunt for Better Radiation Detection," *Science and Technology Review* (January-February 2010): 4–10.

19. Michael Levi, *On Nuclear Terrorism* (Harvard University Press, 2007), pp. 52–61.

20. International Panel on Fissile Materials, *Global Fissile Material Report 2009: A Path to Nuclear Disarmament* (Princeton University, Program on Science and Global Security, 2009), p. 7 (www.fissilematerials.org).

21. George Perkovich and James M. Acton, *Abolishing Nuclear Weapons*, Adelphi Paper 396 (London: International Institute for Strategic Studies, 2008), p. 56.

22. International Panel on Fissile Materials, *Global Fissile Material Report 2009*, pp. 21–22.

CHAPTER 8

1. World Public Opinion, "Publics around the World Favor International Agreement to Eliminate All Nuclear Weapons" (Washington: December 2008) (www.worldpublicopinion.org/pipa/articles/international_security_bt/577.php).

2. International Panel on Fissile Materials, *Global Fissile Material Report 2011* (Princeton University, Program on Science and Global Security, January 2012), pp. 4–7, (www.fissilematerials.org); Daryl Kimball, Peter Crail, and Tom Collina, "Nuclear Weapons: Who Has What at a Glance" (Washington: Arms Control Association, 2011) (www.armscontrol.org/factsheets/Nuclearweaponswhohaswhat); Heather Timmons and Jim Yardley, "Signs of an Asian Arms Buildup in India's Missile Test," *New York Times*, April 20, 2012.

3. See, for example, Richard Burt and Jan Lodal, "A Next Step in Nuclear Arms Control: Securing Fissile Materials," presentation at the Brookings Institution, Washington, June 28, 2012 (www.brookings.edu/~/media/events/2012/6/28%20 nuclear%20arms%20control/20120628_nuclear_arms_control.pdf).

4. International Panel on Fissile Materials, *Global Fissile Material Report 2009* (Princeton University, Program on Science and Global Security, 2009), pp. 21–22.

5. Joint Chiefs of Staff, *National Military Strategy* (Department of Defense, 1992), p. 13.

6. See, for example, The White House, *A National Security Strategy for a New Century* (October 1998), p. 12.

7. "NATO Reactions on No First Use," *Arms Control Today* (November-December 1998) (www.armscontrol.org/print/423).

8. George Bunn and Christopher F. Chyba, "U.S. Nuclear Weapons Policies for a New Era," in *U.S. Nuclear Weapons Policy: Confronting Today's Threats*, edited by George Bunn and Christopher F. Chyba (Brookings, 2006), p. 314.

9. Patrick M. Cronin, ed., *Global Strategic Assessment 2009: America's Security Role in a Changing World* (Washington: Institute for National Strategic Studies, National Defense University, 2009), p. 181.

10. Michael Moodie and others, "Good Bugs, Bad Bugs: A Modern Approach for Detecting Offensive Biological Weapons Research," Defense and Technology Paper 54 (Washington: Center for Technology and National Security Policy, National Defense University, September 2008), p. v.

11. Mark Wheelis, "Biotechnology and Biochemical Weapons, *Nonproliferation Review* (Spring 2002): 48–53; Michael A. Levi and Michael E. O'Hanlon, *The Future of Arms Control* (Brookings, 2005), pp. 76–77.

12. See, for example, Carina Dennis, "The Bugs of War," *Nature* no. 411 (May 17, 2001): 232–35

13. John D. Steinbruner, *Principles of Global Security* (Brookings, 2000), p. 178.

14. Keith B. Payne, "On Nuclear Deterrence and Assurance," *Strategic Studies Quarterly* 3, no. 1 (2009): 45.

15. Michael Walzer, *Just and Unjust Wars: A Moral Argument with Historical Illustrations* (New York: Basic Books, 1977), pp. 269–83.

16. For a similar argument, see Barry M. Blechman, "Why We Need to Eliminate Nuclear Weapons—And How to Do It," in *Elements of a Nuclear Disarmament Treaty*, edited by Barry M. Blechman and Alexander K. Bollfrass (Washington: Henry L. Stimson Center, 2010), pp. 11–13.

17. For a good discussion of this point, see Brad Roberts, "The Nuclear Dimension: How Likely? How Stable?" in *Assessing the Threat: The Chinese Military and Taiwan's Security*, edited by Michael D. Swaine and others (Washington: Carnegie Endowment, 2007), pp. 213–31; Larry M. Wortzel, *China's Nuclear Forces: Operations, Training, Doctrine, Command, Control, and Campaign Planning* (Carlisle, Pa.: Strategic Studies Institute, Army War College, May 2007) (www.Strategic StudiesInstitute.army.mil); Michael S. Chase, Andrew S. Erickson, and Christopher Yeaw, "Chinese Theater and Strategic Missile Force Modernization and Its Implications for the United States," *Journal of Strategic Studies* 32, no. 1 (2009): 67–114; and Michael S. Chase and Evan Medeiros, "China's Evolving Nuclear Calculus: Modernization and Doctrinal Debate," in *China's Revolution in Doctrinal Affairs: Emerging Trends in the Operational Art of the Chinese People's Liberation Army*, edited by James Mulvenon and David Finkelstein (Alexandria, Va.: CNA Corporation, 2005), pp. 119–57.

18. Thom Shanker, "Gates Gives Rationale for Expanded Deterrence," *New York Times*, October 29, 2008, p. A12.

19. Jonathan Schell, "The Abolition," in *The Fate of the Earth and the Abolition*, edited by Jonathan Schell (Stanford University Press, 2000).

20. Bruce G. Blair, *Global Zero Alert for Nuclear Forces* (Brookings, 1995).

21. Although its comments on the subject are offered only in passing, the Obama administration appears to agree with this concept of maintaining certain reconstitution capabilities even after the elimination of nuclear weapons; see Department of Defense, *Nuclear Posture Review Report* (2010), p. 42.

22. See, for example, Frederic S. Nyland, "Exemplary Industrial Targets for Controlled Conflict," in *Strategic Nuclear Targeting*, edited by Desmond Ball and Jeffrey Richelson (Cornell University Press, 1986), p. 215.

23. George Perkovich and James M. Acton, *Abolishing Nuclear Weapons,* Adelphi Paper 396 (London: International Institute for Strategic Studies, 2008), pp. 104–06.

APPENDIX A

1. For a full account of the SALT I negotiations, see John Newhouse, *Cold Dawn: The History of SALT* (New York: Holt, Reinhart, and Winston, 1973).

2. For a full account of the SALT II negotiation, see Strobe Talbott, *Endgame: The Inside Story of SALT II* (New York: Harper Colophon Books, 1979).

3. See Strobe Talbott, *Deadly Gambits* (New York: Alfred A. Knopf, 1984) for a full account of the INF negotiations from 1981 to 1983.

4. See Maynard W. Glitman, *The Last Battle of the Cold War: An Inside Account of Negotiating the Intermediate-Range Nuclear Forces Treaty* (New York: Palgrave Macmillan, 2006) for a full account of the negotiation of the INF Treaty.

5. Eli Corin, "Presidential Nuclear Initiatives: An Alternative Paradigm for Arms Control," Nuclear Threat Initiative/Global Security Newswire, March 1, 2004 (www.nti.org/analysis/articles/presidential-nuclear-initiatives/).

6. Conversation with Russian Foreign Ministry official, December 2008.

INDEX